SELF-INFLICTED
CONFRONTING THE SUICIDE TABOO

DR. KARL T. MUTH

Printed in the United States of America

Hardcover ISBN: 978-1-958714-98-0
Paperback ISBN: 978-1-958714-99-7
Ebook ISBN: 978-1-960876-00-3
Library of Congress Control Number: 2023935613

Muse Literary
3319 N. Cicero Avenue
Chicago IL 60641-9998

Title and Meaning

"Self-inflicted" in the title of this volume refers to the medical examiner's notation often attached to gunshot wounds and poisonings in cases of suicide, but it also refers to the fact that our limited, narrow thinking about suicide from a standpoint of policy and norms is entirely self-inflicted and can be changed at any time.

The fact that these societal guardrails are merely the product of traditions, prejudices, and attitudes gives me hope that prohibitions and limitations on suicide can be adjusted, relaxed, and (ultimately) destroyed.

The arguments in this book are meant to question the *status quo* and to attack the roots of these prohibitions; I hope you will soon see laws and social mores barring or punishing suicide not as a castle built on centuries of sound reason but instead as a wall built on sand.

Acknowledgements and Dedications

I owe enormous debts to so many who helped me think through the arguments and ideas that led to this book around dinner tables, coffee shops, university seminars, campfires, and bottles of whiskey over the years—some of you supported these ideas from the outset, a few were convinced, many are still vehemently opposed—but each and all of you made this book possible, perhaps in ways you do not realize or fully appreciate. (I include in these thanks people who wrote things that influenced my own thinking over the past two years, in particular.) Very special thanks to Brooke and Lillian Scheck, who created the space and support for this book to take shape, even when we were living in tiny cabins or camping in the forest. Thanks to Christina Alfonso, Tom Amenta, Gary Becker, Angela Beckman, Veronica Beckman, Jodi Beggs, Chris Blattman, Temi Bennett (especially for our March 2023 conversation), Vanessa Burrows, Sarah Carson (for pushing and questioning my positions on these topics for over ten years!), Utsunomiya Chiaki sensei (my Japanese mentor), Michael Cholbi, Danielle Citron, John Costello, Ashley D. Cox, Amy B. Danzer, Cristina Desmond, Katheryn DeVelvis, Elizabeth DeWolf (whose content editing on earlier drafts was fantastic and made this final draft possible), Ashkan Emami, Ezekiel Emmanuel, James Fallows, Rachel Furnari, Carrie Goldberg, Sam Goldberg, Pat Gray, Kristin Greenhaw, Jennifer Helgeson, Keisha Howard, Nancy Jack (one of my favorite co-authors and someone who contributed meaningfully to this manuscript's earlier versions in 2022), Christine Kailus, David Kershaw, Tom Kirk, Amira Khatib, Amanda Klonsky, Walter Lamberson, Haruna Lee, Andrew Leventhal, Alice Locatelli, Billy Lombardo, Michelle Mangan, Rachael Meager, Hannah M. Meyer, Kevin M. Murphy, Ed Muth, Griffin Myers, L.A. Paul, Georgie Pearson, Randy Picker, Nadia M. Podolsky, Tim Polder, Richard Posner, Liesel Pritzker-Simmons, James Ramsey, Heather

Repinski, Brooke A.S. Ricketts, Anouk Rigterink, Rachel Riviera, James Schrager, Elizabeth Schutte, Jason Shain (whose technical editing throughout was invaluable), Jamie Shapiro (who taught me how to write years ago and continues to inspire me to improve at this difficult craft), Ian Simmons, Noah Smith, Cass Sunstein, John Sylla, David Tan, Rita D. Tan, Liisa Thomas, Robert H. Wade, Alexander Williams, Benjamin "Beauregard" Dee Winston II, and many authors, discussants, seminar attendees, and students over the years for inspiring, critiquing, and improving my work (and interrogating, and thereby clarifying, my thoughts); though some of these people would not agree with all arguments I make here, I make the arguments more strongly with the benefit of their influence, mentorship, or collaboration. A little different flavor of thanks to Jon and Pete at Getaway (check them out: https://getaway.house/), which provides amazing, remote one-room tiny homes in the forest across North America; big chunks of this book, including what I consider some of the strongest parts, were written over two years in six of these cabins.

This volume is dedicated to everyone making the decision to continue living (or not) each day and, especially and beyond that, to all who listen when people talk about suicide and fight for people to have the choice to die without encumbrance, interference, stigma, or prejudice.

Content Warning

The purpose of this book is not to persuade, convince, or inspire any one person to end life. Rather, it is to advocate for those with the power to set law, norms, and rules to relax restrictions on the decision to end life. In other words, this book is less about suicide and more about the choice to end life. I believe that choice should be more widely available and accessible without many of the present legal restrictions and normative stigmas.

That having been said, this book contains frank discussion of suicide, including suicidal ideation, the relationship between depression and suicide, the relationship between mental illness and suicide, methods for ending life, thought experiments and hypotheticals involving suicide, dreams involving suicide, and other scenarios that may lead to the death of one or more people involved. These can be uncomfortable topics for many readers.

If you are having thoughts that worry you or feel you cannot digest a discussion of suicide right now, I urge you to put down this book and come back to it some other time, or not at all. If you feel you have bought this book in error or cannot, upon further reflection, enjoy its contents, please return it to the bookseller or contact me directly and I will take back your book.

While I believe these are crucial conversations to be had in our society, I recognize not everyone is equally prepared or eager to have the discussions this book is meant to encourage or facilitate.

If you are an instructor (for instance, in a philosophy program) and choose to assign this book or passages from this book for your syllabus, I thank you but also ask you to do so cautiously.

If you are in crisis and need to contact someone to discuss suicidal thoughts, or you are worried you may make an incorrect irreversible mortal decision, contact one of these organizations:

In the United States: Dial 9-8-8 or text TALK to 741741.

For American Veterans: Text 838255, dial 988+1, or dial 800-273-8255 and press 1.

In the United Kingdom: Dial 1-1-6-1-2-3 or text SHOUT to 85258 at any time, twenty-four hours a day.

Globally: Visit https://www.befrienders.org.

Though I believe everyone should enjoy the choice to end life, I believe many people benefit from psychotherapy, informal or community counseling, or family conversations in making the decision to end life. Though I disagree with some tactics and messages groups use in suicide prevention, particularly to the extent they interfere with informed, careful, and lucid individual choice, I do not wish to make the end of life seem less weighty or more urgent; in fact, this book, taken in the spirit it was written, stresses the gravity of this decision and that it should be made with comprehensive preparation for one's death date and deep contemplation of consequences.

Most of all, I want the choice to end life to be widely available, but always made with substantial reflection upon, and consideration of, this unidirectional move. Every day, whether you have thought for minutes or years about ending your life, as you read this your finger is still on that chess piece, and you can think as long as you'd like before the move becomes final. But once your finger disconnects from the piece's surface, there is no taking back that move.

I wish you the best and urge you to make this and other decisions calmly and confidently. May you step boldly into tomorrow or, alternatively, just as boldly, choose to take no more steps.

Citation Errors, Citation Queries

The Internet addresses cited were accurate at the time of publication, but given the nature of hyperlinks and Internet content mutability, they may not be correct or contain the same content in the future; I apologize for any research difficulties this may create for other authors.

In cases where a document is "on file with the author," contact the author at karl.muth@chicagobooth.edu for information on how to obtain a copy.

In cases where a citation error is present (a citation is illegible or incorrect), please contact the author at karl.muth@chicagobooth.edu so the citation can be corrected in subsequent editions.

Run of Show

Tonight's performance contains intentionally provocative concepts and discussion of suicide.

The Origins of This Text

The world is a fine place and worth fighting for, and I hate very much to leave it.
—Jordan[1]

Imagine your ideal death. Is it a peaceful mid-slumber event? Is your bank account healthy for your children or friends to enjoy? Would you have just hours earlier finished a marvelous meal with your closest friends, perhaps delivered a memorable toast? Reasonable minds can differ on what a good final day looks and feels like, but most would classify a good final day as one where bodily and mental functions are in order, where life is still a thing to be explored and enjoyed rather than medicated and endured, and perhaps where certain interactions (intellectual, epicurean, artistic, sexual, or otherwise) are still possible.

And, if you had a date in mind for your good final day, how would that change how you lived your life? With a clear expiration date, you might spend less time cleaning up junk in your work inbox, digging up trivial coffeeshop receipts for last month's expense report, arguing with somebody you don't know on Twitter, or watching something mediocre on Netflix. You might instead be forced to consider what's most important to you, what's realistic to achieve, and what you "really want." But in a world where suicide is generally prohibited, we have little control over one of the most consequential experiences of our existence: how and when we die.

---

[1] Ernest Hemingway, For Whom the Bell Tolls (1963).

13

I ask that you come along on this journey that will often be without comfort and rarely be without controversy, but, as more than one great argument has begun, I beg: *fragilem mecum solvem phaselum*.[2]

If there is a formal intellectual contest this book seeks to explore, it is the conflict between St. Thomas Aquinas's position in the Summa Theologica, "[S]uicide is contrary to the inclination of nature and to charity, whereby every man should love himself," and Arthur Schopenhauer's position in *On Suicide* at page 77 within Essays and Aphorisms, "[T]here is nothing in the world a man has a more incontestable right to than his own life and person." But I hope you'll also wander a bit further afield with me and explore questions blooming at the edges of that battlefield.

This book draws on my perspective both as a former "longevity enthusiast" and as an interdisciplinary scholar at the University of Chicago to consider the importance of the right to choose why, when, and how one's life will end. The book argues that people should have ownership-like control over their own mortality—specifically, that suicide should be a human right—and that this control would enable us to place higher value on our lives, to be remembered as empowered and alert rather than feeble and pitiable, and to leave financial and other legacies with a degree of planning and precision impossible if passing by frailty, disease, accident, or murder are the only options. My proposition, in its simplest form, is that lifespan is precious for each and all of us. My life will end and so, too, will yours. Setting our date of death would help us make better choices with the time we have left. Further, I advance the argument that death through suicide is preferable to natural expiration and that planning a self-directed, consensual death can enhance life.

For years, I was part of a subculture that was fascinated with extending life as long as physically possible using biotech, nanotech, cryotech, and futuretech more generally. These aren't hobbyists or philosophy undergraduates merely contemplating long life—many were taking large doses

---

[2] Embark with me in this fragile boat (of an argument).

of Dasatinib, Quercetin, and Fisetin, which nuke the senescent, or elderly, cells in one's blood, to get "younger median cell life" and trying to boost their klotho levels (a protein believed to protect cells), by flying around the world to see the handful of doctors willing to administer experimental, sometimes dubious treatments. This "quantified self" movement meant wearing a continuous glucose monitor despite not being at risk of diabetes. I was so into this I even invested in the Series A round of Levels Health, a transdermal glucose monitor startup, and was among the first investors in Galen Data, in another startup that increases the speed and accuracy with which future external and implantable medical devices will communicate with infrastructure like ambulances, operating rooms, and wifi hubs. Like many in my longevity enthusiast cohort, I used billing software favored by law firms to track how I was spending my life in six-minute increments, and I worked with a personal trainer to exhaustively critique and redesign my diet, intermittent fasting, and exercise regimens to a point that most people would, correctly, consider an eating disorder rather than a longevity project. I visited startups like Calico (part of Google's Alphabet holding company) and Human Longevity, Inc. (better-known now under its Health Nucleus brand); today, startups like Altos Labs and BlueRock continue work in the same genre: helping people live longer than would be otherwise biologically possible.

My participation in, and eventual rejection of, this subculture led to a deep interest in mortality and various philosophies of living and dying, and a simple question: *Why not make the most of what we've already got?*

Meanwhile, in my economics scholarship, I've long examined the ways in which constraints help us focus thoughts and marshal resources for optimal outcomes. Together, these perspectives have led me to embrace the idea of bounded longevity: that an abbreviated lifespan can enable us to live the best possible life, provided we are able to choose when and how we die. This book advocates thoughtful living followed by planned death. When life loses value for the individual—he or she being the person best positioned to determine that tomorrow is uninteresting, unfulfilling, or unbearable and that today is enough—then it is that individual who should be able to choose to fold his or her proverbial cards.

To continue the poker metaphor briefly: who should be allowed to fold and who should be forced to continue betting on a losing hand? Because this volume's central argument emanates from a traditional liberal[3] (or nowadays perhaps libertarian with a lowercase *L*) argument of individual rights with consent as an important prerequisite, suicide is viewed here not as an illicit act or a depression symptom, but instead as an affirmative, chosen, and consensual death. This also creates convenient and appropriate boundaries around the choice to die, as it is unavailable to those who cannot consent in other important contexts: children, the insane, those in conservatorship and protective custody arrangements, and some but not all of those who are incarcerated or have their liberty bounded by state-administered limits.

Section by section, in bite-sized, nightstand-book vignettes, this book uses historical evidence, challenging questions, and thought experiments—in the manner of scientific and philosophical inquiry—to challenge common arguments against broader acceptance of suicide: that suicide is objectively immoral, that lifespan uncertainty is natural and itself a valid reason for prohibition,[4] that doctors are the only ones who can or should facilitate terminal conversations, that a longer life is always better, and that death is best left up to chance. My hope is you will leave this book with a deeper understanding of the specific cultural, moral, and legal assumptions that dominate discourse about suicide today and, at the very least, a more open mind about whether our society should have a more liberal posture when it comes to the choice to end one's life. Ultimately, the aim of the book is to build support for the eventual societal acceptance of suicide, on the

---

[3] Liberal meaning driven by individual freedom and choice, not liberal meaning virtue-signaling or leftist shuttlecockery or not daring to say anything interesting in San Francisco for fear of offending someone.

[4] This argument suggests suicide is tampering with a natural path, sabotaging nature's course. Interestingly, the only "people" we've managed to create, corporations, can die at our convenience for any reason or no reason at all. See In Bankr. D.N.J., re LTL Mgmt., LLC, 637 B.R. 396, 408 (Bankr. J.N.J. 2022).

grounds that access to suicide can empower us to live with greater purpose and die with greater agency and dignity, having lived the lives we designed and desired.

By anticipating and planning death, we can come closer to an ideal where we live *lives we choose* instead of merely drifting through *lives that happened to us*. And we can end those lives with a choreographed, painless, consensual event rather than an unexpected fatal misfortune.

In the privacy of these pages, far away from the workplace human resources handbook and the red-flag rules of your psychotherapist[5] and the woman armed with a trumpet,[6] we can think about death and talk about death. We can choose that we'd rather die healthy, aware, smiling, and ready than die unprepared, afraid, alone, and feeling ourselves succumbing in silent horror to Nature's deadly schemes.

I plan and intend to die well. And you can too.

You cannot control everything about your surroundings and you cannot plan everything that will happen in life. But, as in Bess's case,[7] the trigger, at least, is yours.[8]

---

[5] Even having thought about death is enough to trigger some safeguards, depending upon the healthcare provider and the interpretation of protocols involved. The prime diagnostic question in the Columbia Suicide Severity Rating Scale ver. 6.23.10 (2010) reads "Have You Thought About Being Dead or What It Would Be Like to Be Dead?" Kelly Posner, et al., Columbia Suicide Severity Rating Scale (C-SSRS) 3 6/23/10 (2010). Clearly, many people would answer "Yes!" to this question without being imminently suicidal or mentally troubled. Cf. Slides: Presentation to the APA (Igor Galynker, 2011) (on file with APA) (claiming a "Suicide Trigger Scale" might be predictive). Over a decade later, no one has deployed this or any similar trigger scale and harvested compelling predictive value from its scoring outputs.

[6] The classical depiction of Rumor (or Fama or Φήμη).

[7] The landlord's daughter in Noyes's classic narrative poem, *The Highwayman*. Bess shoots and kills herself while a captive of King George's troops, knowing the report of the weapon will warn her lover of a trap. The warning fails, however, as the enraged highwayman carelessly rides again to avenge her, only to be shot in the road "like a dog." Alfred Noyes, *The Highwayman*, 180 Blackwood's Mag. 244, 247, William Blackwood, et al., ed. (1906).

[8] Id. at 246 ("The tip of one finger touched it! The trigger at least was hers!").

History and Foundations of Permissible Suicide

SCENE I
From Whence We Came

Death is very likely the single best invention of life. It is life's change agent.
—Steve Jobs[9]

We live in a time of enormous wealth; to deny this is pure folly. The world has never been safer from want and famine, has never held so much knowledge, has never contained so much pecuniary wealth, has never provided for such enormous lifespans. It is important to recognize today we live at the gilt edge of a page recounting gilded ages, a truly marvelous time to be alive. To forget that we live in a golden age is to disrespect those responsible and mis-imagine our surroundings, to mistreat the Staphylas around us.[10]

Particularly if you live in a wealthy country, you likely enjoy a length of life, and a set of choices of what to do with that life, and a level of access to information and education that would have been pure science fiction to a young Jules Verne embarking upon writing his first stories in the 1840s one block from Philip II's palace (then a few decades into its transformation into the familiar *Musée du Louvre*) and a short stroll from two of the finest research libraries in Paris at the time.[11] And we inherit from earlier eras not only knowledge and circumstance, but our chromosomal wealth.

I might inherit superior genetics in terms of longevity to someone else, perhaps in the form of a stronger heart or a substantially lower likelihood of difficult cancer. And these biological windfalls are distributed throughout society in ways even today's brightest Cricks and Watsons[12] cannot yet decipher. Is it not my

---

9   Steve Jobs, 2005 Stanford University Commencement Remarks (June 12, 2005).
10   Alluding to the prologue in *Aulularia*, Plautus's comedy in which Euclio finds a pot of gold but lives in a state of continued "pretend poverty" to disguise his discovery; the pretending requires his mistreatment of his housemaid, Staphyla. See Plautus, Aulularia act 1 sc. 2 (n.p., n.d.).
11   Verne lived on Rue Jean-Jacques-Rousseau at this time.
12   Crick and Watson discovered the structure of DNA in 1953.

21

right to trim this longevity I've inherited (and bolstered through the good fortune of growing up with clean water and plentiful food and so forth) to whatever length I prefer, as I might disclaim and disavow any other inheritance?[13]

The problem raised by detractors is how such trimming occurs, which is not neatly with a scalpel, but messily with a pistol or a needle or a fall, a suicide.

In Buddhist temples across Japan are shrines where people ask for *pin pin korori*,[14] a happy, healthy life that ends with a quick and uneventful death. The latter bit is foreign to Americans and most Westerners, who are told not to speak of death, let alone pray for any particular flavor of it, though when it comes it may have been quietly prayed-for.[15] Death has been made more mysterious, more foreign, stranger in recent decades. Today, fewer than a third of American deaths occur at home and our familiarity with death is more distant than ever.

In the West, we are trained to see death as the villain of the story when it is merely a flash preceding the credits of the film, the climactic closing couplet of an epic poem. So much precedes it that is often worse than death, and this is hardly new.

> *Omni*
> *Membrorum damno major dementia, quae nec*
> *Nomina servoru, nec cultus agnoscit amici,*
> *Cum queis preterita coenavit nocte, nec illos*
> *Quos genuit, quos eduxit.*[16]
> —*Juvenal*[17]

---

[13] Drye v. United States, 528 U.S. 49, 53 (1987) ("Under Arkansas law, an heir may disavow his inheritance by filing a written disclaimer no later than nine months after the death of the decedent.") citing Ark. Code Ann. §§ 28-2-101, 28-2-107.

[14] 病気に苦しむことなく、元気に長生きし、最後は寝付かずにコロリと死ぬこと、To live a healthy life without illness but then to die quickly.

[15] Alluding to *hoc erat in votis*, or that is what was prayed-for. See Horace, Satires, 2-6.1 Roman Republic, n.d.

[16] Worse than being [physically] crippled is the loss of memory, no longer knowing the names of servants, or the face of the friend with whom you dined the night before, or the [faces of] children you bore and raised.

[17] Juvenal, Satires, 10.232–6 Roman Empire, 100–27.

Roughly two millennia after Juvenal, resolution is scarce on the fundamental issue of whether death or its preludes are worse. Undoubtedly, there are varying experiences in life that shape one's approach to death and whether that approach is a smooth driveway or a perilous path. Some will run toward death bravely, others will hide and inevitably be found and slain; our memberships in these groups are likely set early in our lives, our natures rarely transform. A thoroughbred responds to seeing the mere shadow of a whip, but some horses will not run even when bloodied with spurs.[18]

Regardless of which kind of horse you are in the metaphor, *supra*, you get only one life and can spend it in an unprecedented variety of ways. And you have more time and ability than any prior generation to enjoy and explore the world, with an arsenal of discount international airfare and portable supercomputers and free virtual classrooms that Hume or Schopenhauer or Durkheim[19] could not have envisioned. But in the case of suicide, acceptance has lagged behind other liberal progress (e.g., acceptance of homosexual couples in marriages, acceptance of atheism in the mainstream, etc.).

Acceptance is growing for the concept that an orchestrated death may be better than a natural, gradual, suffering demise. However, this acceptance is limited once the word "suicide" appears. For those seeking an affirmative, consensual, painless death rather than eventually mortal, cumulative decrepitude (or simply years of enduring a life whose best days are in the past), choices remain limited, and in the mainstream, suicide remains a whisper word rather than a plenary one.

---

[18] Alluding to (by loosely paraphrasing) Curtius's famous passage on the natures of things: *nobilis equus umbra quidem virgae regitur; ignavus ne calcari quidem excitari potest.* Q. Curtius Rufus, Historiarum Alexandri Magni Macedonis Libri Qui Supersunt, 7–4.18 Roman Empire, 50.

[19] Durkheim's framework, and rebutting parts of it, was a key inspiration for early work on this text. See generally Émile Durkheim, Le Suicide (Félix Alcan, ed., 1897).

Schopenhauer uses "voluntary death" in his essay *On Suicide*,[20] and I often use voluntary death, affirmative death,[21] consensual death,[22] and suicide essentially interchangeably. In essence, I view suicide as a bargain with oneself, and one that we should allow unless the ordinary exceptions to valid contracts are apparent: duress, force, incompetence, and so on.[23]

I view state interference, or the interference of well-meaning spectators, as tampering with the bargain the decedent-to-be crafted in thoughtful, introspective, lucid moments. Particularly harmful and needlessly cruel are state, hospital, church, or normative interventions that force suffering on the individual, whether the person's suffering comes from health woes or recent opprobrium or financial disaster or formal rejection (such as disbarment or defrocking or disfellowshipping) that might sever one from allies needed[24] to accomplish key goals.

Most regrettable of all is the forcing of suffering on the person who cannot fight back: the person imprisoned in a body damaged beyond repair, the person who cannot speak to instruct the doctors to cease care; the person who due to a conservatorship or other protective or custodial or care arrangement cannot express wishes in a way that makes those wishes known via the trustee or guardian or conservator.[25]

Enduring suffering may be noble or brave but should always be optional. Schopenhauer suggests "[t]he innermost kernel of Christianity is the truth

---

[20]   In Suffering, Suicide, and Immortality 25 (by T. Bailey Saunders ed. 2006) originally published by The McMillan Co. (1890).

[21]   Meaning a person affirmatively acts to snuff out life rather than waiting for its wick to drown in Nature's wax or to be extinguished by a random breeze.

[22]   I mean consent in the sense perhaps familiar to attorneys a century ago, not the narrow, modern oft-sexual concept.

[23]   See R.A. Epstein, Unconstitutional Conditions, State Power, and the Limits of Consent, 102 Harv. L. Rev. 4, 8 (1988).

[24]   Again, "needed" is best judged by the person being rejected from his or her cadre of allies.

[25]   To understand all three combined in a particularly troubling fact pattern, see *Guardianship of Grant*, 109 Wash. 2d 545, 547 (Wash. 1987) ("This case involves the situation of Barbara Grant, an individual suffering from the incurable neurological disorder known as Batten's disease. Barbara's mother and legal guardian, Judith Grant, sought a court order that would authorize the future withholding of mechanical or artificial life-sustaining procedures from Barbara.").

that suffering—*the Cross*[26]—is the real end and object of life." Where suffering, and not just any suffering but transcendent mortal suffering, is a centerpiece of a major Western belief system, it is unsurprising suicide (or, more broadly, the avoidance of suffering) is framed as cowardice by Christianity. I suggest the careful avoidance of suffering should be viewed as thoughtful, kind to one's self, and admirable.

To find a new framing, we turn away from *christlichermachisimo* and look to other traditions.

---

[26] Schopenhauer, *supra* note 20 at 29 (emphasis in original).

SCENE II
Looking to the East

十分 [27]

In many Asian cultures, ending one's own life is somewhat less taboo; however, wherever there is power, there is propaganda. Those in power want to use propaganda to their advantage and to prevent rivals or resistance movements from gaining control of the radio waves, the news headlines, the public square, main street mindshare.

In Chinese history, the Han emperors were willing to have Buddhist beliefs and practices (practices included not just religious practices, but also architecture, styles of art, the importation of certain musical instruments and styles) migrate from India to China. And so-called Han Chinese Buddhism (漢傳佛教) flourished during this period (the other historically prevalent kinds of Buddhism in China being Tibetan Buddhism and Theravada).

However, at the end of the Han dynasty, China shattered into a tripartite war among the Three Kingdoms (三國時代). The wars, lasting decades, killed tens of millions directly (through warfare) and indirectly (through famine, disease, and poverty). During this period, well-known historians and poets were often paid, threatened, or manipulated to produce propaganda that praised or supported one faction over another, or portrayed one leader as heroic or wise and another as cowardly or unscrupulous.

Liu Bei, self-proclaimed emperor of Han, wished to be seen as an ideal Confucian monarch, a philosopher king. However, it was during this period that Buddhism in general, and Buddhist monks in particular, began to

---

[27] The *kanji* here, pronounced *juu bun* (or *juu pun*), can mean "ten minutes" (colloquially "a little more time") but can also mean "that's enough." This dichotomy of "ten minutes" and "that's enough" being written identically makes me think of the ambiguity and confusion often present in deathbed requests to doctors and family, which is hardly something unique to Japanese. Thankfully, sometimes, there's more decisive instruction.

cause problems for the Chinese power structure. In the Yangtze delta area, which was logistically vital and strategically important to Liang's (諸葛亮) southern campaign, Buddhism was enjoying popularity, likely originating in Luoyang (in modern Henan province).

At first, leaders of the various factions thought they could use the monks to amplify their messaging and persuade the populace of the righteousness of their causes. This backfired and those trying to intimidate or bribe monks were the first to receive the monks' critiques.

The Buddhist monks felt their higher obligations required them to remain apolitical, and they refused to be bought or to be brought into propaganda campaigns sponsored by the rival states. In certain situations, when threatened with violence, the monks would kill themselves in ritual suicides that demonstrated their peace at a time of worldly squabbles, thereby contrasting their perspectives with the warring factions' obsessions with contemporary, and temporary, power and wealth.

Thus began a 2200-year tradition of tension between Chinese government officials and Buddhist monks, including posthumously after monks end their lives in protest. Today, it is difficult from inside mainland China to understand these deaths as protests, as China suppresses news of Buddhist monks' activities, comments, and deaths generally—and especially suicides in protest. The Great Firewall scrubs this type of content from the intra-China Internet, journalists are discouraged from discussing political speech and suicide, and certainly political speech embodied in suicide!

You may view these monks dying in protest as heroes. You may feel their deaths are pointless. You may think it's a strange thing happening in a land far away.

It doesn't matter what you think. Because that they wanted to die, that they thought they had a reason to die, that dying *made sense to them*, is good enough. Part of the premise of this book is that your reason for dying is just as valid as anyone else's and shouldn't be judged by anyone else. In Japan, this idea of death as an individual decision is more popular.

On a recent visit to Tokyo, I wanted to visit a nearby death café. These are cafés where people gather to discuss death and their plans for dying (including suicide). Some death cafés even provide referrals to lawyers, end-of-life planning, or (in at least one case) a van to 青木ヶ原, one of the most popular places to end one's life in Japan (where gaps in the trees provide occasional dramatic final views of Mt. Fuji to the southeast).

Awhile ago, near Ginza Station in Tokyo, a pop-up death café called シ Café (pronounced *Shi Café*) opened; like the *kanji* at the start of this Scene (十分 pronounced *juu bun* or *juu pun*), シ Café played on the fact that the sound *shi*, or "death," can be written a number of ways. The *kanji* for death, 死, is the same phonetic segment as the *hiragana*, し, and the old pronunciation of the number 4 (pronounced *shi* or *yon* today). The proprietors of the Ginza death café, however, chose to use the *katakana* representation of the syllable *shi*, シ, which sounds like death *yet looks a bit like a smiley face*!

I can think of no better simple symbol (シ) for the complexity of the Japanese philosophy and thought surrounding death and dying.

SCENE III
No Gates, No Gatekeepers

Look back, and smile on perils past.
—Sir Walter Scott[28]

Many want to die as fervently as the previous scene's monks, albeit for different reasons, or perhaps for reasons they are uncomfortable disclosing. We should not through legislation, through inconvenience, or through stigma treat people seeking death as various Chinese regimes have mistreated various groups. It isn't society's job to rank those reasons from meritorious to trivial to insane.

In a free society, we don't scrutinize why people join one religion rather than another, or why people make choices that might result in harm to themselves, from organ donation to skydiving. Such a society doesn't judge the speed at which people end their lives, allowing gradual suicide by ingesting tobacco smoke but disallowing faster suicide by ingesting other mixtures of chemicals.

"But," the prohibitionists interject, "here we're talking about irreversible self-harm. There should be special rules. What if someone has a flash of suicidal thought, acts on it, but this is a regrettable interruption in an otherwise happy and still-inhabitable life?"

Let's leave aside for a moment my core argument that it is the person, and not a bystander or doctor or family member, who is best positioned to judge whether his or her life is still worth inhabiting.

Elderly people in China often kill themselves to prevent mid-career, successful, moved-to-the-city children (who are often only children, thanks to the "one-child" reproductive policy of a generation ago) from having to abandon good jobs to return to the village and care for Mom or Dad. Indeed, suicides among those over seventy years old in China are 400+ percent more

---

[28] Walter Scott, The Bridal of Triermain, London, James Ballantyne and Co. (1813).

common than in the general population with the major drivers being loneliness and the fear of being a caretaking or financial burden to an adult child.

China has seen a substantial decline in its suicide rate as the country has become more prosperous; in fact, China's suicide rate (per capita arithmetic) has declined more than any other country's as the country has become wealthy. Today, China's overall suicide rate stands at nine per 100,000 residents; America's is fourteen. But the rate for Chinese residents over seventy is thirty-five in 100,000. In 2013, in a move to address elder loneliness, China legally required middle-aged people with elderly parents to frequently visit or send greetings.

In ancient times, the West and the East were more similar. While those who died dramatically in battle were saluted and celebrated, many who died by their own hands were also seen as honorable.

In Sparta, many were given the choice between banishment and suicide, and it was seen as honorable to leap from a great height or fall on one's sword rather than walking to the periphery of the realm (often to starve, struggle, or be killed in one's sleep by bandits). In Athens, Socrates was sentenced to public suicide; rather than be silenced by this condemnation, he used this as an opportunity to transmit a definitive statement of his position to his pupils before fearlessly and calmly drinking his poison.[29]

As recently as the late 1700s, the death of Socrates was seen in many quarters as heroic, fascinating, and poignant.

The story's separation of suicide (albeit state-ordered) from modernist constructs of sin, grief, regret, or mental illness is particularly interesting and highlighted in Plato's original account in the Phaedo and countless others in the following centuries. Apollodorus, a loyal student who wept as Socrates prepared to ingest the poison, was sent away for prematurely mourning Socrates's death rather than appreciating the final lesson . . . a truly epic final exam fail.

Socrates approaches death without fear because he does not believe his

---

[29] For a discussion of a modern analogue, see Michael Cholbi, Suicide: The Philosophical Dimensions 35–36 (2011) (discussion of hypothetical character named Dissident).

destination changes according to his means of death.

In other words, Socrates does not believe that he will go to hell having "committed" suicide; rather, he believes he will pass into a different space, and that death is merely the transportation required to reach this postmortem space. Hence, Socrates sees causing his own death as premature in time compared to, but no different in metaphysical effect from, having subsequently died in some other way.

Though Socrates' death could have been a model for how suicide might be well-considered, calm, and resolute, it became instead the edge case. Accounts in the 1700s began to emphasize that his death was punishment and focused on the procedural mechanics of the trial rather than discussing his demeanor.

Jacques-Louis David's painting of the event (showing Socrates defiant and calm), Jacques-Philip-Joseph de Saint-Quentin's painting (showing Socrates reaching confidently for the poisoned cup as one of his dismayed students tries to intervene), and Giambettino Cignaroli's painting (showing Socrates passing peacefully into death while students wail and weep) all highlight a 1700s view of dignified death, a person who, although accompanied, is fundamentally facing death alone and unafraid. By the early 1800s, the sympathetic renderings of Socrates' death surrounded by his students and friends seemed to be nearly forgotten and were no longer widely celebrated (and very rarely created).

The Church in a majority Catholic France saw any initiation or acceleration of one's own death as mortal sin, incompatible with canon law and ecclesiastical command. Paintings showing sympathetic views of self-initiated dying, even those of Socrates (who was given no choice but to die, having been sentenced to swig hemlock), were hidden from view or taken abroad. Jacques-Louis David's famous portrayal of the event, perhaps destined for the Louvre had it stayed in Catholic France, ended up in comparatively liberal America and today hangs in the Met in New York City.

It was not until the revival of stories of death (including suicide) as a dramatic element that discussion of such deaths was again allowed in newspapers and on stage in Europe. The revival (and, in some cases, modernization) of Shakespearean tragedies featuring characters who die by their own hands in the late 1800s and early 1900s (notably Cushman's revival of Romeo and Juliet) helped also revive the idea that characters who cause their own deaths could inhabit high art and the main playhouse stage, rather than being considered a macabre curiosity or too-light parody of a too-serious topic. For more on the cultural conversation underway at this time, I recommend Owen Chadwick's excellent The Secularization of the European Mind in the 19th Century (1975), which presents a sense of how gradual, yet important and radical, these changes of perspective and sentiment were. It is no accident the 19th century campus architecture of the University of Chicago features many sculptures and characters drawn from the grotesque, whether they are deformed limestone faces overlooking the Midway or eerily grinning gargoyles, perched and seemingly ready to glide over campus at dusk.

This period of reviving death[30] on stage inspired the unorthodox thespian structure of this book.

---

[30] Fear not; the irony of "reviving death" as a phrase is not lost on this author.

SCENE IV
In These Pews, Piety

If suicide is allowed then everything is allowed. If anything is not allowed then suicide is not allowed. [S]uicide is, so to speak, the elementary sin.
—Ludwig Wittgenstein[31]

Ahithophel[32] wasn't someone who suddenly, insanely, and impulsively killed himself.

Nor are most people who choose to die. Even in the Bible, suicides are generally deliberated upon, at least for a lucid moment (for the question of how long is needed to contemplate killing oneself or someone else see *infra* Act II, Scene IV). Whether Saul pauses before falling on his sword[33] is not relevant. Nor is it relevant how quickly or slowly Zimri plans or carries out the incineration[34] of the palace, which includes his immolation, ending his one-week reign.

Killing of others or of one's self in the Bible is generally not the result of people being crazy or misled or sick. Judas does not hang himself because he has unmedicated depression or is bipolar or just learned he has inoperable bowel cancer; he hangs himself because he is ashamed after betraying Jesus for thirty pieces of silver.[35]

Yet the Church has chosen to combine one of its most brutal rhetorical weapons (accusations of sin) with a weapon from the modern, secular

---

[31] G.H. von Wright & G.E.M. Anscombe, eds., G.E.M. Anscombe, trans. Ludwig Wittgenstein, Notebooks: 1914–16, 91 (1979).

[32] 2 Samuel 17:23.

[33] 1 Samuel 31:4.

[34] 1 Kings 16:18.

[35] Matthew 26:15 (betrayal); Matthew 27:5 (suicide). Despite having been told by the medical establishment since at least the 1950s that depression is a "chemical imbalance" we know little today about the role of serotonin and other chemicals in the brain (many, like Erik Hoel, correctly question just how little we might know by asking provocative questions like: "if serotonin levels aren't driving depression, why do SSRIs stabilize mood in some patients?").

world's arsenal (accusations of mental illness), creating a new armament against which defense is peculiarly difficult. But before this marriage of instruments, the Church's view toward suicide was one of strict prohibition while the liberal, secular view was more permissive, and even openly curious, on the topic of suicide.

This tension between the Church's view of suicide as mortal sin and a liberal view of suicide as occasionally interesting, romantic, or even heroic continues today (anyone with doubt on this should review recent secular literary scholarship on poet John Dunne's writings, comparing it with philosophy faculty scholarship on the same writings—a non-trivial number of scholars contends Dunne even believed Jesus's death was a type of suicide). The debate synchronizes with other controversies regarding aspects of modern society: societal defaults being set to the more permissive rather than more restrictive belief as groups mix (seen by the Church as dubious, characterized by liberals as inclusive), growing acceptance of drugs and behaviors not tolerated in recent decades (seen by the Church as worrisome, generally welcomed by liberals), and the decreasing importance of family as a social unit (viewed by the Church as tragic, seen by liberals as cosmopolitan).

One of the Church's frustrations is, no doubt, that its enforcement mechanisms are less effective than in the past, when misbehavers could have their bodies imprisoned (by lords or armies loyal to the See), their assets seized (through escheat), their lines of inheritance interrupted (with corruption of blood intervention in the estate process), their voices removed from debate (via banishment and excommunication or, later, book banning/burning), and even their souls explicitly threatened.

Today, only two arrows remain in the Church's quiver: social pressure and ecclesiastical threats, "If you kill yourself, you'll end up in hell!" But it is worth thinking briefly about how severe, and hence how compelling, corruption of blood laws were while in effect.

Corruption of blood is a concept in continental and ecclesiastical law imported across the Channel to the Anglo-American common law in the

1400s, a doctrine binding until the Corruption of Blood Act of 1814. French Catholic judges and Vatican legal doctrines proscribed high crimes and provided corruption of blood among the legal remedies available at sentencing. Its purpose was to taint, or make bitter (*aigrie, aigreur du sang*) the bloodline of the accused, to prevent his bloodline's accumulation of wealth.

The concept of corruption (or attainder) comes from the attinctura that indelibly stained not only the person's character who committed a high crime, but also compromised that person's ability to make bequests or transfers. This meant a man of land and title, once so penalized, would be unable to pass his property, hereditary titles, rights to income (as titled persons typically derived the majority of their incomes from being landlords), and other assets through an instrument of estate (such as a will).

Petty treason (the betrayal of one's superior in the regal hierarchy) and suicide were the crimes where sanctions most often included corruption of blood. The Vatican, which instructed the denial of Christian burials for those who had died of suicide as early as 1533, standardized the punitive denial of burials in 1562. Only recently, in the 1980s, did the Catholic Church again permit Church funerals for persons who caused their own deaths. Nonetheless, the Pope reiterated the Church's prohibition against suicide in September of 2020 and November of 2021, following Italy's first case of legal assisted suicide in 2019, that of a person who was untreatably and irrevocably paralyzed in a terrible auto accident.

What is interesting, of course, is that both corruption of blood (a doctrine created during Europe's economic rise after two centuries of stagnation) and Chinese policies (criminalizing not sending greeting cards to elderly parents) try to motivate against ending one's life by reminding people of intergenerational ties. In the one instance, by interrupting the flow of property and titles downstream to children. In the other, by criminalizing behaviors of children who are insufficiently communicative to their ageing progenitors. Both frameworks are broad-spectrum punitive, large-radius-of-harm weapons: they zoom out from the individual who is seen as at risk of suicide and punish her family.

While ending one's life may be more normatively acceptable in the East, in the West we still see an emphasis on preventing suicide rather than confronting the assumption that all people who end their lives affirmatively and willingly are either themselves insane or part of an insane cult or group.

Where does this judgment come from, our instinct to associate suicide with either individual or group mental illness? A large part of this is not a judgment at all, but rather an assignment of undesirable traits to another group, a partitioning or "othering" of people who contemplate suicide; this step by itself makes suicide something impermissible for "normal" people to consider or discuss (cultural prohibition) and creates distance between people who are "normal" and people who think about suicide who are, in turn, mentally unwell (normative diagnosis).

This combination of cultural prohibition and normative diagnosis intersect to make the typical person confident that (1) suicide is not okay to talk about and (2) anyone interested in talking about, exploring, planning, or carrying out suicide must be mentally unwell.

Once these first two pieces of intellectual scaffolding are firmly bolted in place, martyrdom and bravery in the face of death can be quickly reclassified as suicidal madness. Contemporary accounts suggest waves of Native American warriors throwing themselves before the US Seventh Cavalry were "crazy" and "suicidal" rather than engaged in a gallant defense of their homeland. Similar descriptions of mental feebleness accompany descriptions of the 1864 Battle of Atlanta where Hood's decision to challenge Sherman's dominant force (thereby losing more than two soldiers for each Union soldier lost) suffered accusations of "insanity" and characterization as a "suicidal" decision.

Why do we fixate on the mental health of the person making a decision that will likely lead to death rather than focusing on the decision itself? Is it that the decision to die makes us so uncomfortable that we must classify it as insanity before even considering the actor's rationale or the decision's effect? How did we get to this point of nearly global rejection and revulsion at the idea of suicide, and is that uniformity in perspective healthy, helpful, or productive?

I see in death a daily choice, sometimes a several-times-a-day choice, a valuable and treasured choice.

And I see that choice as central to the human experience.

SCENE V
No False Choices

Faith, as you say, there's small choice in rotten apples.
—Hortensio[36]

People are already making this choice. By 1970, about 50,000 people a year killed themselves in the United States. Over the past fifty years, that number has gradually but steadily increased. About a million people a year affirmatively and intentionally end their lives globally. My worry is not in the number of people, but rather in the freedom of each person to make this choice unjudged and unencumbered.

My argument is rooted in choice, freedom—individual agency.

Yet society wants to prevent him or her from choosing.

Society is intent upon preventing it.

To do this, society has taken up a position near the church and brought along its big-bore gun, the artillery normally reserved only for the worst cultural trespassers: an allegation of mental illness.

The first case is the stereotype, a Shakespearean Enobarbus or Lady Macbeth, haunted by guilt, sadness transforming to madness, unable to wash despair from one's hands, functionally unable to go on living. The second case is the "othering" of suicide, that thoughts of suicide indicate membership in a dangerous or strange group, like the American characterization of kamikaze pilots during the Second World War.

How did we get here? Why do we associate suicidal thoughts with mental illness rather than rational thought? Particularly in a society where planning is generally seen as meritorious, whether it's retirement planning or planning for a child's tuition, why is planning the method and time of our expiration seen as an investment of plenary resources only an insane person could make?

---

36   William Shakespeare, The Taming of the Shrew act 1, sc. 1.

We—the big "we," humans—have stigmatized suicide.

In different cultures and in different periods, it's been thought wrong to abbreviate one's life. Instead, the prevailing narrative argues, life should be one long wandering autobiographical sentence that only ends when its author is struck with a fatal period, perhaps preceded by an Alzheimer's-shaped comma or a metastatic semicolon.

For over two thousand years, people have characterized or classified causing one's own death prior to natural expiration as something that is either (1) evidence of insanity or (2) evidence of one's affiliation with an undesirable group. Sometimes, both—evidence of individual insanity *and* membership in a group of crazy people!

But, as Cholbi correctly points out, "a large number of people suffer from mental disorders such as depression and bipolar disorder and a large number of people suffer from the particular feelings . . . that are associated with suicidal ideation, [b]ut only a small number of those people try to kill themselves, and a smaller portion of those who try actually end up dying via acts of suicide. Therefore, it seems misguided to say that certain mental disorders or feelings of thwarted belongingness and perceived burdensomeness *cause* suicidal behavior."[37]

The idea that mental illness is a prerequisite to suicide or that suicide is strong evidence of the decedent's mental illness during life crumbles when subjected to even a whiff of empiricism.

In the ancient Mediterranean, the *devotio* was a common paramilitary or guerrilla tactic. Today, anthropologists refer to *devotio*-style deaths as "suicide with hostile intent." These were individuals from Greek, Roman, or Hebrew cultures who would infiltrate far behind enemy lines, perhaps sneaking into an important village or military area, and cause harm to the enemy, knowing they would die themselves. They might light strategic supplies on fire or try to kill as many enemy soldiers in their sleep as possible before being discovered.

---

[37] Cholbi, *supra* note 29 at 170.

Like other guerrilla tactics throughout military history, the *devotio* was employed more often by forces that were outgunned or outnumbered. However, it was seen as a demonstration of devotion (hence the etymology) to one's tribe, army, or cause—it was seen as heroic rather than cowardly. A soldier who snuck behind the line at night and killed five soldiers before being killed himself (where it would be difficult for the same soldier to kill five opposing soldiers in a conventional battlefield encounter) demonstrated that great odds could be overcome and that the enemy's numbers were not insurmountable.

The *devotio* is one of the few non-battlefield military practices known from the ancient world because it lives on in multiple contemporary accounts. It was successful in showing enormous devotion to a cause, terrifying the enemy as now even areas far from the line were not safe, and riling up or inspiring the allies who now believed a small unit could take on a larger army. The bravery of those taking on these missions was recorded in song and poetry, commended as not simply a sign of courage, but also a demonstration of savvy and intelligence.

However, as Christianity spread through the region, the stories of the *devotio* were modified.

In these new versions, the infiltrators who went far into enemy territory with the intent of killing a disproportionate number of their foes in spite of the certainty they would themselves be captured, tortured, and/or killed were seen as fanatics. The modern narrative we see today began to develop. The *devotio* was painted as a kind of mental illness afflicting radicals—leading to a reinvention of the term *devotee* (devotion being something that happened *to the person*, not something emanating *from the person*), which suggests the person is not a brave volunteer, but instead someone who has become crazed or been radicalized. Suddenly the motivating devotion involved was not a superpower coming from *the heart of the person*, but instead a defect in *the brain of the person* causing unnatural, illogical, or insane behaviors.

From the 100s BC through 500 AD, we have many stories of people who value their objectives enough to risk almost-certain death to achieve those aims. As with the *devotio* (the saboteurs, infiltrators, and assassins above) they are painted at the time as heroic, but often in retrospect as adopters of hard-line ideology or incurably mentally ill.

Many brave acts by the Jewish martyrs who fought against their peoples' oppression are recorded at the time, including men staying behind and defending holy objects and texts against intimidating hordes. Contemporary accounts suggest these were last stands, more akin to a captain going down with a ship. But these people are later portrayed as being members of a radical group or simply individually insane.

SCENE VI
In Times of Trouble

A rusty nail placed near a faithful compass will sway it from the truth.
—Sir Walter Scott[38]

In the Second Crusade, we read of Muslim martyrs, sometimes a band of five, six, or eight fighters (*najma*) with fewer horses than men, equipped each with only a scimitar, perhaps a dagger, no armor, and a few days' water and rations. But these small groups would organize as raiding parties, striking European troops at all times of day and night, moving seemingly silently within the *sirocco* (the desert wind).

More akin to modern portrayals of the Japanese *ninja* than contemporary retellings of the disastrous Christian Crusades' enemies, the fighters would attack European fighters. Often disoriented in the desert, carrying clothing and armor too heavy for desert warfare, escorting dying European war horses accustomed to limitless drinking water, pauses between combat, and time in lush pastures, these European units must have looked more like stranded tourists than formidable adversaries.

In one particularly famous raid, likely in 1148, a small Muslim squad silently enters and slaughters a camp of Christian crusaders. While they are successful and enjoy the element of surprise, another European camp within sight of the attack notices something is awry and, on horseback and well-equipped, quickly eliminates the dismounted Muslims with a volley of arrows and a mounted charge.

---

[38] Walter Scott, 2 The Fortunes of Nigel 311, Edinburgh, Constable and Co., ed. (1822). First installed in dialogue intended for Lord Glenvarloch in pt. 24, later used in at least two other texts. Originally accompanied by the musing "The nail is, then, reliable in a way the compass is not." Deep thanks to my dear friend Dr. Georgina Frances Coleridge Pearson, who read Scott's tedious and difficult prose with me (via Zoom, no less!) during 2020-21 and who remains my absolute favorite person to visit when in Scotland.

Solomon Bar Simson and Rabbi Eliezer bar Nathan, both learned Jewish chroniclers of history at the time, recount several similar stories of attack and counterattack, bravery and martyrdom. It is more likely Simson who witnesses firsthand many of these violent events and who coins the phrase that would later be loosely translated and (modernized) as "suicide mission."

The term "suicide mission" originates in this mid-1100s period and spreads quickly among German, Italian, and French accounts of the Crusades. It lives on today and carries the same double meaning it did a thousand years ago. It can mean a mission that is unlikely to succeed where anyone who volunteers is extraordinarily brave, or it can mean a mission where the person who undertakes it is very likely to die and hence the only volunteers will be fanatics, maniacs, or fools.

No doubt the presence of tall odds skews the recruiting process. Only certain types of people are eager to join a "suicide mission," to die martyrs, to fly kamikaze aircraft.

Are all of these people part of strange groups or insane? I'd argue against the presumption of unanimous insanity.

A generation after the sands of Aleppo, Mosul, Damascus, and Edessa were soaked in Christian blood of many origins (Flemish, Frisian, Norman, English, Scottish, Germanic, and of the proto-Italianate states), at the opposite corner of the known Occidental world, Icelandic poet Snorri Sturluson wrote his *Ynglinga* saga. In it, he describes in detail a kind of warrior not described or seen in centuries: the *berserker*.

On Trajan's column in Rome, which purports to describe the conquest of Dacia in roughly 100 AD, there appear muscular warriors who are bare-chested, wearing a pelt that covers the shoulders and features the head of a bear or wolf carcass atop the soldier's head like a grotesque helmet. The warriors are fighting alongside Roman legionnaires but use unusual weapons, heavy axes, and scabbarded daggers.

Though he could not have seen Trajan's column, the berserker character reappears in Sturluson's writing. Like the martyrs of the Crusade battlefields, and the fighters holding out against Roman and Greek armies centuries earlier, these men laugh at tall odds and embody the *molon labe* attitude.

The berserkers, sometimes wearing fresh bear heads still leaking blood onto the faces and chests of the warrior, were used by King Harald Fairhair as shock troops. Capable of levels of sudden and intense violence that would intimidate and confuse the enemy into retreat or surrender, they were famously unfazed by minor wounds and were thought to draw power from Odin himself.

"[Berserker] men rushed forwards without armor, were as mad as dogs or wolves, bit their shields, and were strong as bears or wild oxen, and killed people [with only] a blow..." records Sturluson contemporaneously with these events. The mental and physical preparation for the berserker is much debated, and may have involved intoxication, including early use of hallucinogenic mushrooms or teas.

The berserker is perhaps the ultimate evolution of this type of *übermartyr*. Powered by sheer rage, unable to perceive danger, immune from superficial pain, he runs toward death. The idea demonstrates balance: he is a highly trained soldier yet still able to draw upon his primitive rage. A hero, he fights skillfully but can concede defeat gracefully and welcomes death with bravery and grace. His last moments are spent on his back bleeding silently, or even smiling and laughing, admiring the sky above the battlefield and the beauty of the preceding combat.

Yet today, when we say someone has "gone berserk," we mean the person is crazy.[39] We don't mean the person is extraordinarily driven, dedicated, skilled, or invested. We don't mean they can draw on some primitive self and channel that energy into a project they're working on. The person is just nuts—that's what we mean. Why? Why are the "suicide missions" that were once heroism and martyrdom now illness?

---

[39] The berserkers in the Dune science fiction universe take this a step further; instead of being souped-up melee experts and voluntary martyrs, they are people from fish speaker groups under interstellar monarch Leto Atreides II punished by being sent on suicide missions. See generally Frank Herbert, *God Emperor of Dune* (1981). See also generally Fred Saberhagen's Berserker story series, which is not Herbert-designated canon and among fans considered disputed canon. Unlike in Nordic cultures in our timeline, the Dune universe berserkers are female.

All major Occidental faiths distinguish, or attempt to distinguish, between suicide and martyrdom. The first is cowardly, problematic, and forbidden. The latter is brave, laudable, and aspirational. But the man lying on his back, bleeding, smiling at the passing clouds has little use for society's taxonomies.

Mezzanine Champagne Thoughts

I can't stand it to think my life is going so fast and I'm not really living it.
—*Cohn (to Jake)*[40]

Is it a duty of adherents to traditional Occidental religions to not only abstain from suicide, but to advocate through policy or evangelism or other means to prevent others from enjoying the choice to die? In the area of law and policy, should religious people whose religions frown upon suicide use the tools of the state to prohibit and remove this choice (as has been done with abortion)? In the area of normative enforcement, should pious people become normtroopers on a mission to make people uncomfortable discussing suicide (as has been done with homosexuality)?

Or can such people hold their faith dear and reject suicide for themselves while being accepting of others who may want to end their lives affirmatively? Must rejection of suicide reach beyond one's own choices and become evangelical?

Suicide is a mortal sin, while martyrdom is a path to eternal recognition of one's righteousness; yet, they reside within the same entry in a more utilitarian thesaurus. The discussion of suicide or self-killing in Christian,[41] Jewish,[42] and Islamic[43] faiths is similar in that suicide is viewed as a disregarding of life's value (life being a gift from God) while martyrdom is using what God granted (an individual's tangible life on Earth) to advance a righteous cause or message.

---

[40]   Ernest Hemingway, The Sun Also Rises 9 (1926).
[41]   Compare Matthew 27:3–5 with Acts 1:18; see also Leviticus 24:17.
[42]   Jerusalem Talmud Sanhedrin 4:1 (22a).
[43]   Surah Al-Ma'idah 32.

But the lens of modernity blurs these lines. Distinguishing suicide from martyrdom is easy in a simplified parable or a tale architected for the purposes of illustration. What is heroic or not? What is brave or cowardly? These are difficult questions to answer decisively in the gray of life. Perhaps that's why it's easier to be categorical: if you cause your own death, you are either part of a strange culture or you are crazy.

"The Jews who died so that sacred items and texts could be hidden? They were in some weird cult!"

"The martyrs who fought to the last man outside Jerusalem? They were part of a group of fanatics!"

"The berserkers? They weren't brave soldiers; they were hopped up drug addicts killing people!"

"Bess in The Highwayman? She's a crazy young girl who stupidly cut her life short to help a criminal!"

The simplification that people who behave in ways that cause their own demise must either be part of an alien group too strange for us to understand or afflicted by mental illness too severe to be deserving of empathy is not a new view. It runs through nearly all of our recorded history. And, yes, at times of war and times of great strife, these events are more often recorded, but they are ever-present.

Diary entries from Union officers during the American Civil War recount wave upon wave of Confederate soldiers throwing themselves into hopeless charges, often with remarks that the rebels (Confederate units) must be full of crazed men. Ottoman descriptions of later battlefields depict men and horses being cut down with Vickers machine guns just as fast as the weapons could cycle, remarking that only an insane (*majnun*) enemy would continue fighting. Famously, in 1917, Maréchal Pétain (who replaced Gen. Nivelle as Commander-in-Chief of French forces) explicitly promised to order none of his predecessor's "suicidal" attacks as a tactic to quell French mutinies. Accounts of radio traffic from *Bunker Hill*, an American Essex-class carrier present during the invasion of Okinawa, suggest confusion when the ship was struck by a Japanese aircraft, and absolute horror roughly forty-five seconds later when a second aircraft struck the ship; some historians have likened the event to September 11, 2001, as the sailors aboard *Bunker Hill* realize they are being attacked using kamikaze tactics and the planes are crashing intentionally. In the Western press, kamikaze pilots were portrayed as both individually mentally ill and part of an impossible-to-understand crazy alien culture (the Imperial Japanese military).

We are careful where we discuss heroic death in our modern cultural canon; it tends to happen, in popular fiction, in the ancient past or the distant future. Places that are far beyond our reach, scenarios that are unlikely to repeat today. In the far past, we have Zack Snyder's 300; in the distant future, we have Spock's decision[44] to sacrifice himself in Star Trek: Wrath of Khan, and only when absurdly unlikely events are injected into the present-day can we discuss heroic death, as in the death of the Russell character in the set-in-the-present-day summer blockbuster Independence Day.

We can talk about heroism and martyrs. But one cannot profess the egalitarian "every life is valuable" motto without accepting that every decision to end a life is momentous. If one accepts that anyone with sufficient mental capacity to make that decision can make an equally informed, important, respected decision to die, then we should listen to every wish to die. We should take every wish to die equally seriously, just as we take everyone's agency to do things with their own bodies equally seriously. Death is something we choose to do with our own bodies. Jumping on a hand grenade or knowingly injecting a street-purchasable mixture of heroin and scopolamine designed for anticholinergic toxicity both take an instant of intense focus unimaginable to many, but available to all . . . in the right circumstance, the right surroundings, and while in one's right mind. They are equally enormous decisions; they are equally important expressions of resolve; they are equally deserving of society's attention, empathy, and even cooperation.

---

[44] For more on this decision, see Cholbi, *supra* note 29 at 111–13 (discussing Spock's death).

ACT II
Are You Sure
You Want to Die?
How Sure?

If One Thing Is Certain, Certainty Is Overrated

The secret of life is knowing when to stop.
—Alan Watts[45]

Suppose you'd like your life to end.[46]

How can you be sure that's what you want? We all have a sense of what we *want* and what we *want to want*. We *want* French fries. But we *want to want* a salad.

What we *want* is relatively mutable, malleable, and manipulated effectively in the short-term with cheap psychological ruses: a peripheral juicy billboard burger amidst a road trip, a whiff of freshly baked goodies as we pass a patisserie, or a glimpse of pornography that appeals to one's prurient preferences. What we *want to want* is deep, programmed, and cultural. We are told we should *want to want* to live, that even considering suicide is contrary to the most central kernel of self (in contemporary philosophy), is a squandering of God's greatest gift[47] to man (in much theology) or is associated with neurological chemical imbalances (in the sciences, particularly psychiatric medicine).

A common argument opposing access to suicide is the idea that no one who seriously considers suicide can possibly be in the right mindset to be sure it is the right choice and that mentally well people do not ever consider

---

[45]   Alan Watts, remarks (autobiographically recounted by Mary Jane Watts).

[46]   This framework of "consensual death" draws upon, and elaborates upon, thoughts from Jean Améry appearing in his book, J. Améry, On Suicide: A Discourse on Voluntary Death, Indiana U. Press (1999).

[47]   As in Kant, the present discussion does not require a wholesale rejection of God or an unraveling of faith, it merely requires that popular conceptions of God not be the sole moral authority by which actions are appraised.

suicide at all.[48] People considering dying are too impulsive,[49] mentally unwell,[50] or too young to be certain. On this last bit, there may be reasons to end life that are unique to young people[51] and arguably rational; for instance, if a young person is intimately acquainted with the climate literature and believes the world will be substantially less enjoyable, and perhaps even less habitable, during her projected one hundred-year lifespan. She might prefer to expend financial and other resources more quickly, visit beautiful parts of the world before they change, and die before the world sees unlikely-but-catastrophic-if-occurring outcomes (for instance, ice sheet collapse, massive ocean circulation change, and so on).[52]

---

[48] As discussed earlier in the book, this endorses the concept that all people who kill themselves are either individually crazy (the loner, depressed person archetype) or part of a group that is collectively crazy (Western 1940s reporting on Japanese kamikaze pilots or contemporary reporting on Jonestown, which was the first time many Americans had heard the terms "mass suicide" combined with "mass hysteria" or "collective insanity" in a mainstream media context). It also justifies certain quieting or censorship policies that, taken together, mean a person cannot discuss her thoughts at work without risk of a call to human resources, in the therapy setting without triggering a red flag protocol, among friends without being considered mentally ill, and so on.

[49] The pertinent research suggests no connection between the general "trait" of impulsiveness and the occurrence of impulsive or unplanned suicide attempts. See Marianne Wyder & Diego De Leo, *Behind Impulsive Suicide Attempts: Indications from a Community Study*, 104 J. Affect. Disord. 167–73 (2007).

[50] See Thomas Szasz, Suicide Prohibition 30 (2011) ("The 'diagnosis' of dangerousness to self or others' is the ideal tactic for justifying involuntary mental hospitalization: it forms the backbone of the commitment process.")

[51] I do not mean that young people are uniquely insightful in choosing to die; rather, young people may have different reasons to anticipate the present may be better than the future from past generations, whether that is linked to local political instability, climate change, or other factors. The accuracy with which these things can be predicted in the instance of any single lifespan is questionable, but so is the question of whether one will contract cancer or be struck by a bus. For more on suicides of persons under 35, see Louis Appleby, Jayne Cooper, Tim Amos, & Brian Faragher, *Psychological Autopsy Study of Suicides by People Aged Under 35*, 175 Brit. J. Psych. 168–74 (1999). For several insightful discussions of how reasons for suicide may have more to do with rejection of future anticipated conditions than dislike of present conditions, see generally Jean Baechler, Suicides (1979).

[52] The outcomes cited parenthetically are not fantasies imagined by this author; they are proposed as less likely but not impossible outcomes by climate scientists in the *IPCC's Sixth Assessment Report, Working Group 1*, which is accessible free of charge. Intergovernmental Panel on Climate Change (IPCC). Climate Change 2021: The Physical Science Basis. Contribution of Working Group I to the Sixth Assessment Report of the Intergovernmental Panel on Climate Change (2021) (https://www.ipcc.ch/report/ar6/wg1/). Also relevant to a young person's calculation of how long she might want to live, or in what type of world she might want to live, would be social cost calculations related to climate change acceleration, such as Kevin Rennert, et al., *Comprehensive Evidence Implies a Higher Social Cost of CO2*, 610 Nature 687 (2022). My thanks to Jenn Helgeson for pointing me to this lineage of literature.

But statistical forecasts of climate change and other macrophenomena are notoriously difficult to build, maintain, and tune toward accuracy. Wouldn't we want a person to be *certain* before changing her life path, especially if that path involves accelerated death? Certainty feels like a good standard from afar: if someone is absolutely, soberly, ultimately certain, then perhaps we should take plans to end life seriously. Yet what is certainty and how is it developed, gauged, and confirmed? It is at this liminal moment that "certainty" as a standard appears first imperfect, then porous, then fragile.

In the next sections, I set out to illustrate why the standard of "certainty" seems comfortingly clear but, in reality, is both inappropriate and impossible. Alongside this impeachment of the appealing-from-afar certainty standard, I will show that doubting the certainty of the person best positioned to decide implicitly deprecates the mental faculties of the decision-maker or otherwise infantilizes that person.

SCENE I, PART II
100 Percent Certainty Compared to . . . What?

The uncertainty, self-discovery, the unknown, these are many of
the qualities that make life worth living. Well, at least to me.
—*Capt. Jean-Luc Picard*[53]

To presuppose one must be 100 percent certain to elect to die suggests that the alternative mode of death—natural expiration—is totally meritocratic and equitable, something we know to be false. We all know of people who have been irretrievably afflicted by cancer at a young age or struck by a drunk driver while innocently traversing a crosswalk. That we accept randomness in natural death but require unimpeachable justification for choosing death seems odd, especially when natural death can be, and often is, much crueler than euthanasic methods.[54]

This relates to a concept I discuss in greater detail in the next sections: our society's strange relationship with randomness. We are willing to have people who are not "ready" to die, who want to continue living, killed by unexpected events because we accept it as part of living in a society that contains hundred-mile-an-hour-capable motor vehicles or chemical processing plants adjacent to rivers. Yet people who affirmatively express their interest in dying and declare they are ready to die are met with skepticism, interrogation, betrayal, and even sabotage.

This dichotomy where random occurrences are endorsed, but planned events are scrutinized is at least an analogously consistent contradiction across society, even if this author finds it puzzling in nearly every context.

---

[53] *Star Trek: The Next Generation*, The Masterpiece Society CBS (Feb. 3, 1992).
[54] Innovation in euthanasia is nothing new and will no doubt continue into the future. Recently, VR researcher Palmer Luckey invented a VR headset with explosive charges built into the forehead area of the headset and able to cause fatal harm to the person wearing it. See Andrew Griffin, *Oculus Creator Makes Virtual Reality Headset That Intentionally Kills People*, The Independent (Nov. 10, 2022).

We spend over ten thousand pages of legislation explaining our immigration rules, but also run a green card lottery to distribute immigration privileges semi-randomly. We spend countless hours discussing how much CEOs should be paid, but then distribute much larger amounts than the median Fortune 500 CEO's annual pay randomly through multistate lotteries like Mega Millions and Powerball.

Demanding certainty from those seeking death in a world filled with random death is at best curious and in my estimation unjustifiable.

And What Would 100 Percent Certainty Mean, Anyway?

Certain, when I was born, so long ago, Death drew the tap of life and let it flow; And ever since the tap has done its task, And now there's little but an empty cask.
—*Chaucer*[55]

There are two kinds of certainty when we are talking about suicide: certainty that the decedent-to-be wants to die and certainty that the method of death will match her expectations (in its ease-of-use, swiftness, painlessness, or other considered attributes). For brevity, the first concerns the certainty of the mind that it wants to die and has formed an intent to die (the *mens rea*) while the other concerns the certainty a suicide attempt (the *actus reus*) will succeed. Here, I discuss only certainty in the former sense, though certainty of success and reasons I favor widespread availability of very potent suicide methods is discussed in later sections.

To appreciate the impossibility of demanding absolute certainty when it comes to suicide, one need only consider how the American legal system approaches criminal trial verdicts.

In my research on juries, I'm always struck by the fact that we are willing to accept errors from juries in death penalty cases. Twelve strangers are allowed, based on an extremely narrow trove of knowledge about a person, to end that person's life. And because anyone in our society can be accused of a crime (correctly or erroneously), every denizen is constantly at risk of being judged by twelve others in a game with the very highest of stakes.

There are, unfortunately, many cases to which one can point where lives have been ended prematurely and contrary to justice (and contrary to

---

[55] Geoffrey Chaucer, The Canterbury Tales England (n.p., c. 1386–1400).

defendants' wishes to live) by juries. The jury is not a committee of twelve infallible psychics; if such candidates were available, we would neither choose jurors (semi-[56]) randomly nor require so many of them per case. Rather, the jury is a truth-finding machine with twelve moving parts (or, alternatively, a democracy with twelve voters) that exhibits many of the flaws, prejudices, and misperceptions of its dozen members.

Is the level of certainty needed to convict a stranger of a crime one that each juror must attain, or that the twelve of them must merge to create a cumulative community certainty that crosses the threshold?

Now that we are waist-deep in the more serious questions of certainty, we are close enough to the mechanism that we can see the gears are not merely spinning wheels; we can hear each tooth of the drive gear clawing at the next one and struggling to gain purchase, struggling to rotate the final pinion, and dislodge its default setting toward a new position: guilt.

But we notice for all its intricacy this machine is imprecise. We wiggle the gears and see there's a lot of play in the system. We notice its function is lubricated with a slippery mix of uncomfortable truths, including that "beyond a reasonable doubt" is well short of certainty.

> *The accused shall enjoy the right to a speedy and public trial, by an impartial jury.*
> —*US Constitution, Amendment VI.*

If we accept the criminal justice mechanism of juries is imperfect, then we must examine its failure modes, which are two.

The first, Type I error, is a scenario in which a person, who is not in fact guilty, is incorrectly appraised by the jury and found guilty. In another scenario, Type II error, a person who is in fact guilty is found to be not guilty. Most would agree the two are not mirror images; the moral offensiveness of Type I error is grave and, in the criminal justice context, overshadows the

---

[56] See generally Batson v. Kentucky, 476 US 79 (1986).

comparatively harmless Type II error (I argue, however, that *in the suicide context* Type II error of people continuing to live who would have been happier had they successfully died *does present* both a local harm and a social cost).

Type I error, imprisoning an innocent person, has enormous effects: loss of their abode, their relationships, their career prospects, their creditworthiness, and their prior life. To enforce the confiscation of the imprisoned person's liberty, the state deploys its overwhelming resources and exercises its monopoly on violence, to the detriment of the incorrectly convicted person and with harm to the society at large. In some cases and in some jurisdictions, the confiscation of freedom includes confiscation of life: a death penalty.

Thankfully, research suggests juries commit more Type II errors than Type I errors. In other words, it is much more common that a person who was in fact guilty is acquitted than that a person who was in fact innocent is found guilty. This is the balance one wants in a free society; the reverse would ruin countless innocent lives and destroy trust in the criminal justice system.

In courtrooms, we generally (with Japan being a contrarian outlier the OECD) want more Type II than Type I errors; we recognize Type I error in criminal cases as the gravest miscarriage of justice when someone is imprisoned wrongly and an irreversible use of the state's monopoly on violence when a person is executed wrongly.

Yet we accept some degree of error in each direction. One could argue, as I did in 2018 remarks at Oxford, that the range of ratios between Type I and Type II errors deemed acceptable is the foundational aspect of a criminal justice system's design.

Even in questions of Jovian gravity, our society settles for less than certainty. A jury that has heard voluminous evidence in favor of, and sometimes against, life and considered it carefully is disregarded in favor of a bystander's shaky recollections. Perhaps the standard is "beyond a reasonable doubt" or "to a moral certainty" depending on which legal system we examine,[57] but

---

[57] For more on this, see my published research with my friend and mentor Judge James A. Shapiro. See *The Hon. James A. Shapiro & Karl T. Muth Beyond a Reasonable Doubt: Juries Don't Get It*, 52 Loy. U. Chi. L.J. 1029 (2021).

these are incontrovertibly well short of "certainty" in its black-and-white sense; in fact, central to their phrasing is a flexibility, a shaken-not-stirred version[58] of certainty.

We entrust a jury that barely knows a person to use a less-than-certain standard in potentially ending that person's life. To demand a standard of absolute certainty for a person to end her own life is, in every respect, unreasonable.

---

[58] Shaken cocktails are generally weaker than stirred cocktails, thanks to their additional water content.

SCENE II
Are Any "Mistakes" Allowed?

Isn't it nice to think that tomorrow is a new day with no
mistakes in it yet?
—Anne Shirley[59]

Zooming out well past the statistical concentrations that policing practices and probabilities of arrest create,[60] if we are willing to have anyone in our society sentenced to die by any other twelve people in the society with a standard that is undeniably unscientific and would not be described as certainty in any empirical field, why would we impose a far higher standard (certainty) for the individual to electively end her own life? Especially when the individual planning to die is, absent severe mental illness or incapacity, the person best positioned to predict the desirableness and quality of future life?

In the case of suicide, we are currently not willing to allow for any mistakes. If there is any conceivable reason the person could have lived, then he or she *should* have lived, and the suicide was in error. Even more absurdly, the jury who knows the person best (the person's own mind) has its verdict nullified when it comes to this final important decision.

Even people who accept that some desired deaths are acceptable generally fall back to this seemingly tenable argument: that they aren't against an

---

[59]   Lucy Maud Montgomery, Anne of Green Gables 271 (1908).
[60]   The effects of surveillance and policing are uneven. To understand the former, see my published research with my friend and colleague Assistant Attorney General Nancy Jack; to understand the latter, see my published research on traffic stops and roadside ("*Terry* stop" in the legal and policing lingo) interactions between young Black men and white police officers. See generally Karl T. Muth & Nancy Jack, *Watching Watchers: Monitoring Police Performance as Public Servants*, 73 Nat'l L. Guild Rev. 23 (2016); see also Karl T. Muth, *Learning Facts from Fiction in Jay-Z's 99 Problems*, 111 J. Crim. L. & Criminology 1 (2020). And who ends up at the defendant's table in the courtroom is often the result less of uniform policing and some meritocratic prosecutorial calculus and more of a given policeman's attitude toward a given suspect in the wee hours of the morning; see Karl T. Muth & Nancy Jack, Timmsen*: A Crim Pro U-Turn or Just a Detour?* (currently in simultaneous review at U CHI. L. REV., GEORGETOWN L.J., and HARV. J. L. & PUB. POL.) (forthcoming 2023).

option to die, or even a right to die in certain scenarios, but they are against "mistakes," and "wouldn't it be a shame" if someone died who *didn't really mean it*, who wasn't *totally certain,* or who *could potentially have been saved* (while conveniently disregarding whether the person in question *wants to be saved* or if being told to live additional life is being *saved* or *sentenced*). Unhelpful, too, is the '90s cultural trope that suicide attempts aren't an expression of a desire to die but are merely a "cry-for-help,"[61] a provocative and risky mime performance of dying intended to draw the attention of others; yet another way we dismiss the formation and seriousness of suicidal intent: it wasn't a "real" suicide attempt, it was just a "look, ma, no hands!" risky moment, an oops, a moment of inattention/depression[62]/whatever.

When we look at suicide, we see no Type I error is culturally permissible.[63] "Everyone at work liked her," the mini eulogies continue. "I remember our childhood; he was great at soccer." Why should any of these things matter, much less be prioritized, in comparison with the decedent's lived experience, his or her own appraisals of life's value?

Any person who by anyone's account "should have lived" or "had reason to live" or "had so many friends" or blah, blah, blah is deemed to have made a mistake in ending his or her life. I argue that while society fears Type I error in suicide (people who "should not have died" and prematurely departed), the opposite mistake exists but is hidden in plain sight: Type II error (people who should have died and did not). A person continuing to live an unwanted life, prevented from the final act by legal mechanism or community norms

---

[61] "This wasn't a for-real suicide, Marla said, this was probably just one of those cry-for-help things..." Chuck Palahniuk, Fight Club 59 (1996).

[62] We are only now learning how little we know about depression. While most Americans believe depression comes from a "chemical imbalance" (an idea and phraseology popularized in the 1960s), the concept that a chemical imbalance, and low serotonin levels in particular, causes depression is still controversial and empirically questionable. However, the idea that something is chemically wrong has made chemical repairs (antidepressant drugs) hugely popular; today, one in six people in America is psychoactively medicated (and this does not include those who self-medicate with illicit drugs or alcohol). See Jeffrey R. Lacasse & Jonathan Leo, *Serotonin and Depression: A Disconnect Between the Advertisements and the Scientific Literature*, 2 PLoS Med 392 (2005).

[63] This may be subject to cultural variation; suicide is in many years the leading cause of death in Japan among men 20–44. See Andrew Chambers, *Japan*, The Guardian (Aug. 8, 2010).

or physical frailty, is no less tragic than Tithonus, on his mortal plinth, too weak to speak, watching his lover drift away—Francesco Solimena's 1704 painting of these events is particularly moving, if you have a chance to see it at the J. Paul Getty Museum in California.

In our society, any instance in which a person ends life and then with that last gasp, second, or neuron detonation regrets the decision is one too many.[64] This presumes zero deaths are always preferable to one or more. But this preference for zero over one is distinguishable from the demand that each person wanting to die advocate his or her case against a standard of proof (absolute certainty) we do not use in any other context.

Society also vastly underestimates the diversity of reasons for ending one's life and is too quick, in my estimation, to focus on physical pain and medical ailment as the only justifiable reason for ending life. The unanimously terminal cancer patient who "still has a few good months" is considered by many premature in seeking death, no matter how much pain is in play (pain that the critiquing bystander has never experienced for hours that become days, or has never confronted in the middle of the night staring at a blurry ceiling in solitary terror).

Imminent, diagnosable sickness is not the only reasonable scenario for considering suicide.[65] Some people look at life thusfar and declare "mission complete!" with few regrets; some suffer from unvanquishable sadness[66] and prefer death to psychoactive medication or perpetually impaired morale.

---

[64] For a formal explanation of this in terms of option theory, see Professor Avinash Dixit's 1992 paper, which specifically mentions suicides and the concept that a person who waits to end life may enjoy utility from these additional days or years. Avinash Dixit, *Investment and Hysteresis*, 6 J. Am. Economic Assoc. 107-32 (1992).

[65] Though it certainly is *one possible reasonable argument*. Though explicitly not writing about suicide ("[I'm not] talking about ... ending my life through euthanasia or suicide.") in *The Atlantic* in 2014, esteemed physician Ezekiel Emmanuel (who, as an oncologist, has no doubt encountered and pondered a variety of health and illness most humans will not) voiced his wish to die (and not prolong life) at 75. Ezekiel Emmanuel, *Why I Hope to Die at 75*, The Atlantic (Oct. 2014).

[66] I am not talking about people who are temporarily feeling down or momentarily upset. Reports of passing or intermittent depression were rampant during the COVID-19 global pandemic, yet suicide rates in most countries stayed relatively stable or declined during this time period, suggesting that even a communal global malaise shared via Instagram is not sufficient to drive suicide on a whim in any detectable quantity.

Some people have their fortunes transform in dramatic and unlikely-to-re-verse ways,[67] whether on the battlefield or in the boardroom or on the floor of the stock exchange[68] or in the divorce courtroom. The concept that bystanders opportunistically choosing obituarial language or physicians distant from the person's problems are better positioned to make these choices than the person experiencing the hardships is insulting and bizarre; how can these misfortunes possibly be felt, let alone measured, by distant acquaintances and mere spectators?

A person might be outwardly fit as the butcher's but finished with life— or internally broken or in pain in ways not vulnerable to analysis or repair. Yes, psychiatrists and doctors can feel around for hints of these ailments during brief office visits and clinical encounters, but in the best case, it's like trying to make sense of a haiku written about the patient . . . by reading it in Braille while wearing boxing gloves. Instead, I choose to trust the patient's autobiography, written in his or her own native tongue, with expressions of dissatisfaction with life that I see no reason to distrust, undermine, or cross-examine.

But others argue, "it's *crazy* to trust *their* perceptions of the value of life, or the value of tomorrow. People who think about suicide are *crazy*. *They* can't be sure *they* want to die because *they* aren't sure of anything! They're *crazy* people!" If these critics would briefly holster their mental health stereotypes, they'd see the question isn't how certain "we" can be that someone

---

[67] Professors David M. Cutler, Edward L. Glaeser and Karen E. Norberg's economic discussion of suicide in 2001 suggests there may be a value to delaying suicide if it is possible things will improve. See generally David M. Cutler, Edward L. Glaeser, and Karen E. Norberg, *Explaining the Rise in Youth Suicide*, - Risky Behavior among Youths: An Economic Analysis 219 Jonathan Gruber, ed. (2001).

[68] In Japan during the Asian Financial Crisis, many asset managers wrote comprehensive apologetic newsletters to their clients prior to ending their lives; many of their clients also revised estate planning documents, wrote letters to loved ones, and made other preparations prior to suicide. This suggests these suicides were not sudden and unconsidered, but rather planned and reflected upon. Japan's official suicide rate jumped 34.7 percent in 1998 and included both investment managers and investors who lost personal or family fortunes in the regional economic downturn, as well as a (much) smaller number of spouses and children of the affected investors; some scholars who study Japanese suicide suggest the 34.7 percent increase may be an *underestimate* if there are errors in calculation. For more recent analysis of this, see Ryo Abe et al., *Economic Slump and Suicide Method: A Preliminary Study in Kobe*, 58 Psychiatry Clin. Neuro. 213–16 (2004).

is ready to die; that job of arbiter is something we should not covet and should not create for doctors, judges, or others ill-suited to the task. The question is how certain "they" (potential decedents) feel they are, and "sure enough" to them, subjectively, should be "certain enough" for us. As Hume wrote, no one can question "that age, sickness, or misfortune may render life a burden, and make it worse than annihilation"—here, Hume is correctly framing "worse" from the perspective of the person living the life,[69] not the perspective of amateur actuaries trying to guess that life's value.

I recently read a lightweight human interest piece in a major newspaper about a couple where the wife died after fifty-plus years of marriage, and the husband died from a heart attack a couple of days later. This was lauded as mortal evidence of true love. But what if the husband had simply killed himself after his wife was laid to rest? What if he was *very certain* life was not worth living without his spouse's company? Could he ever be *certain enough*? Is only coincidental cardiac arrest worth celebrating and not a planned departure from life after one's work as a human and husband is done? It could simply be a passing sadness or an intense but reversible grief.[70] It could be he woke from a dream about his wife and found it disturbing.[71] Really, *how could he be sure his life is over*, one might ask?

---

[69] David Hume, Essays on Suicide and the Immortality of the Soul 588 London, M. Smith (1783).

[70] Often raised as an argument against suicide facilitation is the concept that suicidal planning is a passing or impulsive tendency or the observation that some who unsuccessfully attempt suicide do not reattempt (occasionally held up as evidence the person's attempt was not serious or was erroneously motivated). In fact, planning suicide is often a long-term project for the decedent-to-be and the fact that some who attempt suicide do not do so repeatedly tells us little about the person's intent or state of mind at the time of the first attempt.

[71] The idea of a person waking from a disturbing dream and being suddenly obsessive or suicidal is as old as the Greek epics and still pervasive in modern storytelling from biography to science fiction. See, e.g., the intriguing contemporary novel Sleep Donation. Karen Russell, Sleep Donation 92 Vintage Penguin ed. (2014) (eleven characters wake from nightmares and then resolve to die by jumping from bridges). Many thanks to my bookworm friend, Kristyn Fons, for recommending Russell's writings to me–I would not have discovered (and fully appreciated) them otherwise.

Can We Test Certainty?

*Attempts to explain the term 'reasonable doubt' do not usually
result in making it any clearer to the minds of the jury . . .*
—*The Hon. Tom C. Clark*[72]

What should we make of the fact that teenagers and women have higher
ratios of "attempts" to "successes" when it comes to suicide? Does it have to
do with their certainty or degree of commitment? Does it have to do with
their competence? Access to, or comfort using, certain tools (for instance,
painkillers versus handguns)? Likelihood of being promptly found, treated,
and revived (far higher for a suburban teenager's afternoon overdose than
for the self-inflicted gunshot wound of a middle-aged widower who lives
alone in a cabin in a rural area).

For millennia, philosophers and physicians and others have attempted
to quantify the depth of despair or gauge when life is no longer worth living. (Note: I do not believe sadness or depression is necessarily the most
important driver of suicide, but rather sober diagnostic consideration of
life's remaining value.)[73] But I argue that "certain enough" is *not the test* and,
frankly, *not even relevant* so long as the genuine intent exists in the decedent-to-be, however briefly. But swapping the word "genuine" for the word
"certain" doesn't solve our problem; it merely diversifies our vocabulary.
In an unbounded space, how would we design a machine that would test
whether the person no longer wants to live?

I've been thinking about, modifying, and discussing with students the
Nozick and Watts machines for years. But thinking about these topics on
morning bicycle rides to my gym in Hyde Park in Chicago, I came to the

---

72 Holland v. United States, 348 US 121, 140 (1954).
73 "I believe that no man ever threw away life, while it was worth having." Hume, *supra* note 69 at 588.

conclusion another machine was needed, my machine, which I'll call the Relief Machine. Want to learn more? Skip ahead to Act V, Scene VI.

One can think of safe spaces and safe periods in which to ponder one's demise. I've done that, but you may create ideas very different from those I've conjured.

The goal of this thought experiment is to illustrate that even with infinite time to deliberate and no distractions or stresses from "real life," we still struggle to be 100 percent certain of what we want (and not only in the context of death). That our whims and hopes at a given moment might indicate more about our preferences than more traditional contemplation of a decision suggests "certainty" is not only the wrong standard, but an unrealistic expectation.

BRIEF DREAM SEQUENCE
A Sci-Fi Interlude

*You hate yourself. You hate yourself so much you think you
deserve to die.*
—*Dr. Julian Subatoi Bashir*[74]

In Star Trek's 1990s franchise Deep Space Nine, Miles Edward O'Brien is
jailed by the Argrathi using a Nozick-like device (see *infra* Act V, Scene V,
Parts 1—3) that lets him experience a twenty-year terrible prison sentence
in only a few hours of real time. Importantly, O'Brien isn't given someone
else's memories of a twenty-year sentence; he actually experiences twenty
years in prison in a matter of hours (similar to the experiential acceleration
theorized in the "life dream" framework proposed by Watts, see *infra* Act
V, Scene V, Part 5). The memories created during this "time" in prison are
traumatic and include many details that "feel" real[75] to O'Brien, including a
memory of brutally killing a fellow prisoner in a squabble over food scraps.

O'Brien knows he did not actually serve twenty years in prison and others, including his best friend, have reassured him he was alone during the
several hours these memories were created (hence there was no cellmate and
no homicide). O'Brien is not insane or depressed; he simply is afflicted by
guilt over events that in fact did not occur, dialogue that in fact was never
spoken, and the terminations of relationships that in fact never existed.
But despite their disconnect from reality, these memories are very real and
genuinely troubling to O'Brien. So troubling that he pulls a firearm from a
weapons locker to attempt suicide.

We, as viewers of this Star Trek episode, empathize with O'Brien. He is
troubled by memories he did not create and that appeared in his brain by no

---

[74] Star Trek: Deep Space Nine: Shattered Mirror Paramount (Apr. 15, 1996).
[75] See generally Philip K. Dick, We Can Remember It For You Wholesale (1966).

fault of his own. He experiences worry, regret, and remorse for things that are real in his mind but not real to others, making it even harder for him to reconcile his thoughts and feelings with his family, friends, and colleagues. Though we see only tiny bits of the twenty-year prison sentence installed in O'Brien's head, we imagine it is awful, both to have experienced and to recall now. And when O'Brien grabs a weapon from the locker to kill himself, we have some understanding of why.

Why, I wonder, are we more sympathetic to this fictional character who has an accelerated, awful prison sentence implanted in his head using alien technology than we are to contemporary real people in our cities who may have similar worries, regrets, or feelings of remorse from "real" or "imagined"[76] sources? Why is the trauma O'Brien experiences during his simulated prison sentence any more deserving of empathy than experiences and memories others may have for reasons beyond their control, such as a violent, traumatic childhood or an accident-initiated brain injury or a false, career-ending accusation?[77]

We see O'Brien consider suicide. We even see the moment at which his deliberation is transformed into an intent to harm himself. No one in this Star Trek episode or any later episode of the series shames O'Brien for considering suicide or being moments from killing himself. No one disbelieves that O'Brien's memories of prison are valid reasons for him to experience trauma or valid sources of emotions, even if they are not "real" to the bystander. No one attempts to disqualify O'Brien from making important decisions in the future, the incident does not interfere with his promotion from Chief (ST:TNG) to Chief of Operations (ST:DS9), and his wife, Keiko, is understanding and empathetic. This suggests an enormously improved attitude regarding suicidal ideation and post-attempt workplace/personal attitudes in the future.

---

[76] Note that an experience during a negative hallucinogenic or opiate episode may seem just as "real" as a naturally formed memory and may be equally, or even more horrifying, to recall when compared to real trauma.

[77] Note that both O'Brien and Budd Dwyer plan suicide with a firearm after being falsely accused of crimes. Compare discussion of Dwyer's suicide following Act III, Scene II, Part IV, *infra*.

But while we're on "life-ending agency in the future" let me turn, very briefly, to the fact that people may in fact enjoy *too much* life-ending agency in the future when it comes to suicide. I'm not referring to the suicide booth in Futurama, which only kills the voluntary participant. I'm referring to suicidal mechanisms that kill others, who may not be consensual decedents, a not-often-discussed and troubling feature of many imagined futures.

Planetary-level self-destruct sequences appear in myriad places in science fiction and future-set fantasy. They range from a suicide in the Krell laboratory in the classic film Forbidden Planet[78] where the entire planet of Altair IV (albeit with only one inhabitant at the time of detonation) can be destroyed with the push of a button to the self-destruct sequence armed by Capt. Picard and Cmdr. Riker on the *USS Enterprise-D*, presumably capable of killing all hands aboard, including civilian scientists and children who had no say in their demise.[79] Similar to the *Enterprise* (but at much smaller scale), there are non-Marines aboard ships like the *Nostromo*,[80] like non-military scientists and civilian colonists, yet the self-destruct sequence is relatively easy to arm and activate (even for someone who presumably would not have valid command codes, like Ellen Ripley), endangering the life of not only the person triggering the self-destruct but everyone else aboard and people on nearby planets/moons/asteroids/stations/ships.

If we believe better or more advanced futures, or even fundamentally peaceful and altruistic Roddenberryesque futures, would feature mechanisms

---

[78]   MGM (1956).

[79]   See, e.g., Star Trek: The Next Generation: 11001001 CBS (Feb. 1, 1988). Some number of civilians are aboard the *Enterprise-D*, though this number is not discussed in detail and seems to vary substantially during Star Trek: The Next Generation. We do, however, occasionally see elderly people, people not in Starfleet uniform, children too young to serve in Starfleet, and personnel with agricultural, diplomatic, scientific, and other roles aboard. Occasionally, the *Enterprise-D* transports substantial numbers of civilians during evacuations, refugee crises, and similar scenarios. In other words, not everyone killed in a self-destruct of the starship would have died in the line of duty. In at least one notable case, the number of civilians aboard is so large that some reside in the ship's cargo hold for a period of days, a la the English rescue of Haitians near Môle-Saint-Nicolas during the Napoleonic Wars, where families took refuge with belongings, children, and even livestock in English warships' lower decks and magazines; see Star Trek: The Next Generation: Up the Long Ladder CBS (May 20, 1989).

[80]   Aliens Twentieth Century Fox (1986).

that kill everyone within a quarter lightyear of the button-presser, then we must at least consider that at least one possible, habitable, good future would include a machine that kills only the button-presser. This book does not advocate for the planetary self-destruct button; in fact, I strongly oppose such mechanisms and believe suicides that endanger nonconsenting others are terribly irresponsible (such as leaping from a rooftop onto crowded, mid-day, midtown sidewalks below or killing oneself by driving recklessly on a busy highway). But this book does advocate for the button-presser's right to, without harming anyone else, press a button and die.

To flip the button pushing to be a button's release, I'll carefully para-phrase comments I once recorded (with his permission) at Camp Lem, Djibouti from one of my dear friends (circa 2011, and this person is still alive today circa 2023):

"It's only two hundred bucks. You buy the stamp and you can buy a machine gun, or a suppressor, or an explosive device, like a grenade [under the National Firearms Act, which requires a $200 stamp transfer tax on machine guns and explosive devices and silencers]. And I plan to lie down in my tent, on a sleeping pad I've used for years, with a pillow that smells like campfires, and I'll fall asleep gripping that grenade under the pillow, holding it tight. But, later, I'll doze off and release that safety lever and the trigger will contact the detonator and that explosive charge will blow right through my pillow and blow off my head in the northern Arizona desert, under all the stars I hope my fellow humans someday get to visit."

Hey, my dear friend: I hope you get to die that way.

I really do.

SCENE IV
Empowerment to Infantilization

Killing one's self is hard to do, requiring courage and fearlessness that few of us possess.
—Michael Cholbi[81]

Discussions about suicide prohibition often center on the irresponsibility or impulsiveness of others and rarely involve concern about one's own ability to judge when to end life. I've never heard someone say, "My worry about permissible suicide is that I'm so impulsive I might just have a bad day and end my life." It always focuses on *someone else's* impulsiveness,[82] whether the teenager after a teary breakup or the middle manager after being told unexpectedly he's redundant or the idiot cousin who decides to end it all after his whelk stall fails. This fits with the framework that *we* need access to maximum latitude/freedom/innovation while *they* need limits imposed via maximum supervision/regulation/guardrails ("rules for thee but not for me").

We (the individual, "each of us" we) are reasonable, thoughtful, contemplative, and unwavering in our sobriety. But everyone else is wild! They pick up hitchhikers on the highway near the prison. (We put up signs to help combat this.) They let their children do and play with dangerous things. (We increasingly make sure their kids only do these things inside videogames or in other virtual spaces.) They push all the buttons all the time. (We put warnings to try to control this behavior.) It isn't the wise and circumspect *we* who need protection; it's the careless and foolhardy *they* who need protection.

---

[81] Cholbi, *supra* note 29 at 173 (discussing Joiner's decision-making framework).
[82] This is true even in the psychological literature, see Craig J. Bryan & M. David Rudd, *Advances in the Assessment of Suicide Risk*, 62 J. Clin. Psych. 185–200 (2006); J. John Mann, Christine Waternaux, Gretchen L. Haas, & Kevin M. Malone, *Toward a Clinical Model of Suicidal Behavior in Psychiatric Patients*, 156 Am. J. Psych. 181–89 (1999).

Above: "We're protecting you from yourselves." A bilingual placard in
Dubai struggles to control the otherwise-unrestrained, feral button-
pushing impulses of the public. Photo taken by the author.

This idea that the autobiographical individual is introspective, deliberate, and empowered while the nameless, faceless others in society are
impulsive, uncontrollable, and rowdy runs through nearly every debate in
today's America.[83] From abortions to alcohol to firearms to foul language for
emphasis, of course *we* use these things responsibly, sparingly, and harmlessly,

---

[83] Empirical research in choice theory shows people will reduce others' range of choices because they
believe others (strangers) cannot be trusted with a wider range of choices, even if that wider range of
choices includes choices preferable to everyone. (Choices that generate economic or social surplus for
the larger group, including the person omnipotently designing the range of available choices.)

but it's the other people who need policing, limitations, and discipline.[84] We can use *the whole fucking dictionary* properly, but everybody else needs to be warned of PG-13 dialogue.

But you may think, "I know someone very impulsive![85] Precisely the kind of impulsive person who would kill herself on a whim after a bad day at work!" But the argument that impulsiveness is a key driver of suicide seems weak: are older men much more impulsive than younger ones, or white people much more impulsive than other racial groups, or doctors dramatically more impulsive than attorneys or chemists or economists or physicists? And, if not, why are these people so overrepresented in suicide statistics?

If impulsiveness is not a significant driver of suicide rates, then what causes us to want limitations on the availability of suicide? It is not the limitation of our own actions, the staying of our own hand, but instead, it's the chaperoning of the hypothetical, intermittently suicidal, problematic person that we perennially imagine yet somehow never encounter.[86]

---

[84]   Often, as Professor Douglass North and other scholars and philosophers of various political persuasions and directions point out, advocacy efforts for enlarging the state focus on the problems others may cause each other or themselves, that the paternalistic bureaucracy is not merely there to detect prohibited activities but to keep order in a much broader sense. "The State is this organized bureaucracy. It is the Police Department. It is the Army. The Navy. It is the prison system, the courts, and what have you; this is the State: it is a repressive organization. *[imitating a participant in a faux-colloquy]* But you've got to have the Police. If there was no Police, look at what you'd be *doing to yourselves.* You'd be *killing yourself if there was no Police.*" Omali Yeshitela: remarks (date of recording disputed) (emphasis added).

[85]   If sudden, impulsive suicides caused by anxiety or unexpected disturbances in one's sanity or situation are the norm, one puzzles anecdotally to understand why the suicide rate during a global pandemic that caused a time of more uncertainty, unemployment, and self-reported mental health issues than any other event in recent memory did not cause the suicide rate to increase. In fact, the suicide rate during the COVID-19 pandemic in 2020 was 13.5 deaths per 100,000, appreciably down from 14.2 deaths per 100,000 in pre-pandemic 2018. Further, despite "Record Levels of Sadness" (self-reported), suicide rates simply do not match self-reported unease; see generally Azseen Ghorayshi & Roni Caryn Rabin, *Teen Girls Report Record Levels of Sadness, C.D.C. Finds,* The New York Times (13 Feb. 2023).

[86]   Some phenomena are, however, legitimately episodic and might cause varying degrees of desire for death. Consider, for instance, a terribly painful, chronic illness that abates intermittently, allowing the person to construct a framework or lived experience during times of calm that might be helpful during times of pain; living through such an illness might have dividends that some might value and others might not. This has been called "learning to live well within physical and mental constraints" and for more it is worth examining and contemplating Professor Havi Carel's essay, Havi Carel, *Ill, But Well: A Phenomenology of Wellbeing in Chronic Illness,* Disability and the Good Life 243 Jerome E. Bickenbach, Franziska Felder, & Barbara Schmitz, eds. (2014).

Our concern about the imagined, impulsively suicidal person suggests that a speedy decision cannot be a considered a thoughtful decision, an argument with which I disagree. These people argue, with emotion but lacking any other compelling aspect, that people should not be allowed to purchase firearms or stand on bridges or order sodium nitrite suicide kits next-day (or perhaps same-day, with the wonders of modern logistics) from online retailers without a waiting period, a cooling-off period, or some other period.

But this imposition of time (a waiting period, for instance) as a litmus test suggests what we really desire is a test of commitment, of certainty.

A person less committed or less certain will not have as durable and perennial a wish to end life, one might theorize, and so suicidal desires might be eroded by time's soft tidal caress, like a teenaged crush. But many are set on the goal of death.[87] One might theorize from the evening news that most suicides are dramatic leaps from bridges, just as that same news source would suggest most kidnappings are carried out by strangers leaping from alleyways; in reality, many suicides are well-planned events and not passing whims, just as most kidnappings are failures of spousal custody negotiations and not "stranger danger" Scooby Doo capers.

Here, it is useful to introduce and explore an unusual dichotomy: *intensive* versus *extensive*. Now intensive and extensive are not colloquially antonyms (unlike interior/ exterior or introvert/extrovert), but they are mutually exclusive in the framework I propose here. *Intensive* thought about death is

---

[87] Some recent research purports to study the characteristics of people who survive a first suicide attempt, regret the attempt, and do not re-attempt or believe in retrospect the attempt was a mistake. This could be for any number of reasons and the reasons a person may attempt or choose not to re-attempt are enormously diverse. In Act VI, Scene III, *infra*, I discuss the hypothetical 1980s HIV/AIDS patient who chooses to die rather than suffer a gradual, terrible death as the immune system fails; however, a few years later, the outlook for such patients improved markedly. It may be reasonable for: (1) a person suffering from HIV/AIDS during this time period to want to die in a painless and controlled way, (2) a person suffering from HIV/AIDS a few years later to want to live with the disease, given treatment advances, and (3) a person in the first scenario, who attempts suicide unsuccessfully, to now want to live and to now consider the attempt a mistake, given new information about HIV/AIDS patient outcomes. Most of the studies in this area are small, sample-size with substantial qualitative taxonomical work, such as use of the very-much-open-to-interpretation Columbia Suicide Severity Rating Scale in Isabella Berardelli et al., *Clinical Differences Between Single and Multiple Suicide Attempters, Suicide Ideators, and Non-suicidal Inpatients*, 11 Frontiers Psych. 1 (2020).

all-absorbing, emotional, jarring, and energy-expending. *Extensive* thought about death can be, and often is, calm and peaceful, perhaps even meditative, and can include feelings of gratitude, consideration of one's friendships and kinships, contemplation of the nature and value of each future day of life as an optional activity rather than a mandatory obligation. Intensive thoughts about death might occur during a skydive; extensive thoughts about death might occur in an *onsen* . . . though, if we're talking about skydiving, I've squeezed extensive thoughts about death into brief freefalls.

People envision suicide being an *intensive* focus on the end of life, a sudden and extreme set of feelings, an insuppressible manic episode of excitement about dying. In reality, however, preparation for suicide can be an *extensive* survey of the available options, of which death is only one. Accepting the certainty of the decedent in decision making is, in my view, only possible when one stops focusing on the imagined *intensity* of the moment of life's termination and focuses instead on the *extensiveness* of one's inventory, contemplation, and consideration of life that makes suicide possible for otherwise rational, thinking, caring people.

Yes, suicide can involve *intensive* thought about death. But it might not include *extensive* thought about life, its nature, its value, and its desired duration.

Remember when we discussed certainty and juries, who do their best, but are demonstrably fallible? Stroll again with me back across campus from the philosophy department to the law school as I would argue even a moment's epoch gives plenty of time for a person to consider a choice.[88]

---

[88] See discussion of the Carroll Rule, *infra* Act III Scene IV.

SCENE V, PART I
Does Death Have Prerequisites?

Nor can a soul die except by Allah's leave; the term being fixed
as by writing.
—*Qur'an*[89]

To talk seriously about the choice to die today or live to see tomorrow, we must dig somewhat deeper than the catchy, deep chorus of Vampire Weekend's *Harmony Hall*[90] (though that song does correctly position dying as a choice to be considered and made).

Beyond merely an impulse, some think suicidal thoughts are always the symptoms of an ailment, rather than the formation of an acceptable set of preferences. Let's explore this line of argument—if there is "something wrong" with people who contemplate suicide that impairs them from forming clarity of intent to carry out the mortal act, that reduces their capacity to form ideas and make decisions, what exactly is it that's wrong?

It could be, to borrow from Professor Meir Dan-Cohen's analysis years ago in Harvard Law Review,[91] either a disease or a disability.[92] A disease is something that afflicts someone, that requires coping, but that can in some cases be cured; many consider suicidal thoughts the symptom of a mental disease. A disability is something that afflicts someone and requires coping but that often cannot[93] be fundamentally "cured" or wholly reversed; instead, the disability is integrated into the person's

---

[89] Ch. 3 (Surah Al-Imran verse 145).
[90] On Harmony Hall Columbia Records (2019).
[91] Meir Dan-Cohen, *Responsibility and the Boundaries of the Self*, 105 Harv. L. Rev. 959–1003 (1992).
[92] I replace Professor Dan-Cohen's somewhat dated term "handicap" with "disability" here with no fundamental amendment as to meaning.
[93] Amazing contemporary advances in machine vision or camera prosthesis for the blind and the advent of various augmentations for those missing limbs or parts of limbs (who in some cases can run faster and leap higher than their track and field peers with natural feet) are beginning, happily, to invalidate this taxonomy in select contexts.

life;[94] many consider suicidal thoughts the symptom of an immutable impairment or disability.

In either case,[95] to suggest that all people experiencing suicidal thoughts are either diseased or suffering from an immutable disability seems a remarkably broad taxonomical (much less epidemiological) brush with which to go about painting the society. But whether suicidal contemplations are something to be managed or cured (as with a disease) or something to be overcome and lived with (as in a disability), eroding and invalidating the person in question's decision making while that person is afflicted with these alleged difficulties seems to disregard all of that person's merits, expertises, and intents, putting all the tools and avenues for that person's agency in setting her own path in the dark shadow of a mental health total eclipse.

In other words, the argument that the very consideration of suicide is irrefutable evidence that a person lacks the capacity (mentally, morally, or otherwise) to make the ultimate decision infantilizes and shames those who even give glancing consideration to ending their lives and creates a false baseline that "normal" people have never considered suicide. (Therefore, anyone who has had even a moment's thought of suicide is abnormal.)

I dislike, and disagree with, this line of thinking because it suggests that (1) there is no person who could reasonably choose or contemplate dying who is not so severely mentally ill as to invalidate that person's ideas and choices or (2) it is impossible to form the intent to end one's life with enough certainty that society should endorse the individual's decision without further review or scrutiny. Instead, I believe we must accept that it is not only possible[96] to form the intent to end one's own life but common. And that

---

[94] For an eloquent description of this, see Dan-Cohen, *supra* note 94 at 996.

[95] For discussion of first disease and then disability and each's implications for self-direction and agency in decision making, see debates in the House of Lords related to the famous case Bedder v. Director, 2 All E.R. 810 (H.L. 1952) (debating murder of sex worker by frustrated flaccid punter).

[96] We accept that, though it is antisocial and distasteful, some are able to form the intent to kill others without being mentally ill themselves; if we did not believe this, insanity would be an overwhelmingly more common (perhaps universal) defense in cases of homicide. Instead, we know some people are able to form plans to kill others and to carry out those plans not in a burst of madness but within an orderly

this intent is worthy of respect rather than pity and deserving of space rather than censorship in the public conversation.

---

execution of a plan. Why should we dismiss the possibility that a person can have the same premedita-tion, planning, and follow-through in ending her own life? See Joshua Dressler, Understanding Criminal Law § 31.03(C)(1) 514 5th ed. (2009) (explaining what terms like "wilful, deliberate, premeditated" mean in jurisprudential settings); see also Julie Engels, *Mens Rea: Purpose to Kill Offenses*, 36 Loy. L.A. L. Rev. 1401, 1403 (2003) (exploring premeditation and plenary processes for homicide).

SCENE V, PART II
Knowing Thyself

You either live life—bruises, skinned knees and all—or you
turn your back on it and start dying.
—Capt. Christopher Pike[97]

Any doubt cast on the individual's position as the person best-situated to gauge the desirableness of future life (and, also, the desirableness of terminating life and thereby avoiding further life) is an attack on the capability and credibility of the decision maker. Why do we doubt the person with the most at stake in a literally life-or-death decision is trying his or her hardest to make the best choice given the information available? We can only expect people to make the best choices possible given the information available and the reasonable expectations they might form from that information. After all, it isn't Robin Williams's fault he was misdiagnosed with Parkinson's, a degenerative and incurable ailment; suicide may have been the "right" choice for him given the information available (and presented as medically accurate)[98] at the time.

We trust people even less to make this decision when they are young. New York lawyer Cheslie Kryst wrote an insightful essay in Allure Magazine[99] perhaps foreshadowing her death (the piece was written a year prior to her leap from a New York building).[100] She wrote not of the norms forbidding planning

---

[97]   Star Trek: The Original Series, The Cage Desilu Productions (Oct. 15, 1988).

[98]   A key principle in decision sciences and in economics is that people attempt to make the best decisions given (1) the possible choices known to that person and (2) the information available to that person. In other words, there may be another choice that was optimal but unseen by the decision maker; equally, there may be hidden or not-yet-available information that would have changed the decision of that decision maker. In the Robin Williams situation, better information (a more accurate diagnosis) might have led to a different decision.

[99]   Various versions of this article exist online, but most are dated during the first week of March 2021. As of this writing, *Allure* offers an archival copy: Cheslie Kryst, *A Pageant Queen Reflects on Turning 30*, Allure (Mar. 4, 2021) https://www.allure.com/story/cheslie-kryst-miss-usa-on-turning-30.

[100]   As I state elsewhere in this text, I disagree strongly with Kryst's choice of method and believe anyone

one's death but instead of other norms that made the remaining years of her life likely to be less fulfilling. Kryst wrote, "Why work so hard to capture the dreams I've been taught by society to want when I continue to only find emptiness?" and noted, "Society has never been kind to those growing old, especially women." After her final birthday, she wrote that she was "searching for joy and purpose on my own terms—and that feels like my own sweet victory" and a few hours prior to landing on Forty-Second Street in Midtown Manhattan, Kryst penned a message to acquaintances: "May this day bring you rest and peace."

If I told you Ms. Kryst was seventy years old and had lived a full life,[101] how would that affect your view of her death? What if she were sixty years old? Fifty years old? Forty years old? Thirty years old?[102] It is natural to create fractions in our heads when we read these numbers, that perhaps forty years of life over a denominator of eighty years of natural life expectancy is dying "halfway"—"what a waste," some would exclaim!

To this, I raise the example of James Knox Polk, the eleventh president of the United States. Polk, a Democrat, had a list of four goals for his presidency,[103] which were communicated on the day he took office to his cabinet and to select others within his close friend group. Due to a combination of managerial effectiveness and luck (especially in the case of Mexican negotiations), Polk managed to achieve all four goals in his first term. As a result, he declared his work done and his contribution to the United States complete, choosing not to run again in 1848, though many historians believe he would have won a second term.

---

choosing to throw themselves into a crowded street (as Kryst and McHale did) is also choosing to endanger the public below and making a fundamentally flawed, awful, and malicious choice.

[101] Whatever a "full life" means, a definitional matter on which reasonable minds can and should differ and debate (but should, in the end, evaluate autobiographically rather than biographically).

[102] The suicide rate in the United States among young people doubled from the 1950s to early 2000s. See Gary S. Becker and Richard A. Posner, *Suicide: An Economic Approach* at *8 Working Paper (Aug. 2004) (on file with author).

[103] The communicated goals were: (1) reducing transatlantic tariffs, which Polk correctly thought hurt American consumers more than European producers, (2) the creation, or in Polk's view the restoration, of the independence of the US Treasury, (3) the annexation of the Oregon territory with a path to its eventual statehood, and (4) the acquisition of California from Mexico, either through a transaction or a treaty or both.

Polk isn't seen as a "quitter" or as a "loser" because he didn't run again; on the contrary, he is seen as a person who thoughtfully limited both the scope and time of his presidency.

The Polk example parallels an example that Annie Duke raises in her newest book,[104] which is to imagine two people: one who sets out to run a marathon and stops halfway, and other who sets out to run a half-marathon and finishes the race. We call the first person a quitter, while the other person is lauded *for having run precisely the same distance.* As in the example of the Polk presidency, it is absurd to say the person who is happy having run a half-marathon should continuing running beyond the goal and run a marathon instead.

Now let's modify Duke's dichotomy. Say a well-regarded medical doctor with the wonderful ability to assess physical fitness from afar witnesses the first person finishing the half-marathon. The person is elated at having finished in a good time and is still feeling fit, not short of breath, but she is ready to leave the race area and enjoy a Sunday brunch. The physician intervenes and says, "Hey, I see you're still in good shape and you look like you could continue running. I don't care that you're happy with your 13.1 miles. I don't care that you've only prepared to do 13.1 miles today. I don't care that you're not interested in running further that or your friends are here ready to meet you for brunch. You should keep running."

That's how physicians interact with people Ms. Kryst's age when they discuss suicide; they are not only dismissive of the accomplishment of the half-marathon, they are insistent the person run the full marathon—a separate thing for which the person has not prepared and in which the person has no interest. To continue the metaphor, the finish line for the half-marathon may be a place of celebration, accomplishment, and victory while the finish line of the full marathon distance may be a gruesome, sad, lonely place . . . but this does nothing to dissuade doctors from ignoring the half-marathon finish line (a chosen suicide date) and emphasizing the 26.2

---

[104] Annie Duke, Quit: The Power of Knowing When to Walk Away (2022).

miles (the maximum possible lifespan) as the only valid goal.

The fact that Kryst was thirty makes her desire to end her life no less valid than if she were a septuagenarian. To think otherwise implies at least one of two things:

- Thirty-year-old people, who we trust to represent multi-billion-dollar corporations in courtrooms, to be the CEOs of those corporations, to command two-billion-dollar Burke-class destroyers representing America's naval might, to represent us at the Olympics, are incapable of considering their own lives and the value of those lives rationally and reasonably.
- Older people are either uniquely qualified to consider the value of their lives or have so little value left in their lives that society should disregard any remaining value and allow them to end their lives more easily than thirty-year-olds—not because of their enhanced competency to make a decision but because of their presumed decrepitude or diminishing vitality.

These sentiments strike me as counterintuitive if viewed in the most charitable light and, more often, deeply offensive. I expect and require more from a system to make sense of the lives lived around me.

I reject any framework whose roots of authority are fertilized only with the presumed ineptitude of the young and the presumed decrepitude of the elderly. And you should too.

If we applied in other contexts the generalization that people move gradually from naïve-and-young to wise-and-elderly, investors would only trust the geriatric to run billion-dollar tech startups and the age of consent for intimate relations would no doubt reside on the far side of typical menopause.

It isn't just people ending their lives that are affected by societal impressions and prevailing ideas. Our ideas about a seventy-year-old ending his or her life, a cancer patient ending his or her life, or a thirty-year-old ending his or her life are formed in part as a result of society's preconceptions and stereotypes of these events and their customary acceptability or unacceptability.

"How," one ponders, "can one be sure she is ready to die at only thirty years old?"

But it is important to recognize that people ending their lives are not doing so in a vacuum. Each is influenced by society. People live and die within a society. Perhaps within a religion too. Maybe at the center of a constellation of Twitter followers. Sometimes among a small, but influential, circle of friends. Each of us will die drowning in a soup of thoughts and feelings no one else sees, a soup of chemical and electrical autobiographical activity inside the skull.

Perhaps it is some mixture, some conflict, of effects from societal pressures that influence some more than others, a matter of degree. Some write publicly about their struggles with finding remaining meaning in their lives, careers, friends, family, and surroundings. Some plan quietly. Some, like Kryst, are aging but are not ill and have years or decades ahead in their theoretical actuarial lifespans. But I urge that we should pay mind not to these theoretical years, which are always, often erroneously, imagined to be costless and happy and healthy, but instead to the wishes of some to end their lives prior to the biological maximum.

SCENE V, PART III
Caressing the Trigger

Our doubts are traitors and make us lose the good we oft might
win by fearing to attempt.
—Lucio[105]

The person best positioned to contemplate and weigh the costs of those additional years was, in her case, Ms. Kryst herself. In my case, myself. In your case, yourself. To assign authority to mere bystanders and voyeurs is to so discount the introspective awareness of the individual that one must ask: If one does not know about that person's life, what, if any, decisions is one able to consider or make (or prohibit) responsibly?

And to be dismissive of Kryst's choice, to contest her agency over her body and life, to call her insane or troubled, is insulting. This is a person who society trusted to handle important matters of legal appeal, to speak to and for women in major media outlets, to represent women on stage at the Miss USA pageant (which she won years earlier). Yet many are quick to strip her of this position once the matter at hand is ending one's life; someone who spoke for clients in the courtroom and for women on a national stage now is unfairly discredited when speaking about her own thoughts and feelings. Why does society dismiss, distrust, and dishonor these people by suddenly discounting the value of these important life-ending decisions coming from respected members of society otherwise empowered to do important work and make important decisions?

When will we examine and unwind our endemic cultural bias that mental illness is a prerequisite to suicide, and instead admit suicide is a choice available to all and a choice most people are capable of making iteratively, perennially, and sanely?

---

[105] William Shakespeare, *Measure for Measure*, act 1, sc. 5.

Above: First-position opinions are stickier than we'd like to admit.[106]

Recent research suggests first-position opinions are sticky, and when people abandon the initial position, they tend to prefer (or even create) middle
positions rather than being willing to move directly (or "flip") to the position
described as at the opposite end of the spectrum.[107] When choices in between
are offered, many will favor an untenable compromise between the two.

Finding these midpoints can be difficult, depending upon how radically different the two ends of the spectrum are. The degree of difference,
however, hinges on how the difference is described ("pro-life" and "pro-
choice" feel almost irreconcilably far apart) even if the substantive difference is much smaller. (A policy of "freer trade" and a policy of "fewer
tariffs" may be nearly identical, though they may be described by politicians very differently.)

---

[106] When test subjects are shown the entire series of drawings one by one, their perception of this
intermediate drawing is biased according to which end of the series they started from. See Gerald H.
Fischer, *Preparation of Ambiguous Stimulus Materials*, 2 Perception & Psychophysics 421, 422 (1967).
[107] This is often cited in critiques of two-party political systems, a debate and topic I will not wade
into here.

Consider, for instance, the difference between the *hiragana*[108] か く [109] and ね こ ,[110] which when seen with Western eyes is very significant; it may be hard for the typical observer to find any similarity between the two—and it would be difficult for the subject to devise an "in between" position.

Meanwhile, consider the difference between the *kanji* 描[111] and 猫[112] (meaning precisely the same things as the *hiragana* supra) which will look similar to most Westerners and could be confused even by native readers in instances of sloppy calligraphy or fast reading without expected context. Here, a person might propose 苗[113] with a slightly bent radical sinister,[114] bent slightly more than for *kaku* (描) but less so than for *neko* (猫). The result would, however, not be a compromise at all; it would be confusing and meaningless, communicating neither "draw" (描) nor "cat" (猫) to the reader. (I've resisted making the groan-worthy "Schrödinger's 猫" joke here.)

Such imagined middle positions are common in policy; I would sug-gest "cannabis regulation is too hard to craft, let's delegate this and make it available through physicians" is an example of a confusing, meaningless, and eventually untenable compromise or middle-ground position. Similar debates of muddy compromise can be seen in numerical form in at what age people should be able to consent to sexual activity, at what age people should be able to drink, what the speed limit should be near a church or school, or in which weeks or months of pregnancy abortions should be available or unavailable. Allowing a person to end life if a doctor, or maybe a (second) doctor after a second opinion, or maybe a quorum of three doctors . . . you

---

[108] *Hiragana* is a modern, standardized Japanese phonetic character set.
[109] Japanese: kaku, to draw or write.
[110] Japanese: neko, a cat.
[111] Japanese: kaku, to draw or write.
[112] Japanese: neko, a cat.
[113] Japanese: nae, a young tree. This seems entirely unrelated, but the *kanji* used here is borrowed from Chinese, where the radical dexter is pronounced "meow" (Japanese: ミ ョ ウ) and the bending radical sinister means "animal," so a cat, if reading the *kanji* literally in Chinese, is a "meow animal."
[114] The vertical sinister is a componentry taxonomy for the left-hand element when a *kanji* character is assembled.

get the idea, these are just imagined middle grounds that merely pile more opinions[115] onto the underlying question.

But these make-it-a-meal, medium-drink-and-medium-French-fry compromises don't match the gravity of the choices being made. If we apply or translate "capacity to contract" as a standard for "capacity to end life" and hence do not permit suicide for those under eighteen, we should take and consider very seriously[116] a decision to deny a freshly minted seventeen-year-old access to suicide arbitrarily when the time between here and an eighteenth birthday may be truly difficult to endure. If we do not permit suicide for those found to be psychologically troubled or those placed in conservatorship arrangements,[117] do we allow trustees or caretakers or conservators to terminate the life of the person governed[118] by the conservatorship? If so, if ever,[119] under what conditions and with what safeguards? How would one go about engineering these safeguards to be reliably sturdier than the mental robustness of the person allegedly protected?

---

[115] And, in the case of medical opinions, these are opinions of nontrivial cost to obtain in time, money, travel, pain, etc.

[116] Special thanks to Cristina Desmond for emphasizing to me the importance of this issue of juvenile choice, where I am not a learned commentator but where I can appreciate the complexity of the issue.

[117] For discussion of the difficulties, moral and legal, of long-term conservatorship, see Marissa Cohen, *#FreeBritney: Why Indefinite Conservatorships are Unconstitutional* (2021) (working paper). ("Popstar Britney Spears, now in her 30s, has fewer legal rights than a child and far [fewer] than those of a woman.") Ms. Spears's conservatorship lasted thirteen years and included accusations of unfair and unnecessary deprivation of various rights, access to financial resources, communication with others, access to legal counsel, and other modes of agency most people enjoy.

[118] I oppose as both unethical and unwise wholesale appointing conservators into this supremely difficult role.

[119] Thanks to law professor colleagues at Chicago, Oxford, and Stanford for raising this conservatorship issue in a seminar in 2021.

SCENE V, PART IV
Making the Trade

A man either lives life as it happens to him, meets it head-on and licks it, or he turns his back on it and starts to wither away.
—*Dr. Phil Boyce*[120]

We should trust in the certainty fellow humans can develop that the dividends of tomorrow are not worth the pains of today. We should also trust that being certain one will die in a given circumstance, on a given date, is limiting but is also liberating—and that taking control of the time and manner of one's demise can let a person live an enhanced, bounded, considered life. This better life with a knowable end[121] is the life for which this book advocates, the goal being to empower a person during life and also as life vanishes. One can think of this planned die-at-a-chosen-horizon framework as in the same genus as political "term limits" arguments.[122]

---

[120]   Star Trek: The Original Series, The Cage Desilu Productions (Oct. 15, 1988).

[121]   Science fiction wrestles over and over with this question, often employing heroes who are time travelers or who know what the ends of their lives look like (and use this knowledge to some advantage, including simply living a somewhat more impactful or rewarding life). These narratives range from H.G. Wells, The Time Machine, where the main character previews the end of human life as we know it to the very first episode aboard the *USS Enterprise* (Star Trek: Strange New Worlds, Strange New Worlds Paramount+ (May 5, 2022)) (Captain Pike, who is Kirk's predecessor as commanding officer of the *Enterprise*, confides to Mr. Spock that he's seen the future and knows the time and mode of his death: "I know exactly how and when my life ends ... It's almost a decade away. Is that soon? Suddenly that feels soon . . . Will [knowing the time and circumstances of my death] make me hesitant? Cautious? Not cautious enough?"). Kirk himself remarks on the merits of considering death carefully years later: "How we deal with death is at least as important as how we deal with life, wouldn't you say?" Adm. James T. Kirk, to Acting Capt. Saavik (LTJG), Star Trek II Paramount Pictures (1982). This concept of bounded life as a driver of more extensive reflection or contemplation also appears in the mainstream "self-help" literature, see Jon Staff, Getting Away 115 (2020). ("If you knew that in one year you would die suddenly, would you change anything about the way you are now living? Why?")

[122]   Interestingly, some faiths suggest God knows when a person will die even before that person is born. (See, e.g., *Qur'an* Ch. 39: Surah Zumar; see also id. at Ch. 4: Surah Nisaa.) Some scholars dispute whether God granting man free will allows him to terminate life at an earlier date than the deity plans or if, instead, God's omniscience includes foreseeing suicide (and hence man's agency in the context of

We should be willing to accept that some people do truly, genuinely, deeply want to die, and we should at least consider honoring those wishes rather than dismissing, mocking, or undermining them. And we should consider that some situations are so difficult[123] for others to meet with appreciation or empathy that it is hard, if not impossible, for us to truly "put ourselves in their shoes," the metaphorical shoes of those seeking to die.

---

suicide is illusory, seeming like a new path from life to death but actually following a predetermined path already mapped by God).

[123] No doubt some people encounter scenarios that lead them to want to end their lives that are hard to imagine: a diagnosis that leads down a painful, terminal path, or the destruction of that person's reputation or financial standing, or a wrongful and defamatory accusation the person is not in a position to rebut. The Model Penal Code, at least in the case of manslaughter, recognizes it is the interaction between a person and her surroundings that leads to difficult choices: "Some instances of intentional homicide may be as much attributable to the extraordinary nature of the situation as to the moral depravity of the actor." 2 Model Penal Code and Commentaries § 210.3 56 (1980) (official draft and revised comments).

ACT III

How Do We Talk
About Dying?
With Whom?

SCENE I
Doctors on the Scene, Know What I Mean?

I consider that medicine may prolong life, but death will take
the doctor, too.[124]
—Cymbeline[125]

While society may have matured into a kinder, gentler creature that does not endorse the Vatican or anyone else calling to punish a paralyzed car accident survivor with confiscation of his worldly possessions or interruption of his ability to leave land or money to his children, taking one's own life (with or without the assistance of doctors) is still frowned upon in much of the world. The opening contemplative salvo of Swedish niche folk act First Aid Kit's *My Silver Lining[126]* apparently never topped charts among senior bishops. The Vatican's Pontifical Academy for Life wrote of physician-assisted suicide in 2021, "What happened to the doctors' oath to care for the suffering? Can giving death to someone else become normal?" I ask, then, not only "why not?" but also that we extend "giving" here to a gift one might give oneself. The Church's lack of empathetic, practical discussion around end-of-life matters influenced in my decision to step down as a regent of a Vatican-aligned university around this time after six years of service.

The first hint of this building momentum in the other direction is the growing availability of physician-assisted suicide around the world, something I find both a promising occurrence and an untenable middle ground. Physician-assisted suicide (a drug, or more often a mixture of drugs, intended to hasten death) is available today in a variety of countries and scenarios to people with and even without (for instance, in the case of Colombia) diagnosed terminal ailments.

---

[124]   Rearranged and modernized for readability.
[125]   William Shakespeare, Cymbeline, act V, sc. V.
[126]   On Stay Gold Columbia Records (2014).

To give concrete examples, today we can detect—with overwhelmingly compelling statistical accuracy—what will happen not simply from an actuarial "you are this old so this might happen to you" perspective, but at a high degree of individual resolution.

We can detect a patient's propensity for developing Huntington's disease, an ailment that is degenerative and incurable. A close friend of mine found out about ten years ago that the odds were overwhelming he would develop Huntington's; it changed his parenting style, his work/life balance, and even how he planned to discuss life and death with his two children.

We can also detect and anticipate cystic fibrosis. Cutting-edge research suggests interactions between viral agents and the immune system cause most, if not all, cases of multiple sclerosis.

I am not proposing that life with these diseases, or in anticipation of these diseases, is worthless. Rather, I'm proposing that a perfectly healthy person at very high genetic (or environmental) risk of certain diseases may want to live differently and do certain things sooner. The list might include climbing Kilimanjaro in one's twenties rather than thirties, choosing early retirement over continued work, and, in some cases, electively dying sooner too.

We should view lives that end with these deaths not as accelerated tragedies, but as thoughtful pieces of choreography. Any other interpretation insults the people living these lives.

As we know more about our bodies, their limitations, their likely ailments, and their expected durability, we will plan our lives with these constraints in mind. In some cases, we will learn things about our longevities that substantially change our plans. This should be respected and not shamed; worshipping natural or accidental death over scientifically-informed, careful end-of-life planning is a species of Ludditeism.

I see physician-assisted suicide as a stepping-stone toward full acceptance of suicide as a tool of end-of-life planning, but a wobbly stepping-stone from which we are well-advised to leap toward acceptance and even encouragement of suicide. (Thus ending the current prevailing policy framework, which refuses to accept suicide as a personal choice and focuses on suicide prevention rather than supplying people the knowledge, tools, and confidence to end their lives quickly, safely, and in a way of their choosing while minimizing any risk to others.)

In the modern world of hospitals and 9-1-1 calls and the final days of life as a profitable event for a healthcare system, if you don't choose, someone will choose for you. And that "someone" might not be the person you want, or would nominate, to choose.

This is one of many factors that led me to a very simple in theory, but complex in practice, conclusion: if my death will be the result of someone's choice, I'd rather choose myself.

SCENE II, PART I
Linguistics

They have been at a great feast of languages and stolen the scraps.[127]
—*Moth*[128]

Over the years, I've discussed suicide in a variety of settings, and students, colleagues, and others have asked a question that, on its face, with no historical context, seems reasonable: if suicide is okay, why do we talk about "committing" suicide when the only other things we talk about "committing" are crimes like arson, carjacking, fraud, or rape?

How can suicide be okay if it's something you "commit"?

Well, language is complicated and "committing" can mean different things. Words over time carry different meanings over time and can become less or more severe in meaning. The cheerful and versatile *ciao* is often the only Italian tourists say with any confidence when visiting. But its versatility as a greeting phrase, a departing phrase, and even to punctuate or transition conversation descends from more sinister origins, the *veneziano* dialect's *s-ciào vostro* or *s-ciào su*, meaning "I am your slave." The phraseology to "commit" a crime has a similarly complex journey from etymological genesis to contemporary speech.

Committing, from the Latin *committere*, meant originally to send or seal something irrevocably. It came to English meaning to put into custody, to entrust. This journey paralleled the journey of *escrow*, from the Latin *scroda* and imported to England thanks to the Norman French. Both meant to keep something of value outside one's own ambit, to voluntarily forfeit agency over something.[129] Many of the oldest English betting games require an ante

---

[127] Phrasing and spelling modernized for ease of reading.
[128] William Shakespeare, Love's Labours Lost, act V, sc. I.
[129] It is important to etymologically segregate this journey from that of *valet*, which is related to *vassal*.

from the players, in medieval times called a "come" (from *committere*) or a "scrod" (from *scroda*). This lives on in the "come line" on the felt of a modern craps table, committing the player to a wager iteratively before or until a seven is rolled.

The Stuart view (under King James I) of criminality, the Victorian view of insanity, and a devolution into colloquial English each thrust the word "commit" into new contexts. This brought the committed clergy (meaning chaste), the committed wife (meaning free of adulterous thoughts), and committed counsel (meaning an advocate without capacity for betrayal). Also introduced were the ideas that someone would "be committed" to an insane asylum and that someone would "commit" a crime.

Interestingly, in the Anglophone Middle Ages, people were said to "commit to" a crime—not to "commit" a crime. So a person would "commit to" murder (forming the requisite thought in one's mind) and then "set to" murder someone (carrying out the physical act of killing). In other words, "commit" was meant as dedicating one's self to carrying out a crime, the formation of a *mens rea*. This is relevant today and I propose is something worth reviving in the case of suicide.

We talk about someone "committing suicide," but we don't mean it in the way we mean "committing robbery"; what we really mean is "committing to dying," trusting one's self to make this choice; in this sense, "committing" suicide is less like committing robbery and is more like committing to a set of marriage vows. And pondering a commitment to ending life should hold a similar gravity and wonder.

To contemplate committing to suicide, even for a moment, is to feel and absorb a great power, to suddenly be a jury of one, a judge immune from appeal, a person whose agency may not be infinite but is more than

---

To *valet* something meant to keep it in the physical custody of a footman or servant, someone who controls that person through an explicit or implicit arrangement of agency. To *commit* something meant to put it beyond reach of you or your agents and to entrust it to another (the "sixth sort" in bailments, an important topic in property law). For more on the use of these concepts during the pertinent period, see Sir John Holt's eloquent thoughts in Coggs v. Bernard, 2 Ld Raym 909, 92 ER 107 (KB 1703) (reciting and explaining six-category taxonomy of bailment).

adequate. And to feel such a power is magnificent, but to realize that we are able to choose in every day and every moment whether to exercise that power to calm the body and free the soul is nearly divine.

We all have that power and that choice; death is an omnipresent option.

We should each—all and equally—enjoy the choice to face life or embrace death.

SCENE II, PART II
The Final Frontier

*Oh, is that what you tell yourself? You're doing it for the
children?*
—Maj. Kira Nerys[130]

I'm a lifelong, unapologetic fan of Star Trek.

But, from an economist's perspective, one flaw in Star Trek is the lack of constraints.

The Roddenberry universe is one of conspicuous, jarring abundance. The replicator produces limitless sustenance,[131] the engine room's di-lithium crystals provide limitless energy,[132] there is no money to limit the crew's consumption. Everything is without bound.

This allows for amusing plotlines but provides no guardrails against which decisions collide; hence, the moral dilemmas and internal struggles of the characters provide the only rules.

The reason Star Trek seems so distant from our lived experience isn't a matter of context[133] or technology, it's a matter of constraints. Our world is one of limits: life is finite, health often more so, many things we desire are practically, fiscally, legally, or otherwise prohibited.

---

[130] Star Trek: Deep Space Nine: Wrongs Darker than Death or Night Paramount (Mar. 30, 1998). The character quoted is Bajoran; Bajorans, like Japanese, use their family names first; above, however, is the conventional name order as a matter of consistency with canon.

[131] Presumably the energy needed to do this molecular-level recombination is substantial, especially as the inputs are vastly different from the outputs, and the outputs are extraordinarily chemically complex, such as Capt. Jean-Luc Picard's earl grey tea, first ordered in Star Trek: The Next Generation: Contagion CBS (Mar. 20, 1989).

[132] The "burn storyline" in Star Trek: Discovery, Season 3 Paramount + (Oct. 15, 2020–Jan. 7, 2021) finally suggests there is a limited supply of these crystals. The crystals themselves cannot be replicated aboard or easily replaced. See Star Trek: The Original Series: Where No Man has Gone Before NBC (Sept. 22, 1966).

[133] At its core, Star Trek is simply a workplace drama (albeit set in an unusual workplace).

In one sense, this is a blessing: people generally make better decisions when subjected to constraints.

You're more careful at the grocer if you only have a certain amount of money in your pocket. You work more efficiently when you must finish a task on a certain timeline, true whether this is a self-imposed deadline or not, as Parkinson's Law and the Apollo Phenomenon attest. Constraints are, generally, good—including constraints placed on one's lifespan.

Decision making around resource allocation subject to constraints is why the question "suppose you knew you were going to die tomorrow, what would you do [today]?" is interesting.

Barbara Fasolo, a behavioral scientist on the panel before whom I defended my Ph.D., shows in her research that when people choose based on fewer attributes or are presented with fewer choices, they make better choices. Other recent research shows also that people operating under constrained conditions make these choices more quickly and are happier with their choices after the fact.

I combine these into the framework in this book, which is also the framework by which I live my life: people make better allocations under scarcity and people sometimes make better choices when they have fewer choices. In practice, they are the same observation, that people perform best when forced to focus their resources within a certain schedule and within a certain budget.

I believe people live their best lives within bounded lifespans.

I've chosen the last day I will live. Yes, it's possible I will die before that date—blindsided in the zebra crossing by a bus or knocked off the treadmill by a sudden cardiac event—but setting that date has had enormous productivity effects in my life, and I believe that, without social stigma or legal hurdle, this choice should be available to everyone.

Yes, I'm talking about suicide.

And I'm talking about how it's *unhealthy* to not talk about suicide.

Whether or not we proactively cause our deaths, I believe planning a high quality life within our lifespans will become less theoretical and more actionable thanks to science and that a known maximum lifespan (whether or not one chooses to utilize the maximum amount) helps one contemplate what might yet fit inside the ever-filling bottom half of life's hourglass.

SCENE II, PART III
Calibrating the Constraint

Has it ever occurred to you that one hundred pianos all tuned to
the same fork are automatically tuned to each other?
—A.W. Tozer[134]

My proposition, in its simplest form, is that lifespan is scarce for each and all of us. My life will end and so, too, will yours. But by setting, rather than discovering, the last possible day of my life, I create a constraint.

By making choices within that constraint, I make better choices.

This is true for two related reasons:

1. I enjoy more information than I did before I set the date, where I had to account for thousands of death dates during a decade(s)-long period.
2. I am able to optimize in certain ways that would be exceedingly difficult if I were thinking in terms of my actuarial lifespan rather than a chosen death date.

A common "what if" is the prompt "what would you do if you had only a day to live" or, alternatively, "only a year to live." It forces people to consider what's important, what's realistic to achieve, and what they "really want."

"Suicide is selfish," critics retort.

Is it, though? Suicide can be selfish but can also be altruistic, much as the decision to have children can be selfish or not. If the goal of life beyond the individual, in the collective construct, is to minimize suffering and maximize happiness, then I can think of few measures we can take as a society that do more to achieve this goal than being more welcoming and permissive toward suicide and the individuals who wish to end their lives affirmatively,

---

[134] A.W. Tozer, The Pursuit of God 97 (1948).

consensually, and on their own terms. Any other policy is bound to create or extend suffering. I further suggest utilitarian concerns about second-order effects, such as confusion or sadness at the passing of the suicide-empowered decedent, are substantially lessened in a world where suicide is less discouraged, less stigmatized, and discussed more openly.

In such a world, people are not dismayed to hear of a friend's plan to end life, are not motivated to call human resources upon hearing of a coworker's suicide plan, and are not obligated to betray their psychotherapy client when she talks about end-of-life matters—in this better world, planned death is commonplace and viewed positively. To suggest a friend's thoughtful and foreshadowed suicide, with financial affairs in order and meaningful conversations had, is somehow worse than learning that friend was unexpectedly struck by a car or a heart attack without the chance to settle debts and make apologies is bizarre to me.

"You can't be serious," the critics continue. But I can be. And I am. Why not think this way in a real, actionable sense?

Before you recoil from this idea, consider that many people you know are engaged in what I might call haphazard, gradual suicides.

We do not generally view gradual self-inflicted terminal scenarios, such as overindulgence in alcohol, food, tobacco, or fast driving without regard for seatbelt laws, as slow-motion suicides; we accept that these consumer decisions are "lifespan planning" choices that individuals in a liberal society may make. We should consider, and perhaps adopt, the same attitudes toward more rapid, even sudden, means of accelerating one's death.

Notably, we allow convicted criminals in some states to plan the circumstances of their deaths. In a sense, these convicts enjoy something most free people do not.

As of this writing, for instance, three of the eight inmates on Utah's death row have selected a firing squad. These prisoners are often unsure on which date their lives will expire—in part due to the labyrinthine appellate procedure that plods a few paces behind death penalty defendants like a loyal hound—but are able to make decisions and preparations we deny to those outside the prison walls.

We allow people to choose gradual methods of lifespan planning, but these have the drawback of uncertainty. It is unclear when one's choices will lead to eventual expiration. One can die from combining habitual cocaine use with poor cardiovascular health or from combining alcohol with a penchant for exceeding the speed limit and disregarding seatbelt laws. But when will such a death occur? There is lingering uncertainty.

This idea of gradual suicide endorses lineages of plenary choices that a civilized society with a thoughtful policy framework likely would not encourage. When one ponders what types of questions a person should be asking to contribute to society, "Am I drinking enough to die before I have to start spending the kids' college money?" is not the kind of question most would cite. Yet it is a flavor of question not unimaginable in modern Occidental societies.

Gradual suicide is less responsible than more affirmative suicide in every way that matters, so long as the latter is carried out with communication, thoughtfulness, and no harm to others.

Whether the effects on others are more modest (a smoker's pollution of loved ones' lungs via second-hand smoke), moderate (an obese person's healthcare costs partially absorbed by the svelte), or severe (a habitual drunk driver's eventual contribution to tragedy), these behaviors have real and significant negative effects (these are negative externalities in economist-speak) to which others did not consent.

If any significant part of the human enterprise is increasing happiness and reducing suffering,[135] then suicide as the end to many or even most human lives should not be overlooked as an option. One need not have

---

[135] I do not believe this is the whole of the intellectual jurisdiction of our species, nor do I think it is even the top priority of our time on our little blue spaceship. However, I do believe many humans embrace an aesthetic preference, if not a moral mandate, that preventing suffering is a good thing and that, *ceteris paribus*, people (and perhaps animals, also) should suffer less rather than more. If true, testing the bounds of maximum human longevity is contrary to reducing suffering while planned lifespans ending in suicide decrease net suffering. Good communication prior to one's planned demise can temper or eliminate the negative effects on loved ones, which often prominently feature in utilitarian suicide-opposed arguments.

first-hand experience with the ravages of disease, the tragedy of geriatric decrepitude, or the gradual decline of the mind to understand these threats to one's physical robustness, social dignity, and cognitive sanity.[136] Nor need one have experienced serious setbacks in life, whether romantic or pecuniary or reputational, to understand these wounds may be stubbornly resistant to healing or even mortal in a way that is very real even if it is not medically diagnosable.

That suicide is a choice a person makes, and is well-positioned to make, is central to this book's argument; suicide doesn't "happen" to someone and people are not suicide "victims." People who end their lives make choices that are the product of intimate deliberations that an onlooker cannot observe or understand or credibly second-guess.

---

[136] .For a heartfelt and wonderful piece on why modern healthcare, and particularly American healthcare, focuses on endless treatment rather than saying good-bye, see Ezikiel J. Emmanuel, *My 92-Year-Old Father Didn't Need More Medical Care*, The Atlantic (Jan. 2020). ("[N]o one had taken the time to ask him about his wishes regarding medical treatment, even though he was competent to make decisions and was himself a physician. No one asked my mother and brother, who were with him in the emergency room and at the hospital, if he had an advance-care directive or wanted to have a do-not-resuscitate order.")

SCENE II, PART IV
Interrogating Stigma

[I]t is indisputable that involuntary commitment to a mental hospital after a finding of probable dangerousness to self . . . can engender adverse social consequences to the individual. Whether we label this phenomena "stigma" or choose to call it something else is less important than that we recognize that it can occur and that it can have a very significant impact on the individual.
—Chief Justice Warren Earl Burger[137]

To say suicide is "stigmatized" is an understatement.

For suicide to be freely available to all who should be able to access it,[138] which is my central position in this argument, it must be a choice protected both legally and normatively. Why? Because rights must be protected by multiple safeguards and these safeguards emanate from different centers of power: law, norms, and education about the underlying issues (which allows individuals to draw similar conclusions independently). As Mill put it,[139] a right is created where "he has the valid claim on society to protect him in the possession of it, either by the force of law, or by that of education and opinion."

We live in a time where suicide is a target of sweeping prohibition and comprehensive disdain, in addition to being regarded as a symptom of mental illness. Meanwhile, longer lives that are difficult or possibly of low quality are celebrated: it's heroic when someone "battles" cancer while the same person deciding to end his or her life "gave in to" mental illness.

---

[137] Addington v. Texas, 441 US 418, 425–26 (1979).
[138] And reasonable minds can differ as to who should have access to this choice. I argue most, nearly all, people should enjoy this choice.
[139] Speaking of rights generally, not this or any other right in particular. See John Stuart Mill, Utilitarianism 970 London, Parker, Son, & Bourn (1863).

This mischaracterizes and recategorizes the day-to-day experience of both example individuals, one being a caricature of a mighty warrior rather than a sturdy patient, the other being a caricature of a strange madman rather than a dignified decedent. People who stop to value their lives are in the prevailing appraisal framework already committing a sin, as all life must be valued at infinity and all death must be feared and avoided.

This moots or avoids all calculus around the actual value of remaining life, something scholars from Howard Friedman[140] to Kenneth Feinberg[141] to Cass Sunstein[142] to Richard Posner[143] to Peter Singer[144] have rightly encouraged us to consider.[145]

Imagine if one week of very painful chemotherapeutic treatment for cancer allowed a person to enjoy a relatively normal one thousand weeks of additional life after the treatment and that, without the treatment, the person would relatively quickly perish. Many people would consider this a good bargain. But now imagine ten weeks of painful treatment that only grants twenty weeks of additional life, and this life is of relatively low quality relative to life prior to the treatment. Now imagine ten weeks of

---

[140] See Howard Steven Friedman, The Ultimate Price: The Value We Place on Life (2021).

[141] Feinberg famously, after much deliberation, drew up the rules for how much lives lost in the September 11, 2001 terrorist attacks were worth in pecuniary terms. The non-economic value of each life was set at $250,000 while $100,000 in payment to a spouse and $100,000 further to each dependent was also approved by Feinberg. Economic value of future earnings was set at actual annual income in recent year(s) but capped at $231,000 if above this—as one might expect, many executives at firms inside the World Trade Center earned substantially more than this and the appropriateness of this arbitrary cap has been the topic of many discussions in recent years. Other recent efforts to value life include how to value relocating climate refugees from the Maldives before that archipelago is damaged or submerged, how to size and value the life (and time within lives) saved (or destroyed) by fully autonomous motor vehicles, and how to estimate and value life lost due to climate change more generally. On the last point, see Environmental Protection Agency, *Report on the Social Cost of Greenhouse Gases: Estimates Incorporating Recent Scientific Advances*, Supplementary Material for the Regulatory Impact Analysis for the Supplemental Proposed Rulemaking, Standards of Performance for New, Reconstructed, and Modified Sources and Emissions Guidelines for Existing Sources: Oil and Natural Gas Sector Climate Review (proposed 2022).

[142] See, e.g., Cass R. Sunstein, *Lives, Life-Years, and Willingness to Pay*, 104 Colum. L. Rev. 205 (2004).

[143] See discussion of pecuniary appraisal of life in Richard A. Posner, Economic Analysis of Law (1973).

[144] See Peter Singer, Rethinking Life and Death: The Collapse of Our Traditional Ethics (1995).

[145] For a general overview of frameworks not only for the actuarial value of life in the strict sense but also other considerations one might reasonably take into account when valuing the human experience, see Cass R. Sunstein, Valuing Life (2014).

painful treatment that only grants ten weeks of additional life and not only is post-treatment life inhibited and burdensome, but the treatment wipes out the life savings of the patient and removes the possibility of leaving needed financial resources to the patient's grandchildren. Of course, we can continue to manipulate the hypothetical to make the treatment more costly and painful and its dividends less enjoyable or interesting.

At some point, some people will consider the bargain unattractive and will prefer death.

This argument holds not only for illness (though illness is an area where physician opinions about mortality risk and treatment options create the illusion of precision),[146] but also for the financial condition of the person, the person's relationships with others, the person's political ambitions, and any other thing a person might hold central to his or her identity. To say that only medical ailments[147] can cause sufficient distress to allow suicide is like saying "we're really good at diagnosing burns, so burns are the only injuries we'll recognize, everything else is just not that serious and people should just be tougher when they suffer any other injury" or some similar arbitrary rule. It also presupposes that only damaged and dying people desire suicide, which is not the case.

We all see minor tragedies that remind us of our mortality or, at least, the passage of time. I recall feeling this the first time I spoke at the funeral of a person younger than me. I feel a twinge of it when I recognize there are things I was good at when I was young that I can perhaps still do at a skilled level—like skiing—but will never again do with the verve I once had. And there are more trivial reminders we all endure, like music we considered rebellious and *avant-garde* as teenagers now playing as ambient noise in second-tier cities' airport terminals or mid-market suburban shopping centers.

To people who say—and there are plenty—that anything short of the most painful, inoperable, imminently terminal cancer is simply an

---

[146] See Renee D. Goodwin, Andrej Marusic, & Christina W. Hoven, *Suicide Attempts in the United States: The Role of Physical Illness*, 56 Soc. Sci. & Med. 1783 (2003).

[147] And, specifically, only medical ailments recognized and diagnosed with current technology.

inconvenience and these people just need to dust themselves off and pull themselves up by their bootstraps, I disagree and offer three cases to consider where real concerns about the value of remaining life are present, but no severe medical ailment is present.[148] These are illustrative and instructive cases, but are not meant to be models for considering one's life and its value; rather, they are meant to show the human diversity in how one might value remaining life.

---

[148] The psychological literature agrees the driver of suicide may not be depression or medical misfortune, but instead can be escape, altering one's environment (or hope of escape to a new environment), or simply wanting to conclude the current persistent state of mind. See, e.g., Gregory K. Brown et al., Cognitive Therapy Treatment Manual for Suicide Attempters (2002); Alexander L. Chapman & Katherine L. Dixon-Gordon, *Emotional Antecedents and Consequences of Deliberate Self-Harm and Suicide Attempts*, 37 Suicide Life Threat. Behav. 543 (2007); Ronald R. Holden, Paula S. Kerr, James D. Mendonca, & V.R. Velamoor, *Are Some Motives More Linked to Suicide Proneness Than Others?*, 54 J. Clin. Psych. 569 (1998); see also Ulrich Schnyder, Ladislav Valach, Kathrin Bichsel, & Konrad Michel, *Attempted Suicide: Do We Understand the Patients' Reasons?*, 21 Gen. Hosp. Psych. 62 (1999).

Brief Illustrative Interlude
Three Suicides

I don't want to cause physical or mental distress. Joanne, Rob,
DeeDee—I love you! Thank you for making my life so happy.
Good-bye to you all on the count of three. Please make sure that
the sacrifice of my life is not in vain.
—R. Budd Dwyer[149]

Life-threatening illness and relentless physical discomfort are not the
only unbearable things that might cause a person to desire life's end. To
quote the Hon. Judge Kaufman, "Severe emotional distress means, then,
emotional distress of such substantial quantity or enduring quality that
no reasonable man in a civilized society should be expected to endure
it.[150] We routinely award damages in cases of reputational damage and
emotional distress in excess of the plaintiff's lifetime estimated earning potential and even in excess of the actuarial value of the plaintiff's
remaining lifespan plus anticipated lifetime earnings. If these pecuniary
awards are to be taken seriously as quantifications of harm, then the damage done to the plaintiff's life can be said to exceed the value of the plaintiff's remaining life. If the damage cannot be repaired with money—as
in the case of a ruined political career or a disgraced excommunication
from the community—then suicide may not be an emotionally charged
overreaction but instead a reasonable, measured response. As Becker and

---

[149] Dwyer's final words before shooting himself on live television with a .357 Magnum revolver.
[150] Fletcher v. Western Nat'l. Life Ins. Co., 10 Cal. App. 3d 376, 397 (Cal. App. 4th 1970).

Posner note,[151] the degree of reputational or other harm to a person may be irreversible and catastrophic, even if to the onlooker the harm appears more minor.

With this in mind, let's explore three cases of suicide that have nothing at all to do with an unexpected medical diagnosis or a constant pain in the literal sense.

In the case of a politician like R. Budd Dwyer, perhaps feeling his wrongful criminal conviction meant his political career was forever stained: "I thank the good Lord for giving me forty-seven years of exciting challenges, stimulating experiences, many happy occasions, and most of all, the finest wife and children any man could ever desire. ... Now my life has changed for no apparent reason. People who call and write are exasperated and feel helpless. They know I am innocent and want to help, but in this nation, the worlds [sic] greatest democracy, there is nothing they can do to prevent me from being punished for a crime they know I did not commit." Dwyer clearly felt even if his conviction were overturned on appeal, aspects critical to his viability as a political creature had already been amputated.[152]

---

[151]   "A businessman [. . .] may commit suicide even though he remains wealthy by most persons standards." G. Becker & R. Posner, p.10 (paginated as "9"), Becker's August 2004 draft on file with the author. Below, Genevieve Roch-Decter narrates on Twitter her confusion as to why someone worth $2B might be finished living (24 Feb. 2023).

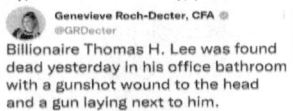

Genevieve Roch-Decter, CFA ⬤
@GRDecter

Billionaire Thomas H. Lee was found dead yesterday in his office bathroom with a gunshot wound to the head and a gun laying next to him.

Why does a 78-year old man with $2 billion shoot himself?

12:21 · 24 Feb 23 · **407K** Views

319 Retweets **71** Quotes **2,278** Likes

[152]   R. Budd Dwyer, news conference (22 Jan. 1987) (available at KDKA Philadelphia Archives).

Above: R. Budd Dwyer holds the Smith & Wesson revolver at a press
conference he convened to profess his innocence. Soon thereafter, Dwyer
shot himself with a single round of .357 Magnum through the roof
of his mouth and, in turn, through his brain, on live television.

In the case of a writer like Yukio Mishima, a right-wing militarist-tra-
ditionalist in postwar Japan with what one might term a fanatical level of
nostalgia for the "old ways" (meaning the ways of imperial Japan), suicide
was planned far in advance to be elaborate, ceremonial, and final.[153] Still in

---

[153] For more on such planned, even choreographed, suicides in the postwar cultural context, see Kirsten
Cather, Scripting Suicide in Modern Japan (forthcoming). Professor Kirsten Cather of UT-Austin has
pondered this particular aspect of suicide and suicide planning substantially more deeply than this
author. See also Alan Stephen Wolfe, Suicidal Narrative in Modern Japan: The Case of Dazai Osamu
(2014) (discussing important case from generation prior to Mishima Yukio-san's planned suicide). For
conceptual imaginations of the transpacific context of Japanese suicide, it is worth reading Haruna Lee's
Suicide Forest, a play which premiered in Brooklyn at the Bushwick Starr immediately prior to the
COVID-19 pandemic. Haruna Lee, Suicide Forest (2019).

For Westerners who have never lived in Japan or read much about its culture around suicide, the life
insurance claims process is perhaps the most informative single datapoint to highlight. Japan is the only
OECD country where life insurance companies will, without protest or appeal or incident, pay in cases

robust health after a career of writing every manner of advocacy for the old ways—including short stories, science fiction, newspaper editorials, and even poetry—Mishima finally recognized that a diet and a head-of-cabinet (内閣総理大臣, who is also the prime minister) would lead Japan, not an emperor or a committee of admirals and generals. Mishima felt he had no place, no tribe, no refuge in this new Japan. He planned a series of photographs and poems to be released immediately after his suicide, arranged for his death in traditional clothing, and disemboweled himself with a short sword before being decapitated with a long sword.

In the case of popular manga artist Yamada Hanako (also Yumi Takaichi[154]), who found fame in her thirties, suicide was perhaps the full-stop after the message sent by so many of her drawings of Tokyo, depicting the city as a dark, black-and-white, threatening monster seemingly supervising the errant, anonymous people below. Hanako's quasi-autobiographical main characters wander Tokyo, having trouble fitting in or understanding a purpose in life. In 1990, she began drawing detailed panels of female characters' suicides, mostly by leaping from tall buildings (though at least one panel shows a nameless character about Hanako's age in front of a train). Eighteen months later, the motif had matured into camera-ready art and the surrounding details became more sophisticated; the final panel, eerily similar to her death, was published in 1992. A few months later, Hanako fell to her death.

Did Dwyer, Mishima, and Hanako feel pain less valid, less intense, or less irreversible than that of a cancer victim? We won't know, but it isn't for

---

ruled suicides. Some policy language has been adjusted in the past twenty years, with the initial policy exclusion being twelve months (suicides peaked in the thirteenth month, unsurprisingly, under these policies); the exclusion was later changed to twenty-four months, which is language present in many policies in force today (which pushes suicides to twenty-fifth month, again unsurprisingly).

Many texts discuss the topic of Japanese suicide, from countless academic papers (from anthropology to epidemiology to law) to nonfiction book-length narrative to how-to Japanese suicide manuals; I tend to favor texts written by Japanese authors with firsthand cultural context rather than voyeuristic narratives written by 外人. For a famous example from the "manual" category, see Wataru Tsurumi, 完全自殺マニュアル (1993), which was a huge success with over 1.2 million copies sold and a bestseller sequel (僕達の完全自殺マニュアル).

[154] Yumi Takaichi adopted a pen name early in her career.

us to judge. And I think reasonable minds may differ as to whether these slights, setbacks, or sadnesses are equal to, or greater than, the physical pain or incapacity felt by a person beset by serious disease.

SCENE III
Of Imagined Lives, Imagined Deaths, Imagined Slaves

If in the first act you have hung a pistol on the wall, then in the following one it should be fired. Otherwise don't put it there.
—*Anton Chekov*[155]

Take twenty-four-year-old Veronika's experience[156] on November 11, 1997:[157]

She believed herself to be completely normal. Two very simple reasons lay behind her decision to die, and she was sure that, were she to leave a note explaining, many people would agree with her.

The first reason: Everything in her life was the same and, once her youth was gone, it would be downhill all the way, with old age beginning to leave irreversible marks, the onset of illness, the departure of friends. She would gain nothing by continuing to live; indeed, the likelihood of suffering would only increase.

The second reason was more philosophical: Veronika read the newspapers, watched TV, and she was aware of what was going on in the world. Everything was wrong, and she had no way of putting things right—that gave her a sense of complete powerlessness.

Does it matter if Veronika is twenty-four or forty-four or sixty-four or eighty-four?[158] If she is real or fictional?[159]

Turning to a somewhat different example, imagine a human settlement culture on Planet *X* wherein chattel slavery (fee ownership of humans as

---

[155]   The translated phrasing of this maxim varies, but this version is borrowed from a recounting of Chekhov's rule in Peter M. Bitsilli, *Chekhov's Art: A Stylistic Analysis*, 43 Slav. Rev. 347 (1984).

[156]   Paulo Coelho, Veronika Decide Morrer (1998).

[157]   The date is fictional and would have been in the future at the time of Coelho's manuscript's creation.

[158]   The very real example of Cheslie Kryst elsewhere in this book deals with this question. See *supra* Act II Scene V.

[159]   Veronika is fictional, but fictional characters and scenarios can be useful in exploring philosophical questions.

property) is the prevailing norm. The settlers of Planet X insist slavery is needed to develop the planet's basic agricultural, mineral, and other resources, and that without it, people on Planet X will be, on the whole, worse off. In this culture, you are the moral arbiter. You cannot "undo" or dismantle the chattel slave economy, but you are asked to decide whether an individual slave should be allowed to end his life. This is a relatively young, healthy man with no detectable physical or mental ailments. But he insists his life is simply an ongoing suffering for the pecuniary benefit of others, with no hope for freedom or individual expression. To allow suicide in this case would terminate the slave's suffering and might inflict financial damage upon the slave's owner, which might be valuable to the slave—the slaveowner is, perhaps, something of an Egyptian, whose wealth it is desirable or even righteous to spoil.[160]

Do you allow the slave's suicide?[161] If so, how do you distinguish the slave's experience from that of a person living in similar daily torment in a less recognizable structure or social schema, for instance a person with no known/diagnosable/treatable medical ailment but mysterious searing chronic pain, or a person who interprets her life to be enormously diminished in enjoyability in ways difficult for a bystander to understand or empathize with? For instance, it may be difficult or impossible for an Alzheimer's patient to describe the degree or impact of her cognitive decline with accuracy, but this lack of narration does not mean the experience is not real.

If we do not allow the slave's suicide on Planet X but allow the suicides of free people, then we implicitly *classify the right to die as a privilege* and deny that privilege to the enslaved group. If we accept that a slave killing herself is an unusual demonstration of her agency, then those opposed to

---

160   Alluding to Exodus 3:22, 12:36.
161   Some will argue allowing the slave's suicide but vetoing Veronika's suicide could come from a competing, objectionable framework; that the slave's life is intrinsically less valuable than the free person's life. That is not the framework proposed or utilized here. Rather, the slave is treated here as equally human and equally potentially valuable, but with a recognition that the slave's expected value from future life may be substantially impaired due to the imposition of slavery. In a scenario where emancipation (through escape, jubilee, etc.) is even a 1 percent possibility, the slave's prospective calculation of the value of future life may be significantly improved.

slavery should support the slave's decision to end life—and should support it as an evidencing of the slave's personhood, not because of the financial loss it inflicts on the slave's owner. In any framing drawn from this lineage of hypotheticals, if suicide is barred for slaves but not barred for free people, doesn't that suggest dying is a fundamental right, or at least a dear choice that we should treasure and defend rather than erode and limit?

How do you, in possession of only the vaguest sketch of Veronika and of the slave, presume Veronika has insufficient clarity in weighing today's journey against tomorrow's reward, or that Veronika has less reason, or a less valid reason, as compared to the slave on Planet X to end the pain of living? Why are such comparisons so tempting? Why can we not simply advocate for a system that might honor Veronika's wishes and also the slave's without judging whose claim to relief from life is more clear, more pure, more valid, more righteous?

Any hierarchy meant to describe the "validity" of one's claim to the right to die is fragile and shatters when exposed to the vibrations of scrutiny.

Imagine, briefly, a terrible regional natural disaster.

Above: Robust lock doors, driven by mighty steel clockwork gears whose sympathetic wear surfaces are measured in square feet, tame the flow of water from the English Channel into inland harbors at Portishead, an area known for flash floods and treacherous tides during Roman[162] and medieval times and the site of countless unrecorded, terrifying littoral moments. The recent episodic drama Liaison (Apple TV Originals 2023) is premised upon a similar scenario (due to locks opened by a cyberattacker) overwhelming the banks of the Thames modern day London. Photo taken by the author.

After the disaster, *A* is now the sole surviving member of her ethnic group and feels ethnically isolated, feels the vacuum left by her pruned family tree and dead messengers of her culture, and constantly wishes to die. Imagine in a slightly different version of the simulation that *B*, from the same village as *A* and having experienced a similar disaster, is the last remaining person who speaks her language, but not the last member of her ethnic group, and constantly wishes to die. Imagine in a different version of the simulation that *C* is the only remaining person of her ethnic group and the only one who speaks the language, and due to genocide rather than due to natural disaster; does this change the calculus? Does forcing *C* to live when *C* does not consent to live reduce *C*'s status to something more like that of an endangered zoo animal rather than a welcomed refugee? How can we possibly compare *A*, *B*, and *C*'s wishes to die to those of Veronika or those of the slave on Planet *X*?

Should *A*, *B*, or *C* be allowed to end life? All? None? Can any of us who has not experienced such a comprehensive and unimaginable loss fairly act as an arbiter of this? Are doctors any better equipped to say whether *A*, *B*, or *C* should be allowed to end life than philosophy professors or ethics experts or the average person on the street?

The idea that we should weigh these questions at all runs counter to my position. *A* is best positioned to choose whether to endure today and receive tomorrow in exchange, just as Veronika is best positioned to choose whether dying today by her own hand, tomorrow by her own hand, or in the distant future from natural causes is best. The idea that one must submit a résumé of suffering to access life's escape hatch is cruel, bureaucratic, and unfair.

---

[162] The lower Gordano Valley is the site of a Roman town built and rebuilt many times due to flooding; ruins and remains suggest fast-moving water rushing through the valley and wiping out the town with incredible force.

It's impossible to destigmatize suicide with a book. It's impossible to change thousands of years of prejudice and prohibition with these pages of advocacy. But my goal is to destigmatize suicide for you, to give you a better life and a better death. I wish you the calm Dickens ensconced in his famous passage on death:[163] "It is a far, far better thing that I do, than I have ever done; it is a far, far better rest that I go to than I have ever known."

Several people close to me intentionally ended their lives prior to their natural expirations, and I spent two and a half years living in a village in a region with one of the lowest life expectancies in the world. These experiences, separately or combined, no doubt influenced my view on death. My conclusion? Death can be horrible or beautiful or something in between, and we have a degree of control over it; *wouldn't it be a shame to exercise none of that control*?

When people can simply hold their breaths long enough to die (including over a dozen people on social media network TikTok who've died this way in the past year or so), are we going to ban breathing slowly? Breathing while on social media? Ban nostrils? Ban diaphragms? Ban lungs? Ban the "idea" of holding one's breath? Ban "discussion" of holding one's breath?[164]

It's silly, but no sillier than the broader suicide-prohibitionist discussion.

The concept that death or dying should be kept secret or kept in a locked cabinet is akin to efforts to restrict access to provocative ideas; they are a silly use of state resources and a misguided ambition of paternalistic *über-regulators*. The idea that words with a "bad tendency," a troublesome and uniquely American legal concept, should be regulated or punished was thankfully

---

[163] Charles Dickens, A Tale of Two Cities London, Chapman & Hall (1859).

[164] For an analogous discussion, see the many examples of fan fiction written in the *Dune* universe on the morality and prohibition of heart-stoppers (variation: heartstoppers), passphrases or secret words that when heard will stop the heart of a hearer appropriately conditioned, similar to a spontaneous cardiac event or ingestion of strong poison. Interestingly, Herbert uses the term "suicide" to describe one such death, suggesting he believed allowing (or seeking) this conditioning was when one chose to die (or chose to place one's death in another's hands). See also many marine veterinary accounts of highly intelligent dolphins diving to unescapable pressures while holding their breaths until brain death, otherwise-inexplicable suicidal behavior (other observed dolphins die from "hunger strike" type behavior and "failure to thrive" but these are more difficult to associate directly with suicidal intent).

abandoned more than fifty years ago. I do not believe content discussing, or even encouraging or instructing, how to end one's life should be restricted, censored, or escorted away from the energetic debate of the public square.

Hiding away suicide in the vaults and safes of society is ineffectual, bizarre, and unnecessary.

To engage with suicide, we must be able to imagine, consider, and discuss it. This includes its merits, its history, its cultural context, and other aspects. And it involves talking about death.

Death was once a *public ceremony*,[165] like a loved one's train leaving a station.

Today, death is almost shameful, something to be whispered about quietly and rarely.

As Justice Brandeis argued in an enlightened concurring opinion in *Whitney*, a general anxiety surrounding unpopular ideas is insufficient to justify government alarm or criminal sanction. In Brandeis's discussion, he introduces a "time to answer" test, where when something unpopular is introduced to the public conversation and the strongest arguments of its merit can be debated in public, adopted by some, rejected by others, but heard by all. This "discussion affords ordinarily adequate protection," Brandeis suggested, even when the proposed thing is "noxious" or highly objectionable.

I adopt this same view of the current discussion. Suicide has enjoyed this period of debate and its prohibition, before by operation of law and now by enforcement of social norms, has outlived its usefulness.

---

[165] To borrow the phrase from Philippe Ariès. See Phillippe Ariès, *Invisible Death*, 5 Wilson Q. 105 (1981).

SCENE IV
Discussion as a Type of Access

*Strange it is, that men should admit the validity of the argu-
ments for free discussion, but object to their being "pushed to
an extreme"; not seeing that unless the reasons are good for an
extreme case, they are not good for any case.*
—*J.S. Mill*[166]

The means of communication in the public square has changed in some ways but not in most. The advent of cellular telephones, online social networks, online forums of various kinds, group messaging services, and other bazaars for the displaying of ideas does nothing to change the fundamental discourse: some people want access to the means to end their lives with peace, pain-lessness (often a desired attribute), and certainty. To the extent technology can offer education, information, and even supplies for this undertaking, I have no quibble with the availability of information and goods. A successful, painless suicide is, after all, simply a first-class upgrade to a destination where everyone is headed anyway.

Some argue, full of passionate intensity, that people should not be allowed to order sodium nitrite suicide kits next day (or perhaps same day, with the wonders of modern logistics) from online retailers. My friend Carrie Goldberg, for whom I have the deepest respect, makes this argument passionately and often. But on this point we disagree. And I argue even same-day airborne drone delivery of suicide kits gives plenty of time for a person to consider a mortal choice.

We live in a world where the deliberation and premeditation to kill (the magic ingredient for first-degree murder in most jurisdictions making that distinction) can be formed in a mere moment; in other words, the quantity

---

[166] John Stuart Mill, On Liberty 39 London, John W. Parker and Son (1859).

of time spent deciding to kill someone is irrelevant (the so-called Carroll Rule) as to whether someone commits first-degree murder.

This means we are willing to subject a defendant, on the basis of a moment's thought, to an enhanced (sometimes life-long or even life-taking) sentence. It suggests to me that we believe people can form elaborate, even conspiratorial, thoughts in a compact period of time, and that we are willing to take those plenary thoughts very seriously.

Why should we take thoughts formed quickly less seriously when someone decides to end his or her own life rather than taking the life of another? I don't think we should. I think we should take both very seriously indeed.

I am skeptical of the society where we celebrate the sudden "aha" of Newton beneath the apple tree or Archimedes in the bathtub but scold and silence a sudden "aha" of the person realizing additional life is not worthwhile, classifying that conclusion as mental illness, or otherwise valuing this insight at zero.

Most people want a painless, regretless death.

Fate sometimes, but rarely, cooperates.

But we can deviate from, perhaps fully outmaneuver, nature's cruel script.

For me, the perfect death is after an evening celebrating with friends.

It's planned; I smile when I think about it.

My friends have invites for it in their calendars.

I'm not terminally ill. I'm not depressed. I'm fit and alert. I've been to over fifty countries, two on the days they became countries. I am in nearly as good shape in my forties as I was in my twenties, own much or most of the art I've ever wanted to collect, and the tough choice in my life is where to drive a sports car on a fair-weather Saturday. Life is great!

But I also believe death can, and should, be great, and that life need not be miserable or pitiful or already nearly over for suicide to be an accessible or acceptable option. There should be no prerequisites for death, no test of *enough*—something I refer to as "pity means testing."

I strongly believe a good death is the end to a good life and that a good death is a planned death. I prefer death to be something I do, not something that happens to me. And if every day I'm spending time, I prefer to know exactly how much I can spend in total.

Any topic of sufficient complexity bifurcates into theory and practice.

Our cultural conversation about death remains at an elementary maturity level; we discuss the basic forces at work, the Newtonian physics of death. The "idea of" death is something we can dream about, sing about, even joke about without discomfort. But thinking about death as an activity in which we participate, as a process, as a task to be accomplished, even as a final achievement . . . this is uncomfortable for many today, deeply taboo.

How strange, as death (or more precisely, dying) is something you and I are doing right now. It is an activity every living human engages in every day. But many do not think of each day living as also containing dying, just as they can admire a sunrise without perceiving or pondering the rotation of the planet.

If we think of death as something to be done well or to be improved, then we need to understand "better" and "worse" deaths. And that means not just thinking about the event of death but rather thinking about the process of death. Here, Sylvia Plath via Lady Lazarus[167] was right: dying is an art. And art is, to paraphrase Damien Hirst, having to do with a mix of process and product.

So what can we learn about the process and how society interacts with that process?

I recall discussing with my friend Cristina Desmond—a fellow London School of Economics alum who focused her research on family and reproductive matters—why Japan has better childbirth outcomes than the US. There are many differences, not the least of which is that Japan is a gerontocracy facing a demographic crisis[168] wherein every Japanese pregnancy is

---

[167]   Sylvia Plath, *Lady Lazarus*, Ariel 14 (1965).

[168]   For more context on the challenges Japan faces, see Florian Coulmas, Harald Conrad, Annette Schad-Seifert, & Gabrielle Vogt, The Demographic Challenge: A Handbook About Japan Pts. III, V (2008). Japan has made a variety of bets to head off its demographic woes, but none has succeeded to the degree hoped. Experiments with increased immigration quotas were met with fierce resistance from those (a powerful bloc of mostly-older voters) who feel strongly Japan should be monocultural from an

viewed not only as a maternal blessing but as a matter of national security.

Japanese women receive more support in pregnancy than US women. They receive better governmental guidance on nutrition and what to expect during pregnancy. They tend to work very little, if at all, during the third trimester compared to American women. Some hospitals run "fire drills" where the woman visits the hospital as she will to give birth and meets relevant doctors and nurses. Typically, women do not work during the final six weeks of pregnancy or the first two months after giving birth and childcare leave, conditions radically different from the US experience.

Cristina and I sat beneath a verdant trellis at the Fort Worth Botanic Garden poking at our takeaway salads. "So they're better prepared," Cristina succinctly summarized. We discussed how Abe Shinzō, in his time as prime minister (a post to which he was elected seven times), was responsible for much of this emphasis on maternal support. In addition to supporting women in the workplace more generally (dubbed "womenomics" in the Western press) and promising 30 percent of Japanese corporate leadership positions would be occupied by female executives by 2020 (a goal not met), he talked often about motherhood.

In 2013, then-PM Abe suggested a three-year, Nordic-style maternity leave, something that split Japanese feminist commentators as supportive of women but also amplifying their gender-specific absence from the workplace. The then-PM went so far in 2017 to make a much-parroted (and also much-parodied) comment that, due to demographic challenges and a low birth rate, Japanese pregnancies are 国家安全保障上の懸念 or

---

ethnolinguistic standpoint. Supplementing the service workforce with guest workers from elsewhere in Asia has not appreciably increased the population, as this mostly male, mostly twenty-something group generally leaves Japan before having children. Strong investments in robotics and automation, once thought to be the best route for a smaller number of Japanese people to operate an economy of comparable size, have borne fruit but have not created a new, comprehensive production infrastructure able to be operated by a small caucus of people from the managerial class. Directly paying young couples to have children (a program currently administered by the Ministry of Health with an incentive of ¥420,000, due to increase to ¥500,000 in April of 2023) has been described as inadequate and insulting when compared to the cost of raising a child in Kyoto or Tokyo or Sapporo, and the real matter of foregone wages or missed parental promotions early in the child's life, given some major Japanese employers' less than family friendly cultures.

concerns of national security. While arguably true in a literal sense, I believe the remark was meant as a prioritization of pregnancies as one of the most important things happening in Japan.

If it is possible to craft such creative, detailed, thoughtful policy around the genesis of life, then it is possible to use policy tools to increase choice, happiness, and support at the end of life. If it is possible to talk about pregnancy in the same breath as national defense, it is possible to prioritize the human lifecycle alongside other major policy and spending decisions. If a society cares deeply about the creation of new lives, then it should care equally about, and take some measure of responsibility for, how each of those lives might eventually conclude.

SCENE V
The Problematic Dichotomy

*Thus we adopt the view of the line of cases discussed in
Saikewicz which would allow Abe Perlmutter the right to
refuse or discontinue life-extending treatment based upon
"the constitutional right to privacy"[169] . . . an expression of the
sanctity of individual free choice and self-determination.*
—The Hon. Gavin G.K. Letts[170]

There are many poetic parallels between the beginning and end of life, but I am drawing a very practical one. For many contemporary Japanese women there will only be one pregnancy; nearly everyone is a first-timer, nobody knows quite what to expect.[171] Death is in this way similar to Japanese pregnancy: it's something important that each of us will only do once. So we should want to prepare fully and do it well.

But why suicide? *Isn't suicide a scary, bad death rather than a good death?*

There is a bothersome and unrealistic false dichotomy often drawn separating natural death from suicide. Suicide is painted as awful and sad. A

---

[169]   For those without American legal training, Judge Letts is not talking about privacy in the narrow Kylloian sense (the lady of the house's freedom from surveillance during her nude enjoyment of a sauna, Justice Scalia's now-famous example, see Kyllo v. United States, 533 US 27, 38 (2001)) but in a broader Griswoldian sense (see the eponymous case, Griswold v. Connecticut, 381 U.S. 479 (1965)), a privacy within which husband and wife can make important decisions or a sphere of privacy within which a person can have thoughts or make plans that may be unpopular or scandalous, free from the thought police. See George Orwell, Nineteen Eighty-Four 4–6 (1949).

[170]   Satz v. Perlmutter, 362 So. 2d 160, 162 (Fla. Dist. Ct. App. 4th Dist.), citing Superintendent of Belchertown v. Saikewicz Mass., 370 N.E.2d 417 at 426 (Mass. Sup. J. Ct. 1977).

[171]   Journalists, anthropologists, demographers, economists, and others have spilled untold barrels of ink on the topic of Japanese demographic change and of the modern Japanese gerontocracy more generally; I will not insult that work by attempting to summarize it here in a quippy footnote. For insightful writing on Japan, I recommend reading my friend Noah Smith (on contemporary issues), John Dower (on the latter twentieth century), and Kume Kunitake's Japan Rising (late nineteenth century). An honorable mention to David Pilling and his book Bending Adversity; David and Noah are both Western journalists who lived in modern Tokyo.

natural death is painted, meanwhile, as virtuous, peaceful, good, and even pious or righteous. But the reality could not be further from this. Your natural death may be peaceful and you may drift off to sleep and never wake; that's lovely . . . and can be engineered via suicide.

But there are many, many worse outcomes if we rely upon natural expiration.

Want your idiot nephew to decide when your life ends because he's the one the hospital was able to reach on the telephone? Want a third-year medical student who got two hours of sleep last night and is multitasking between seven patients, a promising prospect in a dating app, and a borderline-problematic relationship with alcohol to shape your life's end? Want the shoddy health insurance coverage your employer bought last year to help determine the time of your demise?

Because that's how the big, bad world works.

It isn't a matter of idyllic, graceful, optimal natural death versus premature, grim, self-inflicted death. It's a matter of dying unpredictably and possibly awfully, or dying in a planned, orderly, less terrifying way. All airplanes eventually come back to earth;[172] would you prefer a sudden, unexpected crash or a controlled landing?

In the modern world of hospitals and 9-1-1 calls and the final days of life as a profitable event for a healthcare system, if you don't choose, someone will choose for you.

Let me restate that: Part of why I've chosen to affirmatively end my life is because I believe dying is something too important, too personal to leave to chance.

There is another, subtly different, and somewhat worse, lineage of thought about death. I think of it as a species of preservationism.

This is a kind of preservationist philosophy, a hippie Luddite-ism, almost an environmentalism, that some apply to death. That a natural death is a

---

[172]   A modernizing, or at least mechanizing, translation of *wenyo ali malo duogo toa ping, infra* Act VI, Scene II, Part I.

natural wonder, like a sunset or a hatchling, to be admired and cherished. I want to crush the immature, free-of-nuance ideal that a natural death is a dream to be prized, but suicide is a horrific nightmare to which years of pain or purposelessness is superior.

Instead, I believe that perhaps natural death is a natural wonder, but in the sense that an F5 tornado is a natural wonder—something that can be carefully observed and damage mitigated with uniquely human reasoning. Yes, some animals can smell an approaching storm in a way that we cannot, but they can do nothing in response but hide or flee. We can think, plan, and discuss. We can *decide to die* with a complexity and depth of reason no other animal possesses.

The larger natural wonder than natural death, much larger, is human agency. We are able to choose the time and mode of our demise. Suicide is not a tragedy, it is a superpower.

It is our unique ability, and I suggest our duty, to explore how to enjoy life while relieving or preventing suffering; not for the sake of cheap hedonism, but for the sake of maximizing the value of each life and, cumulatively, increasing the quality of human life more generally.

To gather what little information we can to prepare for, and even plan, death requires a great deal of thought and honest conversation. We must interact honestly, reciprocally, and constantly to understand each other's thoughts, experiences, and fears in order to prepare to die.

Yet we live in a time of prohibition, the "thought police" are not just an Orwellian exaggeration in this context. Forget attempting to end your life; even thinking about suicide is framed as problematic.

We are fearful to mention our thoughts about death even to our romantic partners. We fear mention of suicide to a therapist will trigger an emergency protocol. Discussing death with our work friends might result in a workplace training or an escorted stroll to HR. Even Google won't let us ask about death without inserting hotlines, helplines, and other lines prior to our search results. And we're so afraid to talk about death that we prioritized rebranding death insurance life insurance decades before rebranding the War Department the Defense Department.

Our conversations about death are unrealistic, a function of the modern global pandemic of Main Character Syndrome. We find it aesthetically unpleasing and philosophically jarring that, after we die, our little blue spaceship will simply continue doing boring NASCAR-style laps at 67,000 miles an hour with our rotting corpses aboard. I once spoke with a former senior bank executive about the bank's 1980s security protocols around credit card balances, and I found the narrative had less to do with high finance and more to do with our incompetence thinking about mortality.

This particular bank had contracted to rent a disused mineshaft somewhere in Appalachia where someone would drive in a van from the bank's Chicago headquarters to the mineshaft with a box of optical discs carrying ledger data for each customer and current credit card balances, lending terms, interest rates, and so forth. A person or group of people would then unload the van and put this newest box of optical discs in some room or cave within the shaft.[173] Voilà! Even in the event of nuclear exchange between the US and Russia, everybody's Mastercard debts would be possible to perfectly (or at least imperfectly) reconstruct after the conflict.

This ignores the "what next" question of, well, the total destruction of the United States and the fact that people crawling out of bomb shelters having survived full-scale thermonuclear war might not be that concerned about how much they owed on a pre-war credit card. And, what, exactly, was the bank planning to do if people didn't pay off their cards as nuclear winter set in? Sue them in courthouses now reduced to pulverized marble? Threaten their credit ratings? Refuse to extend them another line of credit in a world where bottlecaps[174] are the new currency?

---

[173] This plan was rooted in two beliefs: (1) that a structurally robust mineshaft away from any major city likely to be targeted by a Soviet attack would be a safe place to store something and (2) Soviet nuclear weapons would cause electromagnetic and other effects (collateral EMP detonation effects) that might destroy data on magnetic disk drives or held in memory on computers, but would not affect ledger data already memorialized on optical discs.

[174] A reference to Fallout: A Post Nuclear Role Playing Game Interplay Entertainment (1997).

The bank discs in a mineshaft is an absurd example of how we will do just about anything to avoid thinking about how macabre realities might more realistically play out.

Death seems very far in the future until it doesn't, like those acid-etched warnings on automobile side-view mirrors—death is "closer than it may appear." But thoughts of death are taboo, hidden away, associated with other things we fear (old age, mental illness, etc.). They're confined to our most private moments, our darkest nightmares, unusually deep breaths taken on an otherwise-uneventful afternoon, daydream glimpses of mortal fear after a sudden pain left of the sternum that we dare not mention to anyone.

When we dream of falling, we simply say "falling."

We say, "I dreamt I was falling." It's dishonest, but we all do it. To paraphrase legendary high-wire daredevil Philippe Petit: Anxiety when at a great height (vertigo) is not a fear of falling, it is a fear you will give into temptation and jump. The author, having experienced vertigo on the traverse at Mont Blanc (from the Italian side) and having fallen plenty far enough in a sun-kissed southern-exposure "time stops" experience (from Fisher Towers in Moab), agrees.

We never say that we dreamt of dying—just falling. We never talk about the ground below, a blurry patchwork but no doubt approaching at terminal velocity, the hypothetical people down there deaf to our descending screams. We fall, passing through wind and cloud at a terrifying rate, but we're aware the air passing us is a finite resource of altitude and will be replaced by pavement or soil or water hitting stout as stone.

And we never, ever would confide that before the falling bit of the dream came the rooftop scene, the deepest breath ever, the pause, and the jump.

Were you smiling as you jumped? Did you do a bit of leaning back and forth on the edge of the parapet, have a bit of childish fun before the plunge? I often do, in this dream.

If that interests you, read on.

FLASHBACK, PART I
One Day on the Midway

The individual who hates certain ideas must recognize that if he succeeds in getting the state to bar those ideas, other ideas to which he is attached may also be barred, that censorship once established is difficult to contain, that the censor is almost always somebody else, and that the "somebody else" is generally a tired administrator.[175]
—*Dean Harry H. Wellington*[176]

If there's a place where the concept of "banning ideas" is disfavored, pilloried, and wholesale mocked, it is the University of Chicago. Perhaps no American institution has a stronger reputation for protecting unpopular concepts and debates in the modern age, including holding controversial debates on abortion (when the practice was both unpopular and illegal in the 1950s), a well-attended debate on the creation of a market for the buying and selling of human organs in the 1990s, and one recently the ethics of sending bacteria that can endure extreme environments to other planets as "microcolonists." (This debate occurred in 2019.) To paraphrase Ted Snyder's comments in a C25[177] lecture I attended long ago, the University of Chicago believes in markets, and believes the marketplace of ideas—even unpopular ideas—is among the most important markets.

Many years ago, when I was a graduate student at the University of Chicago, I sat on the Midway only a few hundred yards from where I now teach. I pulled a draft paper from my backpack, still warm from its *naissance*

---

[175] A general critique of bureaucrats but also likely a specific reference to the "tired administrator" who appears as a stock character in Parkinson's 1960s essays.
[176] Harry H. Wellington, *On Freedom of Expression*, 88 Yale L.J. 1105, 1133 (1979). Dean Wellington at the time served as Dean of Yale Law School and Edward J. Phelps Professor of Law.
[177] Gary Becker's preferred lecture hall at Harper Center on UChicago's campus.

in the computer lab laser printer. Earlier that day, I'd attended Advanced Microeconomic Analysis of Policy Issues, ECON33111, which might have been the most "Chicago" course available at Chicago in the 2000s; it was taught by John Bates Clark Medal recipient[178] Kevin Murphy and Nobel Laureate Gary Becker.[179]

The course focused on the economic analysis of difficult policy questions and how markets (often, but not always, auction markets) might be used to find better solutions, from a full week on how patient-recipients should be sorted in terms of priority in a world of scarce organs to a discussion of whether a basic income or some other pecuniary incentive for well-behaved, recently released convicted felons might be a good idea. This course had a profound effect on how I saw the world and was, in retrospect, the key moment when I decided to continue my studies (earning M.Phil. and Ph.D. degrees at the London School of Economics) rather than following some other path.

My lunchtime reading was a draft paper written five years earlier[180] by Professor Gary Becker and University of Chicago legal scholar and appellate jurist Richard Posner. The paper, titled "Suicide: An Economic Approach" with multiple "very preliminary, not to be quoted" notations from Becker, deals with how a rational actor might theoretically (or if one is more quantitatively inclined, actuarially) appraise the value of life and decide to end life rather than waiting for life to reach its maximum medically achievable duration.

Don't worry, I'm not going to bore you with any math symbols or proofs or diagrams here.

However, imagine I ask you, "suppose you knew you were going to die tomorrow, what would you do [today]?" Now I could instead ask, "suppose you knew you were going to die in one year, what would you do [for the next year]?" The latter question gives you more leeway to travel or do certain other things unlikely to be accomplished in a day. Now I could ask the same

---

[178] Awarded to remarkable economists under forty and seen as a leading indicator of later brilliance and perhaps even Nobel-worthiness.

[179] Professor Becker also won the Clark Medal back in 1967.

[180] Story takes place in 2009–10; draft was dated 2004.

question with five years or ten years. Eventually, I ask you, "Suppose you knew you were going to die. What would you do?" Because we all do, in fact, know we will someday die. But we often don't live like it.

When looking at most things, economists will tend to see long-run vertical supply in their right peripheral vision. The long-run money supply, the long-run supply of heartbeats you can conceivably create, it's all vertical and somewhere out there on the right-hand bit of the x-axis (time, t) it's there. Suicide is simply a decision to set the supply of life at some known point on the x-axis rather than wandering rightward on the axis (t) until one is literally or figuratively hit by a bus.

Now this is not some strictly utilitarian Benthamite, trolley-problem position I'm advocating. If it were, this would be a five-page essay rather than a book. I concede that it is very difficult to suppose from a distance, or even with the benefit of intimacy, whether a person's utility (which is economist-speak for what we'll just approach as generalized value) from living an additional day is positive or negative. But this concession is small and leads to the point on which my argument turns: that one's circumstances in life are so difficult for onlookers to empirically observe or reliably quantify that one's own appraisals are best.

Returning to the sunny Midway and my Becker-Posner printout years ago, those two scholars point out (correctly) that not only is the utility one enjoys from a day living rather than dead difficult to estimate, but this is a mutable characteristic. In other words, a person fired from his job today and down on his luck may buy a lottery ticket and win a jackpot tomorrow. (If your utility function is less pecuniary, imagine instead some other windfall of an emotional or medical or aesthetic or other kind.) Professors Becker and Posner imagine an option theory calculus wherein a person makes rational decisions whether to continue living according to the expected dividends of future life, even if present life is very bad. (Every day's expected utility is zero or negative.)

Though this option pricing metaphor—and it's hardly a metaphor as Professor Becker saw it quite literally—is perhaps the most-cited aspect of Professor Becker's thinking on suicide, it is not the most important insight in the paper. That insight is hiding near the paper's end and is that the cost and availability[181] of suicide changes over time. To quote from the paper: "A person who believes but is not certain that he has a fatal disease may wish to defer suicide until he is certain, but may fear that the progress of the disease will render him incapable of doing so at that time."[182] This hints at a moving target problem. In other words, the option to end one's life may have different value over time, the cost to exercise the option and end life may vary over time, and the option may at some time be effectively worthless (impossible to exercise) due to the emotional or physical or cognitive decline of the person involved.

Many modern philosophers begin with the assumption that more life is better. In the Peter Singer model of the world, there is very little life with truly negative utility, and in the broader "effective altruism" framework, ten billion people who are each 1 percent happy is better than one billion people who are each 9 percent happy, assuming people have a common denominator of realizable happiness and that happiness can somehow be measured in a portable or fungible way.[183] In fact, it is possible to read a fair amount of philosophy, including contemporary philosophy, while rarely encountering concepts of negative utility from, or negative value of, additional time serving as a conscripted crewmember on our little blue spaceship. When I read Mill, I see the value of pleasure and the value, too, of reducing pain or suffering. I see agency and self-sovereignty arguments that are the primitives, the essential construction materials, for arguments made here about the individual's rights to treat or refuse treatment for, medicate or not medicate, and even kill one's body (so long as others are not harmed) easily outranking[184] the day's fashions, preferences, and norms. But I do not find in Mill the serious

---

[181] And unavailability of a choice can simply be modeled as infinitely unaffordable cost in this imprecise context.

[182] Becker & Posner, note 154 at *32.

[183] There are both measurement problems and comparability problems when discussing concepts like happiness, oughtness (right and wrong), or broader ethics. See Mill, Utilitarianism, *supra* note 142.

[184] "[T]he only purpose for which [state or societal] power can be rightfully exercised over any member of a civilised community, against his will, is to prevent harm to others." Mill, On Liberty, *supra* note 191 at 69.

contemplation that additional life can have truly enduring, robustly durable, negative utility in the sense that Becker and Posner's thinking allows.

With that, I returned to class and didn't pick up my printout of that essay again until I unpacked it in my flat in London in 2010.

FLASHBACK, PART II
London Calling

*England and America are two countries separated by a
common language.*
—*George Bernard Shaw*

Moving into my new flat, now a London School of Economics masters
student who would soon be a Ph.D. student, I unpacked my books first,
as I often do when inhabiting a new space. Among them, coursepacks[185]
from the University of Chicago (including Becker and Murphy's course)
and several books purporting to express the "Chicago view" or "Chicago
school" of whatever. If I didn't understand that view at this stage, no
book would solve it.

I walked down Curtain Road, cut down Leonard Street which is more
of an alley than a road, and sat down with the same copy of the Becker and
Posner suicide paper once again, my copy defaced with pencil graffiti and
Audi-logo-esque rings of teacups, markings all papers suffer while I make
intellectual investments in them. I recall pausing and smiling when Colin
John's "Karma" played at some point in the evening, off his then-fresh EP
Suicide in Shoreditch.

I want to be clear: I began thinking deeply about suicide as a policy issue
not because I was profoundly unhappy or imminently suicidal, but for precisely the opposite reason, because I wanted to live my life well and be able
to plan to get the most from it.

In furtherance of this, I spent several days in the areas and cafés
Parkinson favored in the early 1950s, when he contemplated Parkinson's
Law (a decade before the Apollo Program, perhaps its most common

---

[185]   These were bound packages of hundreds of pages of reading material, one for each course. In an age
of increasing momentum toward digitization and decreasing fashionableness of deforestation, these are
relics.

in-practice example), including the Black Penny on Long Acre in Covent Garden near the London School of Economics. Many years ago, the Black Penny was a different café but still, as its successor does, served tea and sandwiches to mid-day company men alongside artists and academics and men in dark suits toting unusually square briefcases filled with Freemason paraphernalia.

Parkinson was a contemporary, but not colleague, of Orwell's and came to many of the same views about the ever-more-complex organizational chart, the tendency for firms and departments to hire more yet accomplish less, and the deepest genesis of pyramidal bureaucracy:[186] the innocent desire among all ambitious managers to have fewer peers and more subordinates.[187] Parkinson's Law, however, predicts how people and organizations behave when faced with a deadline.

Parkinson's Law predicts that the amount of work to be done expands or contracts according to the time allotted for the work's completion. This is counterintuitive, as people, even those with high levels of managerial training or management experience, generally experience the world as having tension on the rope from the opposite end of the causal pulley. Put simply, people expect the amount of work to be done will dictate how long the work will take, while Parkinson predicts that, even for complex or novel processes, the deadline dictates the work rather than the work dictating the deadline.

Obviously, it is possible to construct counterexamples. Requiring a ten-year-old to write a thousand pages of poetry in a day will not cause the workload to magically contract. A slothful worker protected by laws and unions and managerial indifference will not suddenly become productive and eager because a deadline is imposed; in fact, from past experience, he may consider deadlines movable or not have any reason to take them seriously.

But it is startling how often and with what sharp fangs Parkinson's Law

---

[186] Sometimes referred to as *the Parkinson proposition* in organizational behavior circles.
[187] The author's somewhat simplified paraphrasing, with apologies to Parkinson.

holds.

In the case of the Apollo space missions of the 1960s, President Kennedy foreshadowed a goal on May 25, 1961 before a joint session of Congress and refined this mandate on September 12, 1962 in a speech at Rice University. Specifically, that the United States put a man on the moon and return him safely to earth "by the end of this decade" (meaning by the close of the 1960s).

Though familiar with the difficulty of bureaucracy as a student of government at Harvard, as a young lieutenant in the Navy, and as the son of a man who had been unceremoniously dismissed as ambassador in London after a series of isolationist statements and diplomatic miscues, this was not training enough to appreciate the complexity and difficulty of the lunar landing mission.

In fact, many at NASA did not fully appreciate the complexity of Apollo's necessary orbiter-lander (CM-LEM) configuration or the difficulties of ensuring the success of such a mission. Kennedy, though certainly bright, lacked the technical training, engineering know-how, and project-based managerial experience to understand whether it was more likely the Apollo mission goals could be completed in 1969, 1970, or 1971—especially when these feats had never been attempted as of September 1962 and only researched theoretically as of the latter 1950s.

AFSWC-TR-59-39

SWC
TR
59-39
Vol I

HEADQUARTERS

AIR FORCE SPECIAL WEAPONS CENTER

AIR RESEARCH AND DEVELOPMENT COMMAND

KIRTLAND AIR FORCE BASE, NEW MEXICO

CATALOGED BY DDC
AS AD No.____
425380

A STUDY OF LUNAR RESEARCH FLIGHTS
Vol I

by

L. Reiffel

ARMOUR RESEARCH FOUNDATION
of
Illinois Institute of Technology
19 June 1959

Above: Armour Research report dated 19 June 1959, discussing lunar missions.

So how did Apollo hit its Kennedy-created arbitrary mandate with only a season to spare?

The answer lies in Parkinson's Law.

With a firm timeline, other items could be prioritized or simplified to fit the timeline.

Contractors and vendors could be sorted with hard deadlines and pertinent milestones in mind.

Astronaut training could move ahead with a focus on a specific mission and particular dates.

A core lodestar objective protected Apollo from mission creep[188] beyond "moon, then home."

Parkinson's Law has many analogues in other areas, such as the observation that a project's costs often expand to fill the budget available, or the observation that teams are hired to the maximum headcount possible (even if some teammates contribute triflingly to the team's total efficacy).

---

[188] Mission creep is the tendency for a complex project to expand beyond its original bounds or specifications to include things that may be valuable in the abstract but were not contemplated as part of the mission's initial goal. Feature creep is the analogous tendency in software, for software to include more and more features, even if fewer and fewer end users find value in these features; the author discussed this at Microsoft's headquarters, which parodied the Pareto 80/20 rule and observed that Microsoft's spreadsheet software includes so much capability and so many features that 99 percent of users use only 1 percent of the software's functionality. Karl T. Muth: Excel and the 99-1 Rule (2014). Creep dynamics in creating things tend to create overbudget and late-to-the-finish-line projects that could conceivably have been finished on time if executed as originally conceived; this is closely related to the 90-90 rule in software and related technical projects, which violates Parkinson's Law (and states it takes 90 percent of the budgeted time to complete the first half of the software product and 90 percent of the budgeted time yet again to complete the second half).

SECOND INTERMISSION
Mezzanine Champagne Thoughts

Work expands so as to fill the time available for its completion.
—Cyril Northcote Parkinson[189]

Another analogue, however, is the one that interested me: If you knew when you were going to die, wouldn't that allow you to plan and enjoy your life more than others? Put in Parkinsonian phrasing: does life expand and contract to fill the time available, if that time is known?

Surely this incremental information about one's mortality has some better-than-zero value. Consider the challenge of planning how much to save for retirement, how often to see one's grandchildren, or whether a trip to Paris at age seventy with one's partner is desirable. Consider now making these decisions knowing the decision maker will die two hours after the birthday festivities conclude on his seventy-fifth birthday.

It is substantially easier, knowing this, to make these decisions and many others.

While one argument in this book is that people should enjoy a classical liberal (today perhaps libertarian or "new liberalism"[190]) sovereignty over their bodies and control their deaths, a related argument suggests life improves in quality and predictability when death is planned—how and why?

Like the Apollo program, life offers few goals reachable via only one path. However, life is full of trade-offs, emotional, fiscal, and otherwise. As an economist, I feel strongly that hard choices are best made within known and understood constraints. Certain things in the Apollo program were

---

[189] C. Northcote Parkinson, *Parkinson's Law,* The Economist (Nov. 19, 1955).
[190] Credit to Jeremiah Johnson and others for thinking deeply about how to describe this policy position.

simply impossible because they were disallowed by the state of materials science, the state of propulsion technology, the physics governing rocket flight, and so on.

Thinking of life's days as a non-pecuniary budget, one might ponder whether a holiday spent at a remote cabin with one's partner is more valuable than time in the city with a gaggle of friends. In a strictly pecuniary sense, one might consider whether a year or two of luxury international travel while still in robust health is more valuable than one's daughter graduating from university without student loans. Or, in a different but very real calculus touched on throughout but explored in depth elsewhere in this text, whether a hundred expensive and painful final days in the hospital,[191] with no realistic hope of recovery to health, are more important than the similarly priced option of buying a first home or a graduate school education for one's granddaughter.

These are real trade-offs made by real people every day, not outlandish, theoretical scenarios or midterm questions for an undergraduate philosophy course.

---

[191] While legal and ethical mechanics allow some people to be "unplugged" in the hospital, the truth is many people can continue to live without mechanical assistance but without much if any prospect for improved quality of life; what to allow these people (who would ask to be *unplugged* if they were *plugged in* – discussions infra at pp. 174, 206) to do is a significant question not given enough attention in public conversations.

ACT VI
Normtroopers, Normforcers, and Prohibitionism

SCENE I
Normative Prohibition

Texas was entitled to place upon Rummel the onus of one who is simply unable to bring his conduct within the social norms prescribed...
—*The Hon. William Hubbs Rehnquist*[192]

Our societal unwillingness to discuss suicide affects our other discourse, sadly.

Well-intentioned but problematic efforts to not mention the word suicide or to offer "trigger warnings" or other self-censorship when discussing suicide make the act of ending one's life seem less prevalent and more alien. These narratives also make suicide seem more violent, highlight particularly violent or unusual suicides, or disguise suicide as homicide.

If you think I'm exaggerating when I say "disguise suicide as homicide," consider first the following tweet from a news outlet in Boston.

Above: A 2016 tweet describes a suicide attempt in an ambiguous manner.

---

[192] Rummel v. Estelle, 445 US 263, 284 (1980).

You would be forgiven for, upon reading this tweet, assuming the woman was threatening someone other than herself with the knife, but this was not the case. Rather, the police were responding to a call from the woman's mother concerned about her mental health and a recent threat to end her own life. In fact, it was not until police arrived at the dozen-unit townhouse development and drew their firearms that the situation escalated.

I thought, "perhaps it is isolated incidents where these things are mischaracterized and, if so, while that's unfortunate and misleading, it is unlikely to sway policy." But sadly, this is not true.

Take, for instance, the public discussion regarding gun violence—a serious matter worthy of debate and plenary policy conversation—which has been consistently and substantially distorted by our inability to talk about suicide. The oft-cited statistic that a record-setting 45,222 people[193] in the United States died "from gun violence" or "as a result of gun violence" (or simply "were shot") during the year 2020 is invoked in contexts ranging from general gun control debate to school shooting aftermath newscasts[194] to legislative and policy and administrative discussions regarding specific measures.

And I don't contest the substance of the number: 45,222 or a similar number were indeed fatally shot in 2020 and many more were shot but did not die, that is true. What I have a problem with is commentators and politicians and others who then claim 45,222 people "died from gun violence" in 2020.

The problem with this statistic is that 54 percent[195] (and perhaps as many as 57 percent[196]) of these 45,222 deaths "from gun violence" were suicides.

---

[193] It is worth noting this number is the highest *number* of gun-related deaths recorded since modern records have been kept but is not the highest *rate* of gun-related deaths recorded during that time. The number of gun-related deaths in 2020 that were ruled unintentional/accidental (535) or occurred under undetermined circumstances (400) is not negligible.

[194] Using the FBI's definitions and excluding suspect deaths, only thirty-eight people died from gunshot wounds suffered in "active shooter" types of incidents in 2020. See Federal Bureau of Investigation, *FBI Active Shooter Incident Report*, Federal Bureau of Investigation Periodic Reporting Documents Database (2021).

[195] In rural states, the ratio can be far larger than this; in New Hampshire, eight to ten gun-related suicides occur for every gun-related homicide. See Madeline Drexler, *Guns & Suicide: The Hidden Toll*, Harvard Pub. Health 24, 33 (Spring 2013).

[196] Three percent of 2020 gun deaths are in the "other" category—for instance, a scenario where it

While dying by shooting oneself is no doubt something that involves a "gun" and is a "violent" route of demise, the storyline most native English speakers envision when they hear "gun violence" is a gun discharged during the commission of a crime or in the environs of mutual combat. This is significantly different from a veteran widower suffering from metastatic stage IV non-small cell lung cancer that's spread to other parts of the body trusting his pistol to end his life. Yet suicides are not a small distortion in the misleading 45,222; they represent more than half the total. People envision the lobby scene in the first *Matrix* film when they should instead envision the lobby scene at the local VA hospital.

Perhaps people were simply depressed during 2020 due to economic uncertainty, a global pandemic, and other factors, leading to more gun suicides. And perhaps during widespread urban quarantines fewer people were interacting at the local saloons or on the street, so there were fewer violent altercations and fewer opportunities for egos and bravado to transit from brain to trigger finger, but more suicides alone at home.[197]

But this hypothesis, like many "2020 was unique" hypotheses in economics, education, political science, sociology, and other fields, fails.

In fact, every single year since the CDC began publishing data on firearms deaths more than forty years ago, suicides have outnumbered homicides[198]

---

is unclear whether the decedent purposely killed herself or accidentally discharged the weapon while handling it or some other situation where the person with authority to notate the event a suicide was not able to reach that conclusion.

[197] This thesis of decreased social interaction and decreased gun violence for 2020, even as a standalone thesis, falls apart. In Chicago, excluding suicides and suicide attempts, 4,174 people were shot in 2020, up a whopping 52 percent from the non-pandemic year before. For comparison, Rahm Emmanuel was mayor from 2011 through 2019 and during his entire mayoral administration only 4,535 deaths were ruled homicides (gun-related or otherwise). Excellent datasets on crime and violence in Chicago are available from a number of sources, including the University of Chicago's Crime Lab. See U. Chi. Crime Lab (2023), https://urbanlabs.uchicago.edu/labs/crime. Visualizations of crime in Chicago are available via crimeisdown.com and heyjackass.com; the former also provides police scanner (radio) access in real-time and archival form, the latter provides visualizations of types of crime over time and sorted by both ward and neighborhood area. Crimeisdown.com! (2023), https://crimeisdown.com/; HeyJackass! (2023), https://heyjackass.com/.

[198] See John Gramlich, *What the Data Says About Gun Deaths in the U.S.*, Pew Research Center (Feb. 3, 2022).

in these data (61 percent in 2010, for instance[199]). And the typical gun suicide isn't a rowdy young man spurned by a lover or a young woman who recently bought a purse pistol; it's a senior citizen who has made a decision to end life and correctly[200] sees a firearm as an affordable, reliable option.[201]

This is not meant to be a book about guns or gun legislation, a topic I've written about extensively elsewhere.[202] However, given that more people kill themselves in the US with guns than by all other intentional means combined,[203] guns do deserve at least a bit of special discussion. Especially because guns represent accessibility to a reasonably priced, generally available means for suicide for people without pharmacological, biochemical, or medical backgrounds.

Just how important is access to firearms for suicide access? Enormously.

If one takes mid-2000s data and divides the states into two roughly comparable groups in macro-demographic terms, but one group is states with higher gun ownership rates[204] and the other states with lower gun ownership rates,[205] the total number of non-firearm suicides in the two states is very similar (9,172 for high-gun-ownership states and 9,259 for lower-gun-ownership states). However, if one looks at the same two categories of states and examines firearm suicides, one finds 16,577 firearm suicides in the first group and 4,257 firearm suicides in the latter group.[206]

If one accepts this framework, then those in favor of access to suicide should also be in favor of low barriers to access to firearms. I believe access to firearms is important (along with access to other reliable, affordable, simple

---

[199] See Drew DeSilver, *Suicides Account for Most Gun Deaths*, Pew Research Center (May 24, 2013).
[200] Firearm-related suicide attempts have a high success rate, estimated at around 85 percent. See Drexler, *supra* note 198.
[201] People sixty-five and older have the highest firearm suicide rate, at 10.6/100,000. Within that group, single older men who are divorced or widowed make up the majority of decedents.
[202] See generally Karl T. Muth, *The Panther Declawed: How Blue Mayors Disarmed Black Men*, 37 Harv. BlackLetter L. J. 7 (2021).
[203] See generally Drexler, *supra* note 198.
[204] Forty-seven percent of households legally owning at least one firearm.
[205] Fifteen percent of households legally owning at least one firearm.
[206] Matthew Miller & David Hemenway, *Guns and Suicide in the United States*, 359 New Eng. J. Med. 672, 673 (2008).

means of causing death), especially since even small added complexities vastly amplify the risk of unsuccessful attempts. (People vastly overestimate the probable lethality of cutting one's self or overdosing on over-the-counter painkillers like Tylenol.)

SCENE II
The Consent Lens

This wasn't a for-real suicide, Marla said, this was probably just one of those cry-for-help things...
—*Tyler Durden*[207]

Consent, and the capacity to consent, is central to any legitimate debate around suicide, but it often disregards the converse observation: natural death is so very rarely consensual.

Natural death often involves many of the crueler tools in Nature's arsenal. The allegedly quiet, peaceful death may not be experienced peacefully; it may be a horrifying series of painful heart attacks or a silent, paralyzed ordeal as one slowly drowns from bodily fluids filling the lungs.

Meanwhile, the planned death allows for greater certainty as to how and when a person will pass from living to whatever lies beyond. It avoids death from ever-worsening decrepitude. It aborts months or years of life the decedent-to-be has deemed painful or worthless or joyless.

Can children ideate, consent to, and affect planned deaths?

Can the elderly, including those who are suffering from cognitive decline?

Can the intellectually disabled or those suffering from severe brain injury?

I propose making both portable and malleable the standards used in contract law, with one exception.

In other words, I would begin with the rather simple principle that a person who would ordinarily be seen as capable[208] of executing a contract

---

[207] Chuck Palahniuk, Fight Club 59 (1996).

[208] *Capable* here means something different from *able*; it refers to having the capacity to contract. "Perhaps no branch of jurisprudence is more elusive than that dealing with one's mental capacity to contract." Henry Weihofen, *Mental Incompetency to Contract or Convey*, 39 S. Cal. L. Rev. 211 (1966). For a discussion of minors' capacities to contract in a very modern context, see generally Benjamin J. Cooper, *Naked before the Law: Reality Porn and the Capacity to Contract*, 11 Cardozo Wom. L. J. 353 (2005).

with another or making a will to dispose of her property would also be seen as capable of making the decision to end life, with a concession that some edge cases exist[209] where it may not be apparent what degree of capacity the person is able to exercise.

The exception I raise is the scenario of conservatorship.[210] While conservators can sign checks, manage accounts, and make medical decisions on behalf of the person within the conservatorship arrangement, I do not believe the conservator should have the authority to end the life he is charged with protecting and resourcing. As with the physician, this seems to unfairly place the good conservator in a position contrary to his central directive. More troubling, it seems to place the nefarious or opportunistic conservator in a position he might impermissibly use to his advantage to unethically enrich himself, mortally threaten the person within the conservatorship, or put in motion any number of easily-imaginable troubling schemes.

---

[209] See, e.g., Primerica Life Ins. Co. v. Brown, 304 F.3d 469 (5th Cir. 2002).
[210] Offered for illustration of conservatorship's difficulty and complexity: Spahr v. Secco, 330 F.3d 1266 (10th Cir. 2003).

SCENE III
A Choice? A Crime? A Sin? Consensual Death?

The time has come to talk ... about personal responsibility for
managing the dying process.
—*Timothy Leary[211]*

Is suicide intrinsically and universally and objectively[212] immoral?

If it is, then we should not allow suicide in any condition; if suicide is itself a kick to society's unstable ladder, a demonstration of *tanquam partic256 criminis rebellionis*,[213] a kind of universally recognized *actus per Legem Juliam*,[214] the discussion can cease here.

I argue, instead, that suicide is not immoral,[215] but instead a route to the inevitable *peremptorie et sine mora*,[216] and that natural death is often needlessly awful—and no whisper for mercy can abort Nature's wrath.[217] I argue at the same time, without conflict, that even if suicide is deemed acceptable, many will not take this shortcut and will choose to live even very difficult days, and my advocacy for suicide as an option does nothing to detract from

---

[211] In Chaos and Cyber Culture (1994).
[212] The history of moral objectivism as to suicide is something that, alone, could arouse the interest of some authors, but this author has no aspirations to be a *Quintus Curtius* of the topic (Roman historian of Alexander). On the question of objective (or at least somewhat objective) argument as to whether suicide can *ever* be ethical, the circa 2006 back-and-forth between David B. Feldman, Antoon A. Leenaars, and David Lester in the journal DEATH STUDIES is worth reading.
[213] The nature of the rebellious among us.
[214] Under Julian law, an act of treason.
[215] Immoral here refers not to some grand theory of morality or the reconciliation of all moral and ethical and religious codes into some binary determination. Rather, it means there is no reason suicide must be universally amoral or positioned so as to be entirely irreconcilable with morality. Exhaustive, encyclopedic determination as to each kind of death's morality or amorality is not the tome I seek to craft and legislating the morality of each kind of death should be very low indeed on society's to-do list; after all, *sed pereunti mille figurae*. (There are a thousand modes of dying.)
[216] Immediately and without delay.
[217] Referencing Proverbs 15:1, "a soft answer turneth away wrath."

their bravery and perseverance; each person who endures another day proves himself a Rowland to Death's Oliver.[218]

In some of my lectures, I integrate the term "consensual death" to describe suicide (but not mythical martyrdom, jumping on grenades, dying to elude capture, and special scenarios[219]).

In every American and British law school curriculum I've had the privilege of reviewing or teaching, we teach our students the esoteric-but-still-relevant difference between *malum in se* and *malum prohibitum*. The former, *malum in se*, is a crime like murder, intrinsically repulsive to civilized peoples and considered wrong since time immemorial. The latter is a crime like driving fifty-five miles an hour on a road with a fifty-four mile an hour speed limit; there is no instinctive moral revulsion to the sight of a car traveling on such a road at fifty-five miles an hour.[220]

While these examples *supra* were admittedly and carefully chosen for maximum contrast, it is no exaggeration to state reasonable minds can differ as to whether suicide is *malum in se* or *malum prohibitum* or even *incivilis minime* (objectionable in even, or only, the smallest degree). There are middle-ground cases where some may believe the activity is prohibited for moral reasons while others may believe the same activity is simply prohibited to preserve economic efficiency or to prevent the erosion of existing institutions.[221]

Pause now your consideration of how wrong, if wrong at all, suicide is . . . and why.

---

[218] Rowland and Oliver were two knights of Charlemagne so expert, tireless, and deft in combat they could duel indefinitely with no victor and with each causing no harm to the other.

[219] This broad exclusion includes mythological tests of bravery or other desirable traits, such as Sita throwing herself into a conflagration to prove her virginity to her husband Rama. See *The Ramayana*.

[220] For more on this particular offense and its cultural context, see Karl T. Muth, *Learning Facts from Fiction in Jay-Z's 99 Problems*, 111 J. Crim. L. & Criminology O. 1 (2021).

[221] To illustrate the fertile ground for disagreement this dichotomy creates: The Hon. Richard A. Posner argues that theft is not *malum in se* but rather a kind of markets regulation and that theft "is [only] punished because it is inefficient to permit the market to be bypassed. " Richard A. Posner, Economic Analysis of Law 68 (1973). In contrast, William Blackstone classifies theft as *malum in se* in one section and as *malum prohibitum* in another (a contradiction Bentham's critique mercilessly seizes upon), and some scholars classify theft of all kinds as *malum in se* without further discussion or explanation. William Blackstone, Commentaries on the Laws of England 377 Oxford, Clarendon Press (1765).

Instead, come with me on a journey that involves a Venn diagram of unkind classification that goes something like this: If you choose to end your life, you are either (1) individually insane or (2) part of an insane group, a social collective madness of some kind. Obviously, it is imaginable that an insane person might also be part of an insane group or that an insane group is composed of insane constituents, so there is a partial, Vennesque eclipse of these taxonomical buckets.[222]

We can talk about these things. But how should we talk about them?

Let's start with committing suicide. It sounds like committing a serious offense. Or at least participating in a serious misdeed. Perhaps conspiring in a serious crime; George Bernard Shaw referred to suicide's perpetrator as being a coconspirator in the devil's burglary of a soul.

But my view is that while someone may be committing suicide in the modern parlance, this is not in the same sense as once commits arson or fraud. As discussed *supra*, it is *committing to* suicide that interests me, and perhaps *committing to* suicide becoming acceptable in polite circles, or really any circles other than those utilizing the Venn diagram above, is what worries prohibitionists most of all.

I think of imagining the flavor and texture of dying in one's mind, not as one imagines the violence of murder when enraged, but as one imagines the savoring of a fine meal after an epoch of fasting. *Committing to* suicide is not merely occasionally daydreaming about that food, but actually opening one's diary and setting a date and time to enjoy the meal.

---

[222] The concept that suicide is only possible when mental illness is present is important to the normative prohibition of suicide and the exile of people who contemplate, plan, or attempt suicide. To understand this cultural prohibition more broadly, see generally Thomas Szasz, Suicide Prohibition: the Shame of Medicine (2011); see id. at 30: "A psychiatric finding of 'dangerousness to self' is the attribution of future '[d]angerousness' to an innocent person. It is an incrimination masquerading as a diagnosis."

SCENE IV
Uniform Prohibition

Moreover, we believe our construction of Article 17 better accords with the Warsaw Convention's stated purpose of achieving uniformity . . .
—The Hon. Thurgood Marshall[223]

We live in a time of unprecedented, and to me, frightening, societal uniformity globally. It isn't just that you can get your usual morning coffee order in every corner of the globe, work out at the same brand of gym (and on the same equipment) in multiple countries, and see the same luxury brands for sale at the same dollar-equivalent prices in Quebec and Qatar.

Our prohibitions are also more uniform than ever.

From which intoxicating drugs are available in alleyways versus pharmacies to automobile speed limits to the age of consent for sexual activity, the rules we live by are astoundingly and unprecedentedly similar globally, to such an extreme degree that any change at all in the rules (or any excess distance to reach an arrival-concourse Starbucks when we disembark from an airplane or vessel) is seen as a curiosity or a quirk, regardless of how far we've traveled.

There was a time before this. One of prohibitive heterogeneity, when one could drink whiskey in Edinburgh but not (legally, at least) in Chicago, when carrying a ten-inch blade in Stockholm was normal but the same blade in Copenhagen an offense, when fishing for certain species was legal in Japan but not along the nearby Korean peninsula, and when what would have been considered playful literature in one part of Europe would have simultaneously been considered prison worthy pornography only a few hundred miles away.

---

[223] Eastern Airlines Inc. v. Floyd et al., 499 US 530, 552 (1991).

In general, the trend of recent generations has been one of reasonableness and liberalization, and I agree with much of what has occurred. I do not believe an automobile barreling down a village lane at a hundred miles an hour is reasonable; nor do I believe a nine-year-old has the capacity to consent to marriage or intercourse.

But this book's purpose is to introduce a few ripples to this relatively calm regulatory sea that spans the globe, to argue in favor of a position that few take in public, let alone loudly or "on the record," so to speak. By reading this text, whether or not you agree with my argument, you're engaging in a type of rare intellectual promiscuity and considering the world could be governed by different rules and norms than those almost every jurisdiction, from monarchies to democracies to theocracies, has tended to adopt.

I'm talking about the decriminalization, legalization, acceptance, and even promotion of the practice of humans planning and causing their own deaths. And I'm talking about framing suicide as a considered, consensual death rather than as a mentally ill, tragic demise.

The more we tamper with or limit suicide, the more we make it a luxury good only available to the few while the many suffer or, at a minimum, distribute rights in a way we'd consider unacceptable for any other right. "Suicide only for Group X" not only privileges Group X but also, and more problematically, denies rights to all non-X individuals. Suicide only for those with three doctors' concurring opinions, for instance, makes suicide only available to those with certain resources and access to physicians; well-intentioned limits unnecessarily restrict access.

To illustrate the importance of eliminating means testing from suicide and having it available to all, consider the issue of money bail in the United States. I have always opposed money bail for a variety of reasons and have funded groups opposed to its use. But one of the striking aspects, or consequences, of money bail not often discussed is to limit access to suicide by serving as a type of means testing.

Access to suicide while "out on bail," to use the colloquialism, is an interesting topic for two reasons:

- A person free on bail has options to end life that are more diverse and more likely to succeed than an imprisoned person.
- A person who dies prior to a verdict in an American criminal matter is never found guilty.

On the first point, preventing suicide among people incarcerated in pretrial holding facilities is a major purpose and custodial duty of those facilities; hence, pretrial defendants who cannot afford bail are essentially denied access to suicide. On the second point, a person wealthy enough to post bail has latitude to visit friends and family, put her affairs in order, and end life on her own terms—and there may be massive benefits to doing so.

Perhaps no controversy better-illustrates the merits of the second point than the case of Kenneth Lee Lay, better known as Ken Lay, disgraced CEO and Chairman of energy giant Enron. Lay was convicted of six crimes. At the time of his death, Lay was convicted but not yet sentenced, an opportune time to die—as Lay died before sentencing and while aspects of the matter were on appeal, the court in Houston was forced to vacate the judgment of guilty, allowing significant assets to pass to Lay's widow and several children that otherwise might have been recouped by investors or obtained by the state in fines and penalties.

Such opportune deaths are accessible to those allowed freedom (Lay's death, which after an autopsy was not ruled a suicide, occurred on an autumn vacation in Snowmass, Colorado while he awaited sentencing) and in some cases hugely financially advantageous. But a person without the resources to be released on bail awaiting trial (or to be at one's multimillion-dollar vacation home in Colorado awaiting sentencing) is forced to live.

Some may claim there is a fairness in this, that people suspected of crimes and captured should be forced to live to face the charges against them. But my take is different, that if part of a criminal trial is being forced to live to face charges, then money bail should not be allowed as an exception to this and all pretrial defendants should be held in pretrial detention under "suicide watch" conditions. If, however, we want to treat people who have not yet been convicted of crimes humanely and as free members of our society (albeit with some reasonable restrictions, such as the obligatory surrender of a defendant's passport), then all pretrial defendants and defendants awaiting sentencing should enjoy the option of suicide—not only those with big bank balances and vacation homes.

Implicit in any narrowing of access that amounts to means testing is the even more offensive, at least to me, argument that people with more pecuniary resources are somehow smarter or can be trusted to make better decisions. I've argued against this in many contexts, for instance, the accredited investor role in the United States, but also in purely moral contexts, like the idea that the daughter of a banker deserves to be able to fly to a location where an abortion is available to terminate her pregnancy while the daughter of an impoverished farmer in some other place with different resources is less deserving of access to that procedure.

My friend (and a policy expert and former advisor to members of Congress on FDA matters), Vanessa Burrows, has monitored a relevant part of the American federalist experiment closely over the last twenty-five years: needle exchange programs. Thought ambitiously (briefly and erroneously) to be a comprehensive answer to the HIV and hepatitis outbreaks of the 1980s, needle exchange programs offer fresh, sterile needles to users who otherwise would be at heightened risk of unsafe injection via needle reuse or needle sharing. The programs, started by Jon Stuen-Parker at Yale (where Stuen-Parker was a 1980s AIDS activist), were quickly hit by a conservative backlash, claiming they were facilitating or encouraging intravenous drug use.

This wariness about the programs and their effects, along with a lack of empirical findings as to their efficacy in preventing the spread of disease, led to blanket bans through the medicalization of needles. Prior to the 1980s, hypodermic needles were routinely available over-the-counter and seen as an ordinary medical item for insulin-injecting diabetics and needed for a variety of ailments in a time before pills and nasal sprays became common administration modes for new drugs (for a typical mode-of-administration evolution, *see* the history of Sumatriptan from its discovery by Glaxo to being available only via vial/needle in 1993, then via prefilled one-time-use syringe, then via autoinjector, then via nasal spray, then via oral tablet, and finally via rectal suppository). Several states, including Ms. Burrows's home state of Illinois, required a prescription to buy syringes (as this book goes to press, Illinois remains the oldest by-prescription-only syringe policy framework in the United States).

After fifty years of research, we know certain things about needle exchange programs. They do not meaningfully contribute to increased injection drug use, to local violent or property crime, or to syringe litter (in fact, most syringe services programs offer safe syringe disposal and reduce syringe litter). And yet Illinois and a handful of other jurisdictions move ahead with policy that all but guarantees clean syringes will be less available and more expensive, creating disease burden and healthcare expense for decades. When one looks at needle exchange programs empirically, it seems obvious there's no need for a doctor's prescription and no need to lock away needles behind the pharmacist's counter. Predictably, the requirement of prescriptions for syringes transformed into safe intravenous drug use for the rich (who tend to have a friend or two with prescription pads) and a return to unsafe needle access for most in Illinois. But, as was true in the "medical marijuana" era of cannabis reform, the policy had less to do with winning a war on drugs than it did with winning elections: the typical voter is more comfortable with a physician in the equation. This physician is not inserted in these instances for her expensive medical training or fine character appraisal, but as a sort of "policy goalie" defending a "policy goal" that constantly changes its shape.

So what if instead of "suicide for the rich" we favor "suicide only for the old?" Is that more reasonable? Equitable?

Suicide only available to the old draws an arbitrary line across the x-axis of life and sprinkles rights on the right side and confiscates them from the left; like statutory rape laws, it creates an arbitrary age at which consent can be formulated, but when people already die at all ages, how old is old enough to die? Suicide only for the ill draws a line between those who've won a strange lottery of illness and those who are "not yet sick enough to die." Suicide only for the wealthy trades doctors for bankers and makes sure peasants die slowly.

These are common reactions I often hear:

"I support the right to die, but only for the very sick."

"Of course I support only physician-assisted suicide."

"To support suicide without doctor approval is crazy."

I've heard these sentiments, in various forms, for years and while working on this book.

When asked why physicians should be the arbiters, perhaps even dispensers, of suicide, these same people reply that physicians are experts on the matter of illness and that suicide should only be permitted for the very ill, and so should only be permitted with the blessing of physicians.

I disagree for three reasons:

1) This position requires that one believes illness is a prerequisite to suicide and that suicides among those who are not ill are problematic or even criminal. Further, it requires that illness be empirically present, manifesting, and terminal at the time of suicide.

2) This position suggests that all illness is fully understood by medicine, that only evident diagnosable illnesses are "real" ailments, and that only the most severe (in other words, already mortality threatening) forms of these are valid reasons for suicide.

3) This position supposes that many things beyond any special understanding of physicians, such as undiagnosable pain, financial woes, worry of religious persecution, completion of one's life's work, and other scenarios are not valid reasons for suicide.

How strange it is that a society would treat disease as a lottery. Stranger still that we would consider contracting (in the case of HIV, for instance) or developing (in the case of cancer, for instance) a fatal disease as "winning" such a lottery, creating a windfall of "special" end-of-life rights.

SCENE V, PART I
The Saddest Lottery

Neither can it be denied that lotteries are proper subjects...
—The Hon. Chief Justice Morrison Waite[224]

But precisely this cynical, cruel lottery has been constructed around the right to end one's life.

As a legal scholar, I take rights and how we distribute them seriously. As a mixed-race Dominican-American person whose refugee ancestors were loving grandparents and living grandparents in my childhood (and not distant lore), I take seriously the fact that it was not long ago that certain people in the United States, be they female people or Black and brown people or indigenous people or people who were not first-language speakers of English were denied certain rights.

As I mentioned *supra* (Act II, Scene I, Part II), I think it is manifestly absurd that the United States, with a carefully defined immigration policy spanning thousands of pages of administrative law and tens of thousands of pages of cumulative legislation then holds a "green card lottery" in which people randomly receive the right to live and work in the country. Similarly, I do not like the idea of sprinkling the right to end one's life randomly among those who develop cancer while denying it to other people who may suffer in other less medically diagnosable ways or those who do not suffer at all but merely want to end life.

There is also an asymmetry in our idea of carefully planning the beginning of life but preferring randomness in death; "family planning" is a phrase customarily invoked when considering the genesis of the family's next generation rather than when discussing when already born members of the family would optimally die.

---

[224] Stone v. Mississippi, 101 US 814, 818 (1880).

This is an asymmetry rather than a contradiction. There is no particular reason life and death need be planned; unplanned pregnancy and unexpected death are common sources of drama in the human experience in real life and in works of fiction. But should there not be room for conversations about the end, and not merely the beginning, of life? And shouldn't the option of planning death at least be available?

Suicide is the tenth most common cause of death in the United States: In a typical year over 48,000 people are recorded as having directly caused their own deaths and many, including me, have believed the correct figure may be double or higher. Among people aged ten to thirty-four, suicide is the second-most-common cause of death behind unintentional injuries and accidents. If this many people are affirmatively choosing death, planning one's death should not remain normatively stigmatized as something only the terribly depressed or irretrievably insane contemplate.

No rights of those who prefer a less predictable date of expiration are infringed, limited, or compromised by allowing suicide for those desiring increased certainty. The suicide route can co-exist alongside the many random routes leading to death; to use a metaphor the gunzels will love, some trains will travel a known distance to a station and stop while others will crisscross the landscape until they exhaust their fuel.

By allowing individuals to choose a date and method for their deaths, regardless of their ages or health, we create an equality in choice and an equality in death. In this section and those immediately following it, I discuss why predictable death should be available not just to the very sick or those suffering from naturally accelerated decrepitude, but also to those who may be facing non-medical challenges, those who find dying on a certain date financially advantageous, and those who are simply finished living.

On the matter of access to death, there is both *polarization* and *factionalization*. Polarization has to do with policy: disagreements on whether medical intervention is appropriate, rules about the availability of over-the-counter fatal compounds, tax and other rules around how we treat the estates of people who ended their own lives. Factionalization is not about policy; instead, it is about identity. The factionalization around causing one's own death might revolve around whether someone is raised Catholic, or if someone lived for a time in Japan, or if someone feels affiliated with a moral or cultural framework that endorses or forbids ending one's own life.

Though it pains me, I feel the Overton window of death must move slowly for this and other reasons, panning from the view of the innocent prairie with a graveyard at its horizon to include a new view, one that includes poisonous trees, great chasms, accessible firearms, and other convenient mortal risks. The change in social outlook must be significant, must be gradual, and must be ratcheted in the more permissive direction. Any slide back toward the current state of prohibition will enjoy cultural, religious, and other momentums that are gravitational in power and Sisyphean in unrelentingness. But once there is momentum in our favor, we must seize it, like the spark does when it encounters a combination of breeze and fuel.

We think an enormous amount about planning our lives and very little, in the case of most, about planning our deaths. On one level, this is reasonable: in an actuarially expected life of 78.79 years in the United States, this is 28,777 days that do not involve dying and 1 day that does. It seems reasonable, in this frame, that one would spend >28,000 times as much effort planning living than dying.

But if one thinks of dying as something special that one will be able to do only once in all that time, then it feels like an occasion in which one's entire life culminates. A special event. Something to be anticipated and choreographed. And this is the way I suggest dying might be in a more perfect world—something not to be contemplated only intermittently or discussed in the abstract, but to be stared at intently, just beyond the foreground of remaining life.

If death is your and my and our inevitable destination, why not treat it as a goal to be accomplished rather than as a menace to be feared?

SCENE V, PART II
A Lottery of Rights?

I don't think you should be overly confident that you know how
to improve other peoples' lives; I don't think we know very much
about that.
—*Russ Roberts*[225]

The "lottery of rights" argument, central to this section's advocacy, focuses on the universal framework of rights (that rights should be universally available and unanimously recognized) and why utilizing medical professionals to screen who has a right (for instance, the right to die) and who does not is problematic. It also discusses, in a Ballantine-esque[226] voice, how having a wrong (suicide) mature into a right (physician-blessed suicide) for some but not all people suggests that people, by virtue of the passage of time or the appearance of a tumor or the whims of a virus, suddenly "get" rights that others don't get to enjoy and may never enjoy.

Worse, the right gotten isn't a trivial prize, it's the existential kernel itself.

But this argument about rights and frameworks begins not at the law school; instead, its origins lie in dusty history books and the hallways of the hospital that have heard so many screams, sobs, and stories as to be voluminously informed on the realities of natural death.

The modern medicalization of suicide begins in the seventeenth and eighteenth centuries in England with the association of suicide with mental illness. Authors like J. Graunt (writing in 1662)[227] and R. Burn (writing in

---

[225] Russ Roberts, Erik Hoel, *Effective Altruism, Utilitarianism, and the Repugnant Conclusion*, EconTalk (Sept. 26, 2022), https://www.econtalk.org/erik-hoel-on-effective-altruism-utilitarianism-and-the-repugnant-conclusion/.

[226] A nod to Ballantine's observations on adverse possession; adverse possession is a strange place in law where a wrong (trespassing) matures into a right with the passage of time.

[227] John Graunt, Natural and Political Observations Mentioned in a Following Index and Made Upon the Bills of Mortality London, John Martyn (1662).

1767)[228] not only associate suicide with madness, but attribute suicide to madness. They suggest the losing of one's mental faculties is a *prerequisite* to even considering, let alone carrying out, harm to oneself. In short, the prevailing view at this time was that any consideration of suicide should not only be stigmatized and discouraged but should be taken as *prima facie* evidence of insanity.[229]

Joseph Bladzer, seventeen years old in 1760, hanged himself by jumping off a barrelhead below a joist in the basement of a disused building off Long Acre down what is now Langley Street in contemporary London's posh Covent Garden. At that time, this was a rundown area in the ecclesiastical and literal shadow of lesser buildings of St. Martin's Parish. Though there were no witnesses or accounts of his mental state at the time he decided to end his life by hanging, the coroner's inquest confidently concludes[230] the young Mr. Bladzer was "not being of sound mind, memory, and understanding but [instead a] lunatick [*sic*] and distracted[.]"

Sneaking into an abandoned building in central London with a length of rope, rigging it up as a noose, and then leaping to break one's neck is something one might do under a variety of circumstances, but it is likely not something one does in the confusion of a distracted moment.

---

[228] Richard Burn, 4 Ecclesiastical Law London, A. Millar (1767).
[229] See Michael MacDonald & Terrence R. Murphy, Sleepless Souls: Suicide in Early Modern England, 121–25, 363–65 (1990) (concluding the vast majority of suicides put before eighteenth- century coroner juries were deemed cases of severe lunatics or death from lunacy).
[230] City of Westminster, Westminster Coroners' Inquests Archives COWAC, BB (1755–67); COWC, CI (Feb. 13–Dec. 1, 1760) (1760).

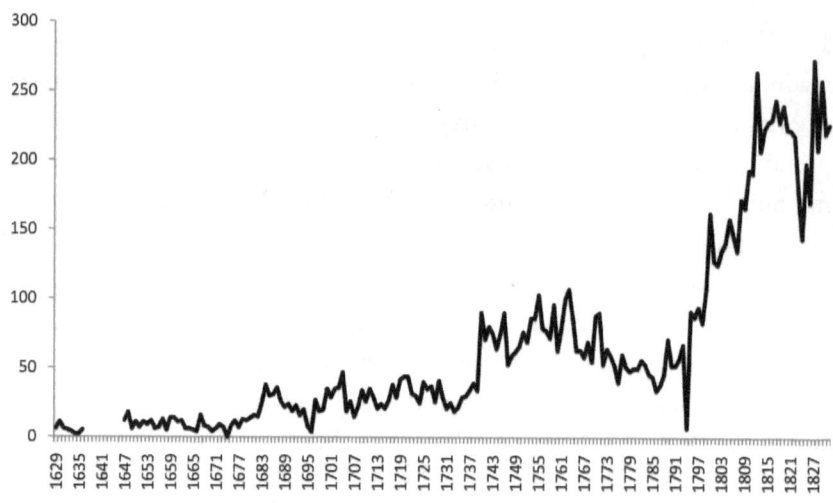

Above: Dr. John Marshall's 1832 analysis of frequency
of "lunacy" as a cause of death in London.[231]

Even if suicide is dispositive evidence of mental upset, which I contend it is not, it is easy to label someone insane after they've ended life.[232]

Diagnosing that same person by seeing madness in the flesh is not so easy, though fictions like Gotham City's Arkham Asylum[233] try to reassure us that anyone can spot the difference between the robustly sane and the vividly disturbed. One need only look to Twitter during the recent Trump administration to see public confusion as to whether *the same person exhibiting the same behaviors* is either a geriatric imbecile or finessing a game of seven-dimensional chess.

---

[231] Dr. Marshall studied the London Bills of Mortality, which were kept in a register in the West End at that time. See generally John Marshall, Mortality in the Metropolis, a Statistical View of the Number of Persons Reported to have Died within the Bills of Mortality in Each of the Years, 1629–1831 London, Treuttel, Würtz, and Richter (1837).

[232] In fact, postmortem shaming by affixing "suicide" or "foul" behavior or "venereal" ailments was a common form of unactionable slander in the eighteenth century. See MacDonald & Murphy *supra* note 232 at 223–86.

[233] A fictional location often featured in Batman-related comics, likely based at least in part (especially its wrought iron front gate and U-shaped footprint) on Bellevue Psychiatric Hospital at Thirtieth and First in New York City.

This demonstrates a diagnosis of madness is not easy, and should not be considered simple; the range of legal rights and other privileges[234] a person lacking capacity loses is nontrivial, and the process is designed as primarily unidirectional and hence difficult to reverse.[235] This means a person perfectly able to exercise his or her judgment as to whether continued life is worthwhile is stripped of any agency in this regard; it is not too severe to state that incorrectly disregarding the wishes of a lucid, thoughtful patient is the mental health equivalent of imprisoning an innocent person.

The modern medicalization of suicide, particularly in the case of physician-assisted suicide, is more sinister than postmortem shaming or mischaracterization of one's life choices as evidence of madness. It transforms suicide into a high-end luxury procedure to end life purchased from the medical bureaucracy rather than seeing suicide correctly as a universal, human choice whether to keep living.

Any medicalization throughout history inserts an expensive gatekeeper, allowing those whose social circles or checkbook entries are full of physicians' names access to a different set of rules (see Act IV, Scene IV, *supra*, for a longer version of this argument). Consider, for instance, Winston Churchill's visit to the United States during the prohibition of alcohol and his use of a New York physician's letterhead to avoid compliance.

---

[234] Affected or limited can be everything from use of one's own accounts and the financial system more generally to voting rights, rights to participate in certain programs (including government-funded programs), and the fundamental right to keep and carry a weapon for one's own protection.
[235] For contemporary commentary on this, see recent voluminous coverage of the so-called #FreeBritney movement and the challenges of removing conservatorship and other safeguards once they have been installed.

Above: Copy of a doctor's note from the No. 10
Archive; original sold by Christie's in 2010.

To understand how we got here requires backing up to a different, more recent branch of history: the use of physicians as arbiters of uncomfortable policy topics, from abortion to puberty blockers to conversion therapy to genital cutting and so on. (This list is borrowed from the abstract of Dov Fox's excellent forthcoming article, *Medical Disobedience*, to be published in Harvard Law Review later in 2023).

Beginning in the 1990s, when I was a teenager, several governments began to explore the legalization of intoxicating cannabis products, and many found a "middle ground" in the concept of the cute, illiterate phrase "medical marijuana." It seemed to put at ease anti-pot hawks who figured only a small number of people would get prescriptions, and this would stop well short of wholesale legalization and wafting clouds of intoxicant in public spaces while also seeming appealing to left-leaning and libertarian folks who wanted a non-carceral approach to regulation.

SCENE VI
Policymaking Logic Up in "Smoke"

Smoke weed every day.
—Cordozar Calvin Broadus

There is no better recent illustration of the flaws inherent in a "suicide is okay but only with a doctor's permission" stance than the recent American experimentation with physician-prescribed cannabis, sometimes referred to as "medical marijuana" colloquially.

Many policy scholars, myself included, saw so-called "medical marijuana" (which I referred to at the time as "medical monopoly cannabis") as a quicksand to be crossed between criminal prohibition and retail, over-the-counter availability. If this patch were not traversed quickly, there was a risk the policy rubber band would snap back to prohibition and stigmatization.

Today, we stand near that quicksand in the conversation about suicide.

While allowing suicide in the medical context *is* a step in the right direction, it *is not* itself a destination or even a place we can safely pause on this journey toward permissibility and, eventually, acceptance. It is *necessary but not sufficient* for access. Inserting boffins and doctors between people and their rights has a very poor track record as a policy maneuver.

We must press on toward over-the-counter, accessible suicide. Rather than "suicide prevention," we must work to make suicide more available, safer (in terms of reducing the suffering of the decedent, more likely to succeed, less risky to people nearby, including family members and first responders), and more desirable.

What do I mean by more desirable?

I mean that the policies we set are not individual or isolated; they interact with one another.

The British campaign in colonial Boston to force the registration of printing presses (presumably to find and imprison the printers of certain pamphlets critical of the king) was not simply a precursor to the campaign one year later to confiscate certain presses, or a prerequisite, *it actually made confiscation a better policy*[236] because the confiscation effort was more likely to achieve its aims once the King's men possessed a list of registered Boston printing presses.

Similarly, we can set certain thoughtful policies that make suicide a better option for more people by emphasizing education, access, and predictability of outcomes.[237]

We can make suicide more accessible and less scary. As we've done in other areas, from abortion to cannabis to needle exchange programs, we can transform these discussions from back alley whispers in shady environs to mainstream, accepted, and supported conversations routinely had among colleagues, friends, and family. We can steer toward a point where an unplanned death is seen as unfortunate while a planned death is seen as responsible and worthy of celebration . . . where our family and society understands a thoughtful decision to commit to ending one's life is something different from, and more than, simply "committing suicide."

---

[236] Thanks to my aforementioned friend Vanessa Burrows for helping me understand this nuance, and the interaction theory accompanying it, many years ago (1998?) in the context of state-specific policy change frameworks.

[237] This includes making tested, painless, very high mortality means very widely available and reassuring people instructions in codicils, wills, and trust arrangements will be respected even in cases of suicide.

SCENE VII
But . . . I Like and Trust Doctors!

Sometimes a man'll tell his bartender things he'll never tell his doctor.
—Dr. Phil Boyce[238]

Let us return to doctors and why their expertise on disease and suffering does not make them ideal referees on the playing field of suicide.

I do not believe disease or suffering should be a prerequisite to suicide. Of the many places suicide can be contemplated or debated, I do not believe the medical field is the right locus among society's many hamlets of expertise or venues for debate.

Simply because people often die in the care of doctors does not mean doctors should preside over deaths.[239]

Advocates for a narrow, physician-endorsed flavor of suicide are both dodging the more fundamental questions surrounding suicide and delegating a choice that should be pondered perhaps more personally and individually than any other: choosing whether tomorrow's price is worth paying in today's experience (which may be bliss or may be suffering). The most basic human transaction is purchasing tomorrow by paying all twenty-four hours of today's costs. This ledger is complex, personal, and to some extent subjective. A physician cannot possibly comprehend every nuance of this transaction's accounting.

---

[238] *Star Trek: The Original Series, The Cage* Desilu Productions (Oct. 15, 1988).

[239] The diversity in patients' degree of interest in continuing life is vast and should not be underestimated. See Harvey Max, H.M. Chochinov, Thomas Hack, Thomas Hassard, Linda J. Kristjanson, Susan McClement, & Mike Harlos et al., *Understanding the Will to Live in Patients Nearing Death*, 46 Psychosomatics: J. Consultation Liaison Psych. 7–10 (2005). People may be in need of help from the medical system but may not be dying from disease; conversely, people may desire to die but be far from maximum natural lifespan. Misidentifying events such as overdose as accidental rather than intentional can have serious implications for the quality and path of care, and for the patient's future trust (or distrust) of the medical system. See generally Kenneth .R. Conner, Peter C. Britton, Luke M. Sworts, & Thomas E. Joiner, Jr., , *Suicide Attempts Among Individuals with Opiate Dependence*, 32 Addict. Behav. 1395-1404 (2007).

Physicians who are burdened with this decision know none of the inputs needed for the calculation. No doctor understands the day-to-day experience of the patient; the litany of scans, tests, and other diagnostics available may adequately describe the functioning of the patient's mechanical, chemical, and electrochemical systems but fails to richly or even adequately portray the patient's *experience* of life.

Requiring a physician to consider and endorse a patient's death when the patient is the one who must endure tomorrow is unfair to the physician (the person not best informed to make these decisions), unfair to the patient (who is denied his or her agency over the matter and whose often superior assessment of what tomorrow holds is unfairly discounted), and unfair to those wanting to end their lives but without financial or logistical access to a physician (who are excluded from these conversations and opportunities entirely).

Indeed, legislatures and courts have struggled with the individual's desire to end one's life and the role a physician might or might not play in that process. In the State of Washington, for instance, one law disallows assisted suicide, and another law defines scenarios where "life-sustaining treatment" is withheld as something other than a suicide. In many states, it is a crime to assist in a suicide, yet patients may refuse treatments physicians reasonably believe are required to sustain life.

This ability for the patient to refuse treatment to sustain life, including a feeding tube, is important. But why is the ability to do so limited to a feeding tube? Is it only in dire scenarios and with a physician's help that we control our destinies? Or is it, instead, that we should control our earthly demises just as we control our earthly lives? If so, the physician is tampering with our agency, not assisting in our decisions.

And there are, in the human existence, disappointments more severe than cancer and misfortunes more severe than a heart attack. These cannot be seen by a doctor and examined for severity, diagnosed for treatment, or placed in some medical taxonomy. They may be rooted in guilt or grief, long ago or recent. And the person who feels that parasite growing within her is best situated to weigh whether killing it is worth sacrificing the life of the host.

Ah, strike that. Perhaps the parasite analogy is too medicinal too.

As someone who taught law students for years and has never instructed a medical student on campus to do anything other than watch where he was walking rather than looking at his iPhone (and the tea spilled on my shirt was Chernobyl hot, mind you) . . . instead, let's discuss something closer to law than medicine: fairness.

The core problem with physician-assisted suicide is not an equality problem; rather, it is an *envelope problem*: at what moment does the demand to die from the patient stop being an impermissible request and begin being a reasonable one? The answer often given is, "when the patient is sufficiently/terminally/irreversibly/untreatably ill." Putting aside the taxonomical nightmare of defining that particular moment, it seems bizarre a wrong (impermissibly ending one's own life) suddenly "matures" or transforms into a right (permissible euthanasia).

How, when, and why does, as Ballentine put it, this wrong "mature into a right"?

This transformation is problematic for two related, but distinct, reasons.

First, it makes access to a sympathetic physician a prerequisite to suicide.

Suicide is related to the individual's most fundamental, existential considerations: whether a particular person's living existence should continue and how that person's life should end. Empowering doctors in this area is no more sensible than empowering accountants or rabbis, each of whom may have ideas about planning the end of one's life that may diverge from, or severely conflict with, the decedent-to-be's wishes and thoughts.

Second, it means that sicker people suddenly have "extra" rights.

Allowing suicide to be incrementally, or perhaps suddenly, more permissible as a person's illness progresses ignores millions of people with limited access to medical care, undiagnosed ailments, or simply a desire to die having nothing to do with illness or injury. Suicide only for the sick means the sick arbitrarily have "extra rights." Illness should in no event be trivialized as a lottery with an extra rights jackpot.

Whether one visualizes sickness as a condition where these extra rights are available or as one where rights are denied to those enjoying better health doesn't matter to me; it's the gust of unnecessary inequality of it that hits egalitarian sensibilities like an unexpected gybe.

Some policies require means testing (poor kids get free or reduced-price school lunches) and that's fine. (To remove stigma from parental poverty, which is no fault of the children, I'd prefer free lunches for all, but that's a battle for another day.) But when we're talking about something as important as the right to live or die, the idea that paying to obtain the fine nuances of a doctor's diagnosis (that may be difficult or impossible for the patient herself to decipher and may poorly align with the patient's own experience) that can allow or disallow this choice—this right—troubles me.

Worse, many of the people suffering terrible discomfort are unable to end their own lives. The envelope of agency has closed and only the sword of mercy wielded by another can cure now what could have been cured by the patient's own hand not long ago. The afflicted have waited so long for this relief that it now requires permission from a doctor or manslaughter from a bystander for life to end. Is this really the situation in which we wish to place some of the most vulnerable people in our society? Warehoused away, connected to machines, begging to die? Begging doctors or friends to kill them?

Is this really the station at which we hope to position our revered physicians?

VIGNETTE I
Decrepitude as "Disease"

Aging is a disease.
—Dr. David Sinclair

There is a Western (and it is almost uniquely Occidental in origin and belief) movement underway currently to classify aging as a disease and old age as a diseased state. I reject and bypass this entire argument because my concept of when someone should have the right to end life has nothing to do with old age—a healthy teenager of nineteen has absolutely equal right to end life as her ninety-year-old grandmother and perhaps more agency to carry out the requisite acts (thanks to more physical mobility, more mental clarity, or more access to a wider range of weapons or chemicals or other means).

Because I do not believe suicide is a solution to illness, but rather that suicide is the most reliable way to create a controlled, consensual, painless end to any life (whether disease is present or not), I decouple suicide entirely from the physician-assisted mercy narrative and join it instead to a universal rights narrative.

Not everyone will exercise the right I envision. Everyone enjoys the First Amendment's safeguards but not everyone is a journalist. Yet, even those who are not journalists, and even those who do not read the newspaper, enjoy a better, freer public square with a greater diversity of ideas thanks to the First Amendment.

I would rather live in a world where a person can say "enough" to life. Perhaps enough pain. Perhaps enough anguish of another kind. Perhaps enough watching as parts of a body fail, leaving an operating machine but one without self-sufficiency, dignity, or hope. Or perhaps enough admiring of life's work, which was done well and amply celebrated long ago. I would choose to live in a world where people have choices about death and can die before they are reduced to panhandling at the hospital for relief, begging to be unplugged.

The world of suicide prohibition is one in which we care more about a physician's malpractice insurance premium payments than a patient's dignity.

Ideally, I would live in a world where disease and dying are decoupled. Where a person who is physically fit, a perfect corporeal specimen, can choose to die, alone if he or she prefers and with help if desired. This would de-medicalize death, recognize that death is a choice that is deeply personal and sacred, and allow everyone access to death whether or not others understand that person's reasoning or motivations.

It is, sadly, often the lowest-quality times in our lives that are the most expensive.

While I believe suicide should be available to everyone, equally, I would be remiss in not pointing out the enormous economic costs that can be avoided by accelerating death. These are not merely "medical bills," but savings that could otherwise be deployed to the benefit of loved ones, to eliminate the next generation's student debt, to start or rescue a family business, to save the family farm or home.

The euphemistic and disarming commentary on "medical bills" suggests that hospitalization and medical intervention are attached to accounting matters that are at worst inconvenient. This outrageously privileged perspective discounts that medical bills exceeding a few thousands of dollars, let alone into the hundreds of thousands of dollars, are crushing for most families.

Recent studies suggest 25 percent to 40 percent of an American's lifetime healthcare costs[240] will come in the final six months of life. In cases where a person relies on mechanical assistance to live, perhaps not even in a fully conscious or aware state, the costs of an additional month can be staggering.

---

[240] It is worth noting, and the author concedes, such studies are skewed toward those whose healthcare costs are more observable, and hence are skewed toward people in the care of the traditional healthcare system, who tend to die while hospitalized, and who tend to have expensive-yet-low-quality final months.

If families (or insurers) are able to shoulder these costs and value the additional duration of life for an unconscious loved one, that's fine.

But those who want to die, or have expressed a wish to die, should be allowed to do so whether hospitalized or not. Just as a patient can be kept barely alive through feeding tubes and machines, a person outside the hospital can be kept barely alive with antidepressants and lateral moves at work, or with alcohol and intermittent pitying support from a rich uncle or former spouse.

Who should be allowed to choose to die?

As you know by this point in the book, I think the answer is nearly everyone.

But in many cases there are real financial costs (not that other non-financial costs aren't "real," they are simply less vulnerable to accounting) to delaying or disallowing death for the majority of the population. They are, most tragically, borne not only by the person forced to live longer than he or she would like, but also by that person's siblings, children, and other loved ones who are forced to witness an approaching simultaneous bankruptcy of money, optimism, will, and life.

We already live in a pecuniary world where he who survives the next downturn may simply be the one with the best attorney. Do we really want to live in a world where having to watch all of your friends and contemporaries die is a sign you were the one with the worst doctor?

VIGNETTE II
Brief Economic Thoughts

The cost of the [Metronomoni's] policing is not merely [or only] the cost of the policers.
—Aristotle's subsequent comments in re the Constitution of the Athenians

In economic terms, prohibitions impose costs on both sides of the line of legitimacy.

In other words, if I prohibit not paying 10 percent of the sales from your shop in taxes and make noncompliance a crime (tax evasion), I impose compliance costs on those who are doing their best to comply and impose other costs (for instance, the liberty cost of a risk of prison or the pecuniary costs of inefficiently operating under clandestine conditions) on those who do not intend to comply.

By making suicide impermissible, costs are imposed across society that otherwise would not be suffered, and inequalities are created that otherwise would not be experienced.

If a physician must be involved before one can permissibly end life, then the cost of the physician (and her various pro rata facilities' costs and malpractice insurance premiums and so on) is added to the cost of suicide; for those who do not intend to comply, the costs are also enhanced, whether of obtaining the needed chemicals under false pretenses or elaborately planning a death that will not be immediately recognizable as a suicide.

People think of suicide in frameworks that invite paternalism: involvement of the church, examinations by doctors, exceptions made by politicians. But what if we start from the other end of the spectrum, the end that accepts that death is a universal to which we are inexorably drawn as a consequence of life? That every soul will, at some point, taste death?[241] From that beginning, shouldn't death be an experience we participate in equally and fairly?

What if the problem with suicide is not how to regulate it, but how to ensure equal, easy, affordable access?

Once we begin to consider suicide a right or public good where "how to ensure access" is the dominant priority rather than "how to regulate," then we begin to see how uneven and difficult the access problem really is.

In the US context, access is restricted by normative rules (such as disapproval in one's friend group or community), guild rules or professional rules (such as those governing the participation or conduct of physicians), and legal rules (such as restrictions on the operation of everything from life insurance policies to one's estate plan in the case of suicide). These rules can be circumvented in some cases but only with contortionism and expenditure I suggest should be necessary.

The result is a plutocracy of dying.

If you talk to people, they may favor a technocracy of death where the experts, usually doctors, control access to death. Or perhaps a gerontocracy of death where old people, closer to their natural deaths, know best. Or perhaps a theocracy of death where the clergy, enlightened from intimate colloquy with the divine, can best set the rules for how and when death should occur. But very, very, very few people would tell you that death should be controlled by the wealthy.

Yet that's exactly the situation we've created.

Today, to access suicide while abiding, even cursorily, by any of society's rules requires enormous financial resources. Second and third opinions. More medical tests. More psychological and psychiatric conversations. Ability and conveyance to visit hospitals. Debates about whether you're really "ready" or "fit" or "lucid" to make the decision and then, separately or relatedly, whether you're really "sick enough" or "hopeless enough"[242]

---

[241] Surah Ali 'Imran 3:185.

[242] Many suicides are not, contrary to the prevailing media narrative, associated with hopeless depression. See Lyn. Y. Abramson, Gerald I. Metalsky, & Lauren B. Alloy, *Hopelessness Depression: A*

or "[medical term] enough" to die, often requiring the patient to bring a medical advocate or even an end-of-life attorney.

We scrutinize, expensively and endlessly, whether we are ripe for Death to take a bite.

But, in the meantime, life ticks onward. And this time, too, is not cost-less. Or painless.

Theory-Based Subtype of Depression, 96 Psych. Rev. 358 (1989). But see Aaron T. Beck, Gary Brown, Robert J. Berchick, Bonnie L. Stewart, & Robert A. Steer, *Relationship Between Hopelessness and Ultimate Suicide*, 147 Am. J. Psych. 190 (1990); Aaron T. Beck, Robert A. Steer, Maria Kovacs, & Betsy Garrison, *Hopelessness and Eventual Suicide: A 10-year Prospective Study of Patients Hospitalized with Suicidal Ideation*, 142 Am. J. Psych. 559 (1985).

VIGNETTE III
More Isn't Better

One thorn of experience is worth a whole wilderness of warning.
—James Russell Lowell
(likely alluding to the Bard's "thorn of love" in
the first Act of Romeo & Juliet)

Ending one's life can be achieved through the inaction of the person (ceasing resistance in the midst of battle or refusing to move as a train approaches), through the affirmative acts of the person (stepping off a ledge or ingesting a poisonous substance), or through some combination of inaction and action. In this book, I draw no moral lines between the decisions or methods used to end life, except to apply the moral lens that people should end life in ways that create as little harm, strife, and danger to those who remain alive. Evelyn McHale traveled to New York City with the express intent of jumping off the Empire State Building;[243] in that scenario, my concern is twofold: that she should have had other nearby and painless options to end her life, and that by choosing this method, she endangered the people and property below.

Ms. McHale, on her way to New York City, had already made a choice to end her life—if suicide is something to be *committed to*, rather than something *to commit*, she had already *committed*.[244]

Predictably, media coverage was focused on what "despair or misfortune" could drive an attractive young woman whose corpse was captured

---

[243] At the time, this suicide garnered national attention. While accounts of McHale's final days vary, it is clear she departed for New York City with the specific intent to end her life.

[244] McHale wrote a suicide note that was later published due to national interest in her case, though it is unclear whether the publication of the note was consistent with the decedent's wishes. I purposely do not suggest or critique the drafting of "suicide notes" *per se* in this text but intratextual and anthropology-of-language research suggests drafting such notes may reveal something about the authors and their intentions. See Alison Brevard, David Lester, & Bijou Yang Lester, *A Comparison of Suicide Notes Written by Suicide Completers and Suicide Attempters*, 11 Crisis 7(1990).

in a famous photograph[245] to want to end her life? Because being young or being attractive is a guarantee of happiness (*insert sarcasm here*).

The suggestion in such cultural narratives and the journalism adopting them, of course, is that all suicide stems from depression and that suicide is a poorly chosen or crazy solution to depression, like caring for a property's greenery by doing a rain dance rather than running the lawn sprinkler. But depression is not, in many cases, what causes suicide nor, often, what suicide is meant to address.

Rather, suicide is a choice of route to a destination where we each and all are headed on our own schedules and at our own paces. Viewed through this lens, waiting for the supernatural spirits above or the ambient terrestrial perils to chill our bodies to room temperature looks more like the rain dance and suicide more like the sprinkler.

Suicide isn't a crazy choice. Or a bad choice. It's simply a choice.

Though explicitly not writing about suicide ("[I'm not] talking about… ending my life through euthanasia or suicide.") in The Atlantic in 2014, esteemed physician Ezekiel Emmanuel (who, as an oncologist, has no doubt encountered and pondered a variety of health and illness most humans will not) voiced his choice to not live past seventy-five. He described how his preference "drives his daughters crazy" and causes concern among his friends and family.

Though we disagree in several areas, where Emmanuel and I are dead-on aligned is his sentiment that longevity for longevity's sake is not a worthwhile or meaningful goal and that thinking not generally but instead specifically about one's preferred lifespan is helpful. I recommend (and commend aspects of) his essay, but the essence is contained in my two favorite passages from that essay:

> [D]eath is a loss. … But here is a simple truth that many of us seem to resist: living too long is also a loss. It renders many of us, if not disabled, then faltering and declining, a state that may not be worse than death

---

[245] See *The Most Beautiful Suicide*, Life Magazine 43 (May 12, 1947).

but is nonetheless deprived. It robs us of our creativity and ability to contribute to work, society, the world. It transforms how people experience us, relate to us, and, most important, remember us. We are no longer remembered as vibrant and engaged but as feeble, ineffectual, even pathetic.

. . .

But [choosing a date] defines a clear point in time: for me, 2032. It removes the fuzziness of trying to live as long as possible. Its specificity forces us to think about the end of our lives and engage with the deepest existential questions and ponder what we want to leave our children and grandchildren, our community, our fellow Americans, the world. The deadline also forces each of us to ask whether our consumption is worth our contribution.

Emmanuel makes a compelling argument, parallel but in some ways non-congruent to my own. I want to be clear that Emmanuel's argument is one of "enough" while mine is one of "choice" and that's an important distinction. I strongly believe we have, should value, and should take seriously a choice to end our lives at any point, a choice to walk away from the table, a choice to say "game over" on any day and at any age, whether Dr. Emmanuel's favored seventy-five or Lenny Bruce's forty or Kurt Cobain's twenty-seven.

Suicide can be a declaration of "mission complete," a final act in a life well-lived and thoroughly enjoyed. For others, planned death acknowledges that not every cookie crumbled as expected, but what was possible in this life is done and tomorrow's rewards are simply not worth today's costs. Many suicides are fundamentally altruistic, if not in the stricter Durkheimian sense, then in some slightly broader one.

"The world is better off without me" is often dismissed as a musing common among the depressed, but it may be an honest—if unpopular—analysis of the state of play. Many can visualize a happy world where they are absent, where children or friends enjoy their resources, where their art resides in museums for others to enjoy, where their vital organs benefit others.

The reason I emphasize "choice" and not "enough" is that "enough" still bends to social norms, acceptability cues, and popular measures. As in their spiritual beliefs, sexual identities, and favorite films, I think people should feel comfortable or even invited to be "weird" in choosing when to die. The choice is yours, and it's okay if it's peculiar, arbit, or even inexplicable to others.

The idea that this choice is something we own, hold, and control is vital. It must reside in the firmest clutches of our sovereign, *étroit* ambit.

And if others control, censor, or even slightly narrow our ability to choose, then it is not our choice at all. Dying must be a personal choice that belongs to *each*, not *all*, of us.

And that choice enjoys growing popularity in the contemporary United States and around the world. The World Health Organization estimates one million people per year die from suicide and many, including me, believe there is every reason to presume this estimate is low rather than high.

The concept that suicide is an individual, anomalous act of madness rather than a popular choice for end-of-life planning is central to the prohibitionist framing: in this narrative, each person choosing suicide is alone, separate, sad, and crazy (or part of a group that is cultish, weird, and dangerous). This is not only argumentatively disingenuous, it's empirically false.

The US suicide rate has been rising for some time and doubled in the ten years leading up to the COVID-19 crisis. (Interestingly, suicides actually dropped during this global pandemic,[246] despite press coverage of mental health concerns and supposedly widespread feelings of anxiety, depression, and isolation, suggesting that the drivers of suicide often are not simple "sadness" or "loneliness" but instead complex feelings driving planned behavior.)

---

[246] This was true in the US and in other developed countries and across several demographic factors.

Mezzanine Champagne Thoughts

The complaint seeks damages based upon an actuarial life
expectancy of plaintiff of more than seventy years — the life
expectancy if plaintiff had been born without the Tay-Sachs
disease.
—The Hon. Bernard Jefferson[247]

Outside of academia, I spent much of my career advising large banks and insurance companies and thinking about insurance products, including life insurance products. There is significant evidence US suicide statistics are conservatively reported (when empirical) and conservatively computed (when extrapolated or inferred), and this has been true for at least fifty years.

Like the line between suicide and martyrdom, the line between accidental death and suicide is easy to draw in the abstract and difficult to discern in real life.

An executive in her mid-fifties who usually wears her safety belt and has a well-known affection for fast sports cars is found dead after a single-vehicle, unbelted collision at ninety miles an hour in her vintage Porsche wherein she crashed the vehicle into a concrete bridge support and was instantly ejected head-first into the bridge's superstructure, eventually ending up in the river below. Suicide or an unlucky spirited drive after watching the 1981 classic *King of the Mountain*?

Single-car, ambiguous, unintoxicated, vehicle crash fatalities are difficult to rule suicides. Without a note or other indications of intent, it can be impossible to discern the circumstances of the scenario. Many suicide

---

247   Curlender v. Bio-Science Laboratories, 106 Cal. App. 3d 811, 830 (Cal. App. 2d 1980).

incidents are architected to look like home or workplace accidents or accidental poisonings. In some cases, the possibility of a plausibly accidental overdose leaves the possibility of a life insurance windfall to the decedent's loved ones.

And there are often both pecuniary and social incentives to lean toward a/any finding other than suicide; delivering news that a loved one has passed is already difficult; combining it with news that the death was a suicide and there will be no life insurance payout makes this news even harder to deliver and even less palatable to the listener.

As I write this, there are state- and national-level policy pressures that may *en masse* reclassify tens of thousands of opiate overdose deaths, many of which may have been ruled suicides, as fatal product defect events or incidents involving criminal misconduct. We are so afraid to talk about death that we cannot even be honest about the places from which it originates. We lament society's obsession with youth, but we never speak the second half: that youth is desirable not just because it is aesthetically pleasing, but because it is often distant from death.

Rach Against The Machine @econ...
by the way an obsession with youth and thinness is an obsession with ignorance and obedience, send fucking tweet.

Karl T. Muth 🌐✈️📊 ✅ @KarlMuth
Replying to @economeager
Obsession with youth (and thinness e.g. if one associates weight with morbidity) is just a preference to feel (erroneously) like one is further from death or to feel like one is exempted from seriously considering one's own mortality. It is a hoax vaccine re mortal contemplation.

Above: The author discusses related themes with economist Rachael Meager.

At least in the mainstream of society, we are so afraid to discuss longevity that some of our most complex, euphemistic narrative tools are reserved for stories dealing with death.

ACT V
Making Sense of Metaphors and Machines

SCENE I
Vampires as Narrators of Death

We learn from failure, not from success!
—Prof. Abraham Van Helsing[248]

For over five hundred years,[249] both European and Asian writers have explored the question of death and dying with the use of vampire stories.[250] The question of whether to become a vampire is a cousin to the question of suicide, and it is often depicted similarly to suicide: irreversible and tempting, even seductive. Of course, one (vampirism) is a route to immortality, the other (suicide) an exhibition of mortality.[251]

Note this section discusses becoming a vampire as a consensual decision to be bitten while acknowledging much vampire literature includes non-consensual elements or scenarios wherein people become vampires through some elaborate series of events. (E.g.: "Gaunt has vampire characteristics because his mother was bitten by a vampire when she was pregnant."[252])

As L.A. Paul highlighted,[253] the question of whether to allow a bite presents the so-called "vampire problem." It's hard to make an informed choice to become a vampire; you don't know much about what it's like to be a vampire before you've become one, it's hard to just ask around and find

---

[248] Bram Stoker, Dracula 59 London, Archibald Constable & Co. (1897).

[249] This book does not put forth cultural, ethnographic, or evolutionary theories that humans choose suicide for population control or other reasons; I focus instead on an individual-centered, rights-based approach. But it is worth acknowledging that other approaches and lenses exist. See, e.g., R. Michael Brown, Stephanie L. Brown, Aron Johnson, Berit Olsen, Kristen Melver, & Mark Sulivan, *Empirical Support for an Evolutionary Model of Self-Destructive Motivation*, 39 Suicide & Life Threat. Behav. 1 (2009).

[250] Many problematic themes have also been explored using vampires and I acknowledge but do not explore those here; they include antisemitic policy, economic isolationism, gender violence, immigration quotas, rape discussed as seduction, and quarantine policy. It is important to recognize and call out these problems. However, in this section, I am talking about the vampire as a stock character or creature, not as a canon or *genre* of material.

[251] See generally Roy F. Baumeister, *Suicide as Escape from Self*, 97 Psych. Rev. 90 (1990).

[252] Hogan v. DC Comics, 48 F. Supp. 2d 298, 312 (S.D.N.Y. 1999).

[253] This section is influenced heavily by Paul's recent book, Transformative Experience (2016).

out how people feel about being vampires, and all of the cues we normally use to make a decision are missing in the "should I let a vampire bite ('turn') me?" decision.

It is a situation where the result is severe, important, and transformative but wherein our normal mechanisms to make informed decisions fail us.

I'm going to extend the vampire problem here as applicable more broadly. In the vampire problem, the path to becoming a vampire seems disgusting. Once you have become a vampire, however, especially in the eastern European literary traditions, life seems pretty great. You stay young and fit and attractive forever and can accumulate vast fortunes, what would otherwise be intergenerational levels of wealth. Faust, but *la vie nocturne* rather than hell.

Modern vampire stories embrace a certain thought, choice, and consent as people become vampires—a post-Victorian fanged SPF500 gentleman (or, in some storylines, a slender caped seductress of similar complexion) romances the convert not only into the bedroom, but into the ways, customs, and culture of the vampire. Modern zombie literature is the opposite—a horde of mindless, unfortunate former humans overruns and infects nonconsenting people in the wrong place at the wrong time.

To me, choosing suicide is much like choosing to be a vampire. It is not a fully informed choice, as dying is by definition something the living have not yet experienced. Yet dying "naturally" (meaning in a manner or at a time that the decedent did not specifically choose) is more like becoming a zombie than choosing to be a vampire; it is something that strikes, afflicts, and overcomes you rather than something you've chosen, selected, or consented to.

In this framework, at least to my eye, suicide is inevitably more desirable than natural expiration because it creates a comforting certainty and stems from an affirmative consent, both of which are often missing in nature's crueler route to death.

The question of knowing consent to die, or to live longer, is complex. It is not obvious or clear that a person who wakes up should continue and complete that day, nor is it self-evident when a person should not continue living.

The kind of considered, careful consent that we see in vampire literature (but not zombie tales) is perhaps analogous or even informative. Especially where the choice is not simply to breathe or eat or live, but whether to adopt technological aids[254] without which we could not breathe, eat, or continue life.

Many life-extending technologies and therapies currently being researched, including implanted robotic organs, periodic injections of symbiotic microorganisms, blood cleaning and modification chemically or through "onboard" dialysis (implanted filtration or the "filter backpack") sound unappetizing to a substantial portion of the population, and likely would not see universal adoption even if cost were not a concern. Like becoming a vampire, these things seem repulsive at first blush, but perhaps are wonderful.

Many are unwilling to admit that prevailing norms and popular vanities already limit life extension. Some portion of people will refuse oncological chemotherapy[255] for dislike of hair loss or superficial lesions, or perhaps because they are "foodies" and fear that their senses of taste and smell may be damaged or altered by radiation, an effect reported by many radiotherapy patients. To the onlooker, the idea that death is better than never again being

---

[254] The question of whether to adopt these kinds of technologies is more complex than it seems at first blush.

Consider, for instance, the fact that many top golfers have undergone LASIK surgery to improve their vision (including superstar Tiger Woods). In many cases, their vision improved 3x to 5x compared to their natural vision.

Imagine another world where, instead, LASIK was never invented but instead a robot eyeball was invented with precisely the same effect (3x to 5x increase in visual acuity). But looked weird (think "Terminator").

One can imagine a world in which people with the robot eyeball are banned from activities like professional sports (because of perception issues) even though the benefit is *precisely the same* as today's LASIK surgery.

Perception of technological aids and futuretech upgrades to biological abilities will be very important for adoption. Ideally, technology will be seamless and symbiotic, but at early stages of experimentation this is unlikely.

[255] As this book goes to press, the French are beginning a nationwide debate on end-of-life options and what people should (and should not) be allowed to do to end their lives. See generally *France Starts a Debate on Legalising Assisted Dying* The Economist, 24 (Dec. 20, 2022). France already allows people to refuse treatment and refuse heroic efforts to prolong life but does not yet allow the affirmative ending of life in hospital settings; it is the first major European Catholic country to create a citizens' assembly to debate these topics.

able to discern the quality of one's sashimi is absurd. But who better to judge that than the one seated at the omakase bar?

The expiration of our physical vehicle is a timeless worry and a limitless trove for storytelling. In ancient tales, the immortal goddess who falls in love with the mortal suitor is a recurring theme (or, in less frequent cases, the reverse in terms of gender); these romantic adventures are the distant ancestors of the kinds of vampire stories we read today. When Eos requests that Zeus make her love interest, Tithonus, immortal, she forgets to also request that he enjoy timeless youth. As a result, he outlives the limits of his physical body and cannot lift his limbs or do anything to interact with Eos meaningfully. Eventually, he begs for death to come.

In more modern literature, the extreme of quantity of life at full expense of quality is explored, in a lineage that includes everything from Dorian Gray to the latest blood-sucking romance.

In the opening essay of The Myth of Sisyphus and Other Essays, Albert Camus states, "There is but one serious philosophical problem (in the myth of Sisyphus), and that is suicide. Judging whether life is or is not worth living amounts to answering the fundamental question of philosophy." The next task is always for Sisyphus to push the boulder once more, to gather his breath before pressing his shoulder to the task, to choose to allow the boulder to hit, harm, or kill him. It is more complex than the simplistic portrayal of moving an object uphill; it is a question of whether to continue in life.

People often talk about "one more day." What they are really talking about is anticipated regret—what if I reach the end and there's one more thing I want to do, a friend I didn't get to say "good-bye" to, or a brilliant idea that comes too late? The problem, of course, is that we don't know what the quality of that last marginal day would be like. Would you be able to form and remember and communicate that idea? Would you even be conscious?

A question I often raise with my graduate economics or finance students is something I call the "last drop" problem. Knowing everything you know about the petroleum market (a well-understood, thoroughly studied market), do you think the last drop of naturally occurring petroleum oil on Earth that is extractable and available to burn will be worthless or very expensive?

The classroom debate that then ensues is like watching a table tennis match. "Well, maybe everything will be electric and renewable by then, it'll be worthless." Then someone else replies: "There are cases where oil will never be replaced, it'll be very expensive!" Then another: "It won't even be extracted, we'll just leave it in the ground because burning oil will be seen as so environmentally harmful." And another: "But there are other uses for natural oil than fuel to burn, like making certain plastics and non-synthetic rubbers."

And we understand the market for oil vastly, vastly better than we understand what our last day (or last-day-plus-one) of life will be like. So I bristle at the idea that a person at age X can really understand what life at age X-plus-one-thousand days or plus-five-thousand days will look, feel, and be like. And even if you know what your life plus one thousand days looks like (you don't; Heraclitus was right about men and rivers), you certainly don't know what someone else's life today, let alone plus one thousand days, looks like.

Returning to the last drop problem, I know that in my case I'd prefer to leave the last few gallons of life's oil in the ground, unextracted, unburned. And that's all I need to know to make this decision.

Put simply, more isn't always better.

SCENE II, PART I
Seductive Incrementalism

Today, we hit the bottom of the slippery slope. I would find a
place to draw the line higher on the hillside...
—The Hon. Thurgood Marshall[256]

The "just one thousand days more" slippery slope is where the gradient argument flourishes. It then becomes the "just one hundred days more" argument, an argument that drives many Americans to spend a double-digit percentage of their *lifetime* healthcare expenses in the final months of their lives.

If one talks to economists and policy wonks—as I do nearly every week—a recurring theme is early investment. Empirical studies suggest early interventions are a good deal. Preschool education, infant nutrition, and other things along these lines are all incredible bargains, paying back many times their cost in later dividends.

It isn't surprising that these things lead to healthier, more successful people; if you're sending a rocket to the moon, starting off aimed in the wrong direction is really, really hard to remedy with later course corrections.

But hardly anybody talks about the flipside of this. It's taboo to discuss, even in utilitarian economics circles, but let's break that taboo: as you get older, buying more life is a bad deal. Each dollar buys fewer years of additional life and years of comparatively lower quality. At the very end of one's natural tenancy on Earth, a low-quality day or hour can be enormously expensive while being not particularly enjoyable.

But it's always tempting to want one hundred more days, ten more days, one more day. Let's be clear: I'm not immune from these temptations or overly eager to die.

---

[256]   Florida Star v. BJF, 491 US 524, 553 (1989).

Yet rather than sliding with limited agency down that slippery slope's hypotenuse, I'd like to choose a point where my control over the situation still enjoys some purchase on the incline; I plan on using the remaining traction to decide where, when, and how my life ends.

When I am asked in the inevitable after-dinner debate among friends: "So you've got this all figured out, when is the right age to die, Karl?" my reply is never a number. Rather, I think it is useful to consider when the last "good day" will be. What might you look like in the mirror that day? What might the day's agenda contain? What might you be able to enjoy, alone or together with others, in those chosen waning hours?

The last day need not be magnificent or remarkable. For most, it will be a series of good-byes, firm eye-contact handshakes throughout, a final check that things are in order with calm calls to the accountant and the attorney, a favorite meal at a favorite restaurant or at home, a time to finally toss the bucket list into the fireplace at the end of the night.

If you can hold that last good day in your head, and modify it, curate it, consider it, accept it, grow toward it . . . now you're planning. Isn't that better than rolling the proverbial dice and dying when a heartbeat grew too erratic to sustain or a tumor grew too large to be benign or a nearby motorist grew too tired to stay awake?

SCENE II, PART II
When You've Done Enough

[H]e indicates that he is ready to retire ... that is his choice.
—*The Hon. Mary Muehlen Maring*[257]

I want to, and plan to, end my life. That means if I do not die prematurely (meaning before the date I've chosen), I will choose when and how I die.

I acknowledge there is a risk that fate (which I do not capitalize, as I do not use it as a deity's euphemistic pronoun) will snatch my life from me before I intend to relinquish control of it, perhaps in an accident[258] or an unanticipated failure of my body's systems.

But if that does not occur, I will choose the date and manner of my death.

At that point, I will have done the things I aim to do in life and will be at peace with the things I have not achieved and, indeed, will never achieve.

Many people who win Nobel Prizes are elderly, but the ages at which they make the pivotal underlying discoveries are not geriatric. The average age for a physicist to make the Nobel-worthy breakthrough is under fifty. In economics, the John Bates Clark medal is awarded to an economist who made "significant contribution to economic thought and knowledge" by age forty (and is an interesting, though imprecise, predictor of Nobels decades later).

There is no surge of economist suicides on their fortieth birthdays and no detectable concern at the American Economic Association that all but one economist turning forty each year will end their lives.

My point is that while achievement is concentrated in a certain period of life in many vocations (especially areas like performance of pop music

---

257 Krueger v. Krueger, 748 NW 2d 671, 675 (N.D. 2008).
258 For a detailed discussion of accidents and deadly misfortunes through a nuanced utilitarian lens, see Guido Calabresi, The Cost of Accidents: A Legal and Economic Analysis 17–18 Yale (1970) "Ventures are undertaken that, statistically at least, are certain to cost lives ... [w]e take planes and cars rather than safer, slower means of travel and perhaps most telling, we use relatively safe equipment rather than the safest imaginable because—and it is not a bad reason—the safest costs too much."

and promulgation of economic theory), the anticlimax of not having a hit album by age twenty-five or not developing a theory that describes a given economic phenomenon by age forty is not, in my view, a good reason to end life. That said, the people who have not made huge contributions to their fields by age X are unlikely to by age $X+10$.

It isn't that it never happens. Nor is it that professional achievements or academic laurels are the fairest or best benchmark of one's life's value. On the flipside, I doubt Sir Lawrence (Bragg) of Cambridge's famed Cavendish Laboratory felt his life was over at age twenty-five when he won a Nobel Prize; he did not promptly declare "mission accomplished." He instead continued his work and went on to mentor Francis Crick, who would win his own Nobel for discovering DNA.

In my own life, I've found mentoring the next generation is a meaningful way to spend much of my time, whether that mentorship is professorial or more casual. People can discover meaning in life in all sorts of things and no doubt may stop finding meaning in further life for a similarly wide variety of reasons: Is the latter (losing meaning) not very reasonable if one accepts the former (finding meaning)?

Lebbus Woods, an architect whose portfolio after decades of work contains relatively few designs that were ever built, once said on a panel that he saw his portfolio as a success. I would be dissatisfied with this and would not have felt like a success. But it *isn't my job* to figure out if Lebbus Woods (d. 2012, RIP) lived a good life or should have felt satisfied with his life. That's Lebbus Woods's job, because it's *his life* to celebrate or critique or treasure or terminate.

To me, life is forward progress. This can be maintaining or improving one's own abilities, knowledge, physical fitness, or other attributes, or adding to the capabilities and experiences of others through teaching, philanthropy, culinary generosities (preparing food for others is a wonderful way to enjoy company and conversation), or simply listening. Once forward progress halts, life no longer contains these very special things that make us uniquely human.

A well-known acquaintance of mine remarked, truthfully but very politically incorrectly I suppose, in March of 2020 as the world was shutting down thanks to COVID-19, that if there's something you wanted to do to improve yourself (in terms of fitness, learning, or some other area improvable during a global pandemic) and you didn't achieve it during COVID, it wasn't because you didn't have the time, it's because you didn't have the discipline.

I embraced this fully and, quarantined at a dear friend's home in northwest Wyoming, completed about one certificate class on Coursera every forty-eight hours during May of 2020, many at leading universities that had offered few opportunities to take one-off courses online prior to the pandemic. These ranged from a course marginally improving my Arabic (thanks, Northwestern) to a mathematics refresher called Data Science Math Skills (thanks, Duke).

Did I apply for a new job because of this? Did I get a raise? No.

But I enjoyed learning about these topics and felt it was deeply important during this unique window of opportunity, when the world was in so many ways "on pause," that I was enjoying life and not simply watching time pass. (Though if one is observing passing time thoughtfully or meditatively, this can also be forward progress.)

My friend's assertion can be expanded and extended to capture much of my view of life more generally, COVID-19 or not. There is an age at which those things that are "on the bucket list" or that "we'll do some day" turn from grand ambitions to small tragedies; they develop the mold and moss of inaction. We must either accept wanting but not obtaining them or maintain a fantasy that wounds us each time we contemplate these un-done to-dos. When one's regrets swamp her ambitions in size or number, it is time to inventory what is left of life.

At some point, more life isn't the reason you haven't done that thing.

SCENE II, PART III
Perils of Imagined Ambition

*Thou wouldst be great Art not without ambition, but without
The illness should attend it...*
—*Lady Macbeth*[259]

You haven't done that thing because, even given limitless time, you wouldn't. It is easy to say you won't win the Boston Marathon because you don't have the ability; it is harder to admit you didn't learn calculus simply because you don't have the tenacity, direction, or focus.

Let's talk yet more bluntly about quality of life and quantity of life, who gets what and why.

If you believe additional days and months and years are points awarded in a grand meritocracy that rewards cardio and punishes croissants, that's fine. If you believe life is forfeited in an unfair and fatal lottery, that's fine. Both are true, each in some but not all cases. That's not the debate I'm agitating.

The debate that interests me is far simpler: When life loses interest for the individual—he or she being the person best positioned to choose that tomorrow is uninteresting, unfulfilling, or unbearable and that today is enough—then it is that individual who should be able to choose to fold his or her cards.

While I agree with the first two lines of Billy Joe Shaver's *Good-bye Yesterday*,[260] I disagree with the two lines that follow; making it through today presents a different price for each person and, for some, it's simply too high a price when an unwanted tomorrow is the thing on offer.

No person who would rather pay her daughter's law school tuition than live another few months of painful, lonely life in a healthcare setting should

---

259 William Shakespeare, Macbeth act 1, sc. 5.
260 Billy Joe Shaver, *Good-bye Yesterday*, Highway Of Life Justice Records (1996).

be forced to live those months or be told she is insane or delusional because she prefers to die a few months earlier with a larger bank balance.

One's philosophical reflection can require a lifetime or a moment. One can think about one's achievements, vices, and regrets while the mechanism offers barely detectable resistance, during the spring's tightening and, finally, as the trigger breaks with sudden ease. One can reflect on life while falling. Some fall—screaming, others silently. Or fall into a final sleep. That, too, screaming or silently.

In recent years, I've wandered in and out of an interesting subculture and it has led me to think deeply about life and life planning. Perhaps it's crypto anarchism, perhaps it's the newest libertarianism, perhaps it's a society wide reignited discussion of the existentialist absurd. Today, many people are deeply interested in experimentation and self-sovereignty, people who want to have control over themselves and their bodies and their destinies. To own those things. To own themselves.

These people who've thought deeply about longevity (as a philosophical challenge, a curse, a problem to be solved, or in some other way) are, in my experience, polarized into two groups on the topic of life.

The first group is interested in maximizing longevity using biotech, nanotech, cryotech, and futuretech generally. They are maintaining the fitness(es) of their physical and cognitive selves until the singularity[261] or until UC.[262] But if every moment of life is a moment in which one can choose to die, then medicinal contributions to longevity also mean more choices for dying in new contexts. I am deeply interested in those choices.

The second group is interested in "bounded longevity," the idea of living the best possible life within natural—or even abbreviated—bounds. This philosophy views life not as something to be stretched to its limits, but

---

[261] The singularity is a vague unscientific shorthand for some degree of human-machine symbiosis that may be as simple as physical prosthetic augmentations or as deep as integrated biomechanical (cybernetic) technology without which the person cannot survive.

[262] UC is Bay Area techbro slang for uploadable consciousness, the idea that we will eventually be able to take a person's conscious self and put it into a computer where it can live on separate from the body.

something to be treasured as a scarce resource. It often integrates the idea that people value life in part due to its scarcity and that known scarcity is better than arbitrary, unpredictable, or surplus supply.

I am part of the latter bounded longevity group. I will someday touch death and I want to do it on my own terms. I want to own the decision to die. Strike that. *Ownershipesque*, not strictly in the sense one owns property, but perhaps in the sense one owns a fond memory. In the sense that, in the robust vault between our ears, we can grasp things so tightly that no one can tear them from our grip. When it is death's hand we choose to hold, no one should weaken our grasp.

I make this argument from a fundamentally liberal tradition, one of self-sovereignty and auto-agency. I believe strongly that people have control, an ownership-like control, over their bodies. I strongly believe people should be allowed to try experimental therapies and drugs, to sell blood or organs for profit, to partake in high-risk activities that present little harm to other members of society, to volunteer proudly for what they know will be one-way missions to Mars and beyond, where they will die far away, having built something and having helped future colonists.

I believe that we should control ourselves, be responsible for ourselves, be the product of our choices.

Even if one of those choices leads to one's demise at a time of her own choosing rather than fate's.

SCENE III
I'm Not a Suicide Advocate, I'm a Recovering Longevity Enthusiast

For in this sleep of death what dreams may come...
—Hamlet[263]

I soured on longevity as a personal fixation, then as a uniting goal in my friend group and the tech community, then as a focus of society's resources. I value life and don't believe it's something to be discarded lightly, but I don't value the accumulation of life as a goal.

It is popular to deride those who accumulate wealth throughout their lives. "You can't spend it in the next life," people muse. The "he who has the most toys wins" attitude so popular in the 1980s is today out of vogue. But is it any more virtuous to accumulate years? Especially if those years are decreasingly meaningful? Decreasingly enjoyable?

My view is that everyone is dying. The person who will die if disconnected from the machine is no different from the person who will not; both are dying, just at different rates and with different degrees of mechanical intervention.

There is some research suggesting certain interventions can (1) materially modify intentions to end one's own life, (2) meaningfully extend periods between attempts to end one's life, or (3) dissuade a person from attempting to end life by causing the person to engage in different calculations as to the speculative value of that person's remaining life. I don't oppose these interventions, as I believe a person should engage in autobiographical preparatory arithmetic that is as informed and precise as possible; I do, however, object to interventions that interfere with the attempt itself or are likely to cause a successful attempt to fail, resulting in a damaged person with

---

[263] William Shakespeare, Hamlet act 3, sc. 1.

even-further-decreased quality of life and, importantly, perhaps harming the person's position or capacity to take affirmative steps to again attempt to end life in the future.

Whether we think about it philosophically, contractually, or in some other framework, suicide is a type of commitment to oneself.

When we talk about "looking death in the eye," we are talking about looking ourselves in the eye, looking in a mirror.[264] Whether in the polished slide of a handgun, the freshly honed blade of a knife, the calm water below a bridge,[265] or the driver's side window of a car filling with odorless danger, looking death in the eye is looking at ourselves and contemplating life's ending.

The surface　　　　　　　*Samazama na*
of the water mirrors　　*kage mo utsurishi*
many things.　　　　　　*mizu no aya*

—*Masumi Kato (Yoel Hoffmann trans. in Japanese Death Poems at 236 (1986))*

Bukowski's *An Almost Made Up Poem* discusses the measuring of future difficulties and injustices between people, not only as incidental or inevitable, but as able to be anticipated and avoided, including through suicide.[266] The extent to which someone is attracted to death versus finished with, or even repelled by, life should be tallied only in autobiographical accounting.

---

[264] I see this nowhere as clearly as in Charles Jackson's Don Birman character in that writer's best-known novel.

[265] As of this writing, it's taken more than four years (still not finished) to build a suicide barrier on the Golden Gate Bridge, the estimated cost at completion? $400 million. For comparison, it took four years to build the Golden Gate Bridge in the 1930s at a cost of $35 million (about $600 million today).

[266] Charles Bukowski, *An Almost Made Up Poem*, Charles Bukowski, Love Is A Dog From Hell 47 (2002) ("If I had met you I would probably have been unfair to you or you to me. It was best like this." Capitalization in quotation *supra* conforming to traditional rules, differing from the original...)

SCENE IV, PART I
When the River Asks for a Kiss

The calm, Cool face of the river Asked me for a kiss.
—James Mercer Langston Hughes[267]

The question of "when" to commit, and when to deliver on the commitment, brings us to the topic of time. Just as we talk of death in euphemisms mystical, we speak about time in euphemisms monetary.

We talk about time in a way that suggests an economics of time. We spend time and waste time. We ask whether someone can spare a minute or whether we can borrow an hour of someone's time. In the economics of time, we are all Al in Bing Crosby's Brother, Can You Spare a Dime?

In these contexts, time is used as the murky, sanitized proxy for what we're really talking about: can your boss spare a minute of her life to listen to your idea? Can he or she spare a moment of life while hurtling toward death, approaching the pastoral surface like so many falling dreamers.

We are all falling, our "time accounts" are falling in value, we are falling into an irreversible bankruptcy from which no court can design escape or relief.

And the creditor-in-chief, wielding a cane and called Osiris in Egypt, or armed with a scythe in dressed in black rags in Europe, or hiding in a chart full of bad news in a fluorescently illuminated room known only by a letter and a number, is unforgiving.

So frightening is this interpretation of daily life that we resort to monetary metaphor; as uncomfortable as it makes many to speak of money, it does not rise to the level of discomfort felt when discussing mortality.

This gilded language dilutes time's link to mortality but also emphasizes the opportunity cost of spending minutes, hours, and days in ways that

---

[267] Langston Hughes, *Suicide's Note*, Langston Hughes, Collected Works 62 (2002).

could have been spent in other ways.— Each unit is now lost forever, having been immutably expended in one particular way and not in another.

We can think of the heartbeat as a pump distributing oxygen needed for life or as a timer counting beats until death; I suggest it doesn't matter which we choose. The quantity remaining is unknown. But by setting a budget for the time we have, we better understand what we can, and might choose to, afford.

Affording, a word we use allocatively or budgetarily, is itself a euphemism in this context. It puts beyond view the things we will not do in life, hidden by the curtain of analogy though they are not beyond the horizon of possibility. As one of my linguistics mentors once said, in every phrase there is both description and advocacy.

Perhaps, then, if we apply this budgetary lens, life's length is not prescribed by what we can endure, but rather defined by what we can afford.

SCENE IV, PART II
The Truth About Dying

Death, a necessary end, will come when it will come.
—Julius Caesar[268]

People don't find things in the places people expect. If you want to know the right questions to ask, don't go to church or a guru, take a statistics course. But if you want to understand the alleged answers to questions, work from empiricism forward and not theory backward. And if you want to learn about death, don't read books or medical studies—talk to dying people.

The good news is it's easy to find dying people to talk to, as we're all dying.

The speed of death is rapid. When it arrives, it can be slowed but not stopped.

Death, whether in a hospital or in one's own home or bleeding and convulsing next to the stop sign deemed less important by a local soccer mom than finding the right emoji to reply to her kid, isn't as gradual as spectators perceive. It's gradual until it's not, painful until it's not, with a prosthetic-limb-beige machine beeping next to you until it's not.

Death is like some bizarre futuristic railyard, each life a bullet train being carefully loaded with a life's worth of baggage, being jockeyed around. But then, once aimed in the right direction and ready for departure, they shoot off toward the horizon, onward to a futurescape Imperial-Boy-imagined Japanese city . . . or a traditional heaven . . . or whatever it is you believe in.

People don't like honesty, and not just because it's less entertaining than fiction.

It's anticlimactic.

---

[268] William Shakespeare, Julius Caesar act 2, sc. 2.

My favorite ten-letter thing (oh yes, I have more than one . . .[269]) is that "'accounting' is eighty percent 'counting.'" It's funny not just because "counting" is eight of the ten letters in "accounting" and not just because it underplays the importance of the most important thing invented[270] in Italy;[271] it's funny because there's a chocolate chip of honesty in that cookie.

There really is a lot of accounting that can be reduced to, well, just counting.

My goal in this section is to discuss death in the tone of that joke.

One of my closest friends is a qualified trauma surgeon who has saved lives and watched people die. We, humans, have invented some really, really cool stuff to save lives and ease pain and I love that technology and the IQ points and brilliant midnight ideas ensconced in those gadgets and techniques. But we've also found ways to prolong suffering, isolate life from living, and manufacture what I can only describe as Wachowski-grade slo-mo'ing of tragedy.

If I had to sum up this section thematically, it would be: "More is not better, full-stop."

But why isn't it? More seems tempting, even seductive. We are trained to lust after "more."

In the case of life, I argue, "more" isn't just selfish and costly, it's dangerous and cruel.

It isn't a case of *confusing* quantity for quality, it's a case of *trading* quality for quantity.

The Swedish have a word for moderation in these larger lifestyle questions: *lagom.*[272]

---

[269] Like many economists I know, I have obsessive mental fetishes and weird little games I play with myself. One of my favorites, when I was flying internationally two to four times a week in my late twenties, was to spend time on airplanes and in airports thinking of English words with precisely ten letters and no repeating letters. Some examples to get you started are "porcelains" and "upholstery." You'll drive yourself nuts, but it's fun. There are well over a hundred such words, but I haven't yet reached two hundred.

[270] Thank you, Luca Pacioli.

[271] The engine of my briefly owned, still fondly recalled 2018 MV Agusta F4/1000 being firmly in second place.

[272] English lacks this piece of vocabulary aside from Goldilocks' metaphorisms. One of the better

211

If part of living a good life is reducing or preventing suffering—and this is true whether one's decision-making framework is biblical[273] or the recent "effective altruism" movement[274]—then supporting a broad right to end one's own life is one of the best things for which to advocate. But there are many reasons to end life that do not involve terminal illness, painful suffering, financial ruin, or even any detectable kind of discomfort.

And people making the decision to end life should not have to justify it to anyone.

I call the contrary argument "pity means testing" and I find it one of the most offensive, useless positions one can take in this broader set of conversations. Pity means testing argues if you are in *enough pain*, if you are *pathetic enough*, if you are *depressed enough*, then maybe society's gatekeepers or onlookers or Mildred Ratcheds[275] will permit you to end your life.

---

explanations I've read came from a somewhat unlikely place, a now-quite-old interview with Stockholm-born Johanna Jussinniemi.

[273] Some cite the promise of salvation as sufficient for them to endure nearly any interim misfortune or discomfort. See Romans 8:18; see also Revelation 21:4. Earthly suffering may even be prerequisite to ease later, in the interpretations of some. See 1 Peter 5:10. ("And after you have suffered a little while, the God of all grace, who has called you to his eternal glory in Christ, will himself restore, confirm, strengthen, and establish you.")

[274] I disagree with many of this movement's views, including that more life per person and more lives in total means more total happiness—firstly because I disagree that any precision can be reached in "happiness accounting," and secondly because many lives may either have negative current happiness or negative expected happiness in all future years.

[275] One Flew Over the Cuckoo's Nest United Artists (1975).

SCENE V, PART I
Enter the Machines

You have the look of a man who accepts what he sees because he
is expecting to wake up.
—Morpheus[276]

Thought experiments about death and dying, including self-initiated death, date to at least ancient Greece. The modern frameworks discussed in this section are part of a lineage of philosophical thought much more modern.

The premise of this section is not that we should be building suicide machines, but rather that we should carefully consider the role life plays in how we perceive death. Conversely, we should consider the role death plays in how we plan and enjoy and value our lives.

Central to our concept of the fairness or oughtness of death is the question of quality of life. To a lesser, but not irrelevant, degree, the quality of death and the time before death (and after death, if your beliefs embrace that sort of thing) often influences our lives.

In economic terms, this makes a great deal of sense. The opportunity cost to be weighed in the case of death is the value of the highest and best use of the alternative expenditures of any remaining time. This is, at its essence, the reason some initially prefer hospital assisted death for the ill and infirm to assisted or over-the-counter (or from-the-vending-machine) death being available to healthy twenty-five-year-olds.

However, if one envisions that twenty-five-year-old in prison for the rest of her life, having exhausted appellate possibilities,[277] if one envisions a twen-

---

276   The Matrix Warner Brothers (1999).
277   As of this writing, twenty-seven states practice the death penalty, and in every one of these states, life without parole is available to judges as a sentencing option; this is also true of federal courts and US military courts (courts martial).

ty-five-year-old in Mauritania in chattel slavery with no hope of escape,[278] or if one envisions that person in any number of other situations limiting enjoyment of life, people are generally more willing to allow that person to end his or her life after an interval that is biologically premature than a white collar twenty-five-year-old in Brooklyn who recently involuntarily left an investment banking job or similarly involuntarily left a relationship.

In essence, it is easier for the bystander to accept death that would otherwise be deemed premature when certain contextual details are present. Society is generally more comfortable with the death of a sick person than the death of a well person, the death of a slave rather than the death of a free person, the death of a prisoner[279] rather than a person on the street, even though the person observing the sick person often does not know how consuming the deep, cellular-level burning pain of chemotherapy feels or how waking to do the physical labor of slavery under threat of violence feels.

This is like other areas where the observer infantilizes the observed, reducing the agency of that person. In the case of observing a person who wishes to die, the observer may do this by imposing laws or restrictions or waiting periods, by impeaching the person's sanity, by questioning the

---

[278] Slave masters as masters one might only be able to escape by dying, and hence a slave's life as an example of a life one might end affirmatively, dates at least to biblical times, see Timothy 1:10; see also biblical discussion that seems to suggest slavery is itself a gravely unrighteous and inequitable imposition of hierarchy, as slaves, too, are made in God's image (see, e.g., Genesis 1:27, Exodus 21:1–11). The Qur'an in several instances suggests slavery is inequitable and that slaves who die in righteous moments may in fact be martyrs; in one case, freeing slaves is compared to feeding the poor; in another case, mistreatment of slaves is likened to other kinds of unnecessary and impermissible cruelty. These prohibitions against mistreatment may have been embraced less as a human rights matter and more as governance advice for the ruling class; many scholars believe mistreatment of slaves may have fermented, or even directly caused, the unrest that became the Zanj Rebellion, ثورة الزنج, leaving tens of thousands dead by the time dusk came awaiting a new autumn moon in 883 AD; in that martial action, hundreds of slaves killed themselves or chose to die in groups northwest of ٱلْبَصْرَة rather than being forced to fight (or, often, being marched through the desert in states of thirst and starvation before reaching the enemy).

[279] The valuation of lives, particularly comparatively, is a delicate thing and difficult to discuss in terms that are precise or polite. This having been said, suicides among slaves, prisoners, and others are not erroneous datapoints and remind us some lives are difficult in ways that are not related to deadly illness or geriatric decline. See generally Emda Dooley, *Prison Suicide in England and Wales 1972–87*, 156 Br. J. Psych. 40 (1990); see also Lindsay M. Hayes, *National Study of Jail Suicides: Seven Years Later*, 60 Psych. Q. 7 (1989).

person's motives, or by calling into question the magnitude of the person's pain, sorrow, or other feelings.

In 2021, I published a piece with Professor Rachael Meager discussing laziness.[280] Many of the arguments invoked in discussions of laziness apply to people seeking death. The longevity-above-all-else advocate professes: "If I were in that situation, I wouldn't make those choices. I would be more tough, more perseverant, more driven. I would endure what that person doesn't because that person is weak and I am strong."

Okay, you're so tough and brave. *Brah-fucking-voe.*

But why does being tougher or braver empower you to take choices away from others, even if those people are less tough or less brave?

Isn't that a kind of theft? Isn't victory of the strong over the weak[281] simply a regressive transfer tax on opportunity? Is it impossible for us to celebrate and appreciate your bravery and robustness while still providing choices to the timid and meek? And if you think courage or vigor is an innate characteristic, I urge you to briefly consider the etymology of "encourage"[282] or "invigorate."[283]

And it is easy to "other" people and imagine how our behavior in their circumstances would be superior. The other is permanently, perennially, immutably inferior.

Those caring for young children think their childless friends having fun in the city are selfish. The friends in the city may equally believe the suburbanite parents focused on breeding "mini me's" are selfish. The person playing with the child thinks the person playing with the dog across the park is lazy. The person playing with the dog, in turn, thinks the person in a nearby house playing videogames is lazy. The person playing videogames looks at those on the scoreboard below her and deems them lazy.

---

[280] Rachael Meager & Karl T. Muth, *People Aren't Lazy*, Noahpinion (Oct. 21, 2021).

[281] Samuel Colt believed the pistol would protect the weak from the strong and the few from the many; it was not long before the strong and the many had pistols, however.

[282] From the Middle French *in-corage*, to give or stimulate courage, *cor* in *corage* coming from the Latin (meaning heart). See also corāticum.

[283] From the Latin *in-vigorare*, to make strong. In Medieval Latin, *invigorat* meant "made strong" (compare contemporaneous Middle German: *starkgamacht*).

Accusations solve nothing, whether of selfishness or laziness or any other critical observation. Because this book focuses on the decision making and agency of the individual as primary, only secondarily asking how the individual's choices are narrowed or limited by others, it is important then to first ask "by what mechanisms do individuals make choices?" and then to ask how the variety of choices available might be limited by others.

Thought experiments allow us to visualize unlikely, or even futuristic and technologically impossible, situations to test the limits of our empathy and reason. They present a necessary, but not by themselves complete, vantage point from which to consider these questions.

A few comments on these thought experiments, machines, and simulations, first. For the purposes of the following discussions, I do not believe it matters whether we are living in a corporeal world or are brains in jars living in a simulated reality; we are experiencing a life that we have the authority and means to end, the "realness" of what is ending need not be appraised and is not particularly relevant. I don't know and don't particularly care whether my suicide will result in a "game over" screen or a meet-and-greet with St. Peter or eternal darkness or a contribution to local soil quality.

It also does not matter, at least to me, if we opted into a simulated reality, which we cannot remember opting into (Nozick), as we are now in that simulation and can choose for it to continue or terminate.

And, finally, it does not matter if the reality we are in was constructed for the amusement or profit or exploitation (Wachowskis) of another (whether that is a god, capitalized *G* or not, or someone else) because the simulation's creator or owner is invisible to us and we do not have the choice to join other simulations; hence our only choice is to continue or terminate the current simulation.

It is a choice to continue or, in the prescient words of Pfc. William L. Hudson, "game over, man."

SCENE V, PART II
Nozick and Variations

Plugging in [to a Nozick machine] is a form of suicide.
—Ben Bramble[284]

In the classic thought experiment, the Nozick machine, the moment a person is plugged into the machine, the machine reaches into that person's memory and deletes all memory of having chosen to be plugged into the machine; as a result, the visceral experiences feel completely real and the person has no desire to leave the simulation because the person has no knowledge there is a simulation (the Matrix problem[285]). The person might even measure his or her self-worth or his or her life's worth in this synthetic context (the stamp pad nightclub problem[286]).

While plugged into the machine, the machine directly stimulates the brain in such a way that its simulated surroundings appear real to the user. Meanwhile, the user is physically immobilized (usually depicted as face-up and prone, coma-like[287]) and connected to the machine (presum-

---

[284] Ben Bramble, *The Experience Machine*, 11 Phil. Compass 136, 141 (2016).

[285] For an example of a person contemplating dying while *knowingly* and *consensually* hooked up to a Nozick machine, see poignant discussions of this question in the in-progress Jackpot trilogy by William Gibson. See generally William Gibson, The Peripheral (2014); William Gibson, Agency (2020). For those not wanting to read 1,500 pages to get the gist of this, the larger discussion of whether a person might choose to *voluntarily* live and die inside a Nozick simulation rather than enduring the balance of one's corporeal life is elegantly summarized in the porch conversation between Burton Fisher (who would choose real life) and Conner Penske (who would prefer to die while hooked up to a Nozick machine) in The Peripheral (which takes place in the universe created in Gibson's Jackpot trilogy); The Peripheral: Fuck You and Eat Shit Amazon Prime (Nov. 18, 2022) (at forty-eight minutes).

[286] This is similar to the invisible ink hand stamp nightclub proposed in debates recently at the University of Chicago, wherein a big-budget hedonistic nightclub stamps your hand and the stamp is invisible and contains an advanced transdermal drug that scrubs your memory of entering the nightclub and a period beforehand, separating your reality in the nightclub from the reality outside. In such a situation, one might appraise his or her life's value in terms of the interactions in the nightclub; for instance, his or her perceived attractiveness or interestingness in the nightclub environment, rather than in the context of prior, outside achievements.

[287] See H.R. Giger, Notebook #3 21 (1975) for what a wasting-away Nozick patient might look like.

ably electrically or perhaps electrochemically with direct machine-to-brain stimulation[288]).

While the user enjoys every whim in the machine's simulation, his or her real body is starved of the water and nutrients it needs to survive. Some discussions of the machine include an intravenous fluids bag for the user (so he or she does not die of dehydration) or even a feeding tube (so he or she does not die of starvation), but in all instances, the user dies connected to the machine. There is no "off switch" reachable by the user because the user does not realize there is anything to turn off.

To review, the characteristics of the machine are these:

(a) Once the simulation is operating, the person is unaware of the boundary between real life and the simulation. The initial decision to enter the simulation is difficult or impossible to remember.

(b) The machine can simulate scenarios that are impossible or improbable in real life and does so at such a high visual resolution and such high tactile veracity that it seems "real" in every way.

(c) The machine's simulation is so compelling and tangible that people are distracted from attending to their needs to eat, drink, sleep, exercise, and so forth, or these things are replaced with simulations.

(d) The machine operates seamlessly from start to finish, never glitching or hiccupping, always delivering a similar or superior user experience to what is possible for the person in real life.

(e) The person, once immersed in the simulation, cannot unplug from the machine and inevitably dies plugged into the machine's simulation absent severe intervention from another (unplugged) person.

When Nozick theorized the machine, he suggested that, if the machine were indeed invented, no one would use it. Who, he asked rhetorically,

---

[288] Whether this machine-and-brain singularity is purely electrical is unclear in sci-fi and as of this writing has not yet been achieved in any quasidisk I/O or logical file system sense. For an optimistic account of how one such symbiotic technological intervention might function, see, e.g., Elon Musk, *An Integrated Brain-Machine Interface Platform with Thousands of Channels*, 21 J. Med. Int. Res. 16194 (2019).

would choose to be a superman (or -woman) in an imagined software simulation rather than achieving things in the real world? Surely even the mediocre life in the real world, well-lived, is better than a simulated life where one has no meaningful contact with others, no lasting achievements, and no benefit to friends or family?

But I argue many would choose the machine. And some do today.

Heroin (or perhaps another opioid of your choice) is the chemical version of the same machine.

SCENE V, PART III
Nozick Reloaded

*Like a narcotic. Because when dreams become more important
than reality, you give up travel, building, creating.*
—Vina[289]

Opiate addiction is very similar to the Nozick machine, though its mechanism is chemical rather than virtual reality. It meets or exceeds all criteria (a) through (e) above and creates an almost-inescapable alternative reality that is often described as superior in every way to the real world in terms of contemporary user enjoyment. Also similar to the Nozick machine, it actively attacks the health of the person's body, making the real world less attractive as a destination and making the simulation or fantasy more attractive as a place to spend the rest of one's life.

Even for high-functioning opioid addicts,[290] it's difficult to decouple from the machine for more than a day or two. Fantasy and reality merge, stitched together with moments of clarity and smiles to oneself, the satisfaction of knowing a deep and valuable secret. Other times, the link between fantasy and reality feels stretched and one's confidence oscillates between fortified boldness and timid haze. The real world feels colder, harder, stricter than it did before; the simulation feels infinitely alluring, freeing, and wonderful.

Unlike Nozick's prediction, many people do choose to be plugged into the machine, and those people usually die connected to the simulation because reality is no match.

---

289 Star Trek: The Original Series, The Cage Desilu Productions (Oct. 15, 1988).
290 Thanks to a friend, who I will anonymize for obvious reasons. This friend was a Ph.D. candidate at the University of Chicago while I was a law student and educated me more than anyone else on what the reality of high-functioning heroin addiction looks like; how and to what extent it parallels so many aspects of the Nozick machine; and where incremental choices can accumulate to replace one's life in reality with, in some cases, augmented or distorted reality and in other cases completely detached dream. Without her help, I would not fully appreciate this analogy.

Scrub the disturbing Nozick machine from your mind for a bit and let's return to the beginning of the book, to why I wrote this book, to the movement I examined and then became disgusted with: the lifespan maximization movement.

SCENE V, PART IV
Imagining Mechanical Maximization

Gone was the strong and healthy beast who had led the
Farthing Wood party . . . In his place was a weak and starving
creature.
—*Whistler's Thoughts Via the Narrator*[291]

Imagine now a machine that we'll call the maximization machine.

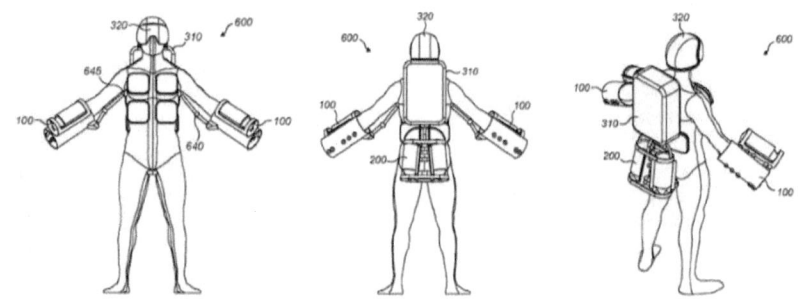

Above: Drawings of a suit design from UK Patent GB2,559,971.[292]

In this machine, the machine is worn like a backpack with supplementary garments for the head, wrists, and pelvis to allow mechanical access to cognitive, endocrine, respiratory, cardiopulmonary, and other functions, and combines a comprehensive biosensor loadout with advanced logic to trade off various functions to absolutely maximize and supplement the longevity of a given body. Customized from minute-to-minute to respond to

---

[291]   Colin Dann, The Animals of Farthing Wood 4 (1979).
[292]   Propulsion suit patent issued to Gravity Industries, Ltd. US Patent No. 7900867B2 (issued Mar. 8, 2011).

the weaknesses, strengths, and current health of each user, it makes difficult decisions and interventions that might not occur to, or be attractive to, the user or her physician. Like the Nozick machine, once someone opts in, the decision is essentially permanent; after a relatively short period of human-machine symbiosis, users cannot survive without the machine.

Over time, the user offloads more and more biological "work" to the machine. As the user's kidneys fail, the machine shoots cannulas into the rotting kidneys of the user to remove the afflicted tissue and then finer tubes to perform the filtration dialysis functions the kidneys once contributed. As the liver fails, the machine invades that part of the abdomen and replaces areas of the shrinking liver with biocompatible sponge material synthesized in the machine for the user. As dementia sets in, the machine downloads memories from the user's brain and duplicates them locally and in cloud storage for seamless access, granting backup storage plus superhuman recall.

With confidence mimicking Nozick's, and perhaps equally as misplaced, I predict no one wants the maximization machine.

People want longer *healthspan* (as opposed to *lifespan*), longer enjoyment. People want to rewind to being twenty-five when they're sixty. People want the thirty-fifth year to last three years. For "forty to be the new thirty" as we used to say in the nineties.

But people don't actually want maximum longevity. People don't want to be a brain in a jar depending on an AI-controlled therapeutic backpack for essential functions, a robotic exoskeleton for transportation, and a speaker for communication. That's my position. That even if you have unlimited financial and engineering resources, you would not choose this type of maximum longevity.

You would instead prefer an optimized, shorter life.

Maybe I'm wrong. About you. But I know I'm not wrong about me and my preferences.

SCENE V, PART V
Today's Hardware and Software Loadout

The meaning of life is just to be alive ... yet, everybody rushes around in a great panic as if it were necessary to achieve something beyond themselves.
—Alan Watts[293]

Now that we've talked about Nozick's fantastic machine (and I mean "fantastic" to mean "drawn from fantasy" not "really wonderful"), which seems very far in the future, and my concept of a maximization machine, which seems within the imaginable future, let's examine the software and hardware already available today.

The Watts machine, as in philosopher Alan Watts, is already invented, in a sense. You were born with it implanted inside you.

You dream.

Because you dream, I know you have the hardware and software needed for the Watts machine.

Of the many provocative constructions Watts created during his life of writings and lectures, one has always struck me as both fascinating and disappointing, which he called the "life dream," but which I'll call the Watts machine.

Before we begin, we should acknowledge that Watts was well-read in Eastern traditions and poetry and almost certainly did not come up with this concept himself. Japanese poet Rokushi writes of such a mechanism in 1881, and mentions it in reference to a much older tale.

---

293 Alan Watts, The Culture of Counter-Culture: The Edited Transcripts (1988).

I wake up	*Awa no meshi*
from a seventy-five-year dream	*samete shichiju*
to millet porridge.	*gonen kana*

—*Rokushi (Yoel Hoffmann trans. in Japanese Death Poems at 259 (1986))*

In the scenario Rokushi refers to, the narrator puts a pot of porridge on the fire and falls asleep, dreaming of a seventy-five year adventurous life of intrigue and fortune. When he wakes, the porridge has not yet boiled, showing his dreaming mind simulated a whole life in a brief period.

In the very similar Watts construction, each night you can have a dream in six to eight hours that, in experienced time, is something like seventy-five years in length. In other words, each night you can live an entire life.

The Watts machine is a brilliant construct because it takes hardware and software that already exists (body and brain and whatever is within them) and an experience already familiar to the "user" (dreaming) and applies them to an experience machine framework.

As a result, the suspension of disbelief and sci-fi-ism of the Nozick machine is removed from the experiment. Most people have had strange things happen in dreams, or dreams that seemingly lasted much longer than the dreamer slept, so the premise is not itself objectionable (or rejected at first blush).

In the Watts machine, like the Nozick machine, the dreamer can make choices about arbitrary aspects of the world and relax limiters and rules that normally exist. For instance, one can relax the influence of gravity. One can move faster than is normally humanly possible or be stronger than human musculature normally allows. One can dive deep below the surface of the sea with no ill effects.

Watts argues that you have a few amazing lives like this, like Keanu Reeves's character in The Matrix, free from the barriers of the conventional world. But then you find it boring. You begin to erect certain barriers to your omnipotence. You create problems for yourself to solve, or find problems in

225

your environment to solve, like Bill Murray's character in Groundhog Day.

You find you crave resistance from life, a few walls to bang up against, some hurdles to clear, that accomplishment is impossible without it.

Isn't it possible, argues Watts, that eventually you create a life that is very complex, nuanced, filled with challenge, and this creation contains more than a dash of randomness also . . . isn't it possible that, given the god-like power to create whatever you like each night that you eventually create a life that is very much like the life you are presently living?

That eventually you begin to dream about your real, ordinary, waking life.

This convergence is maddeningly worrisome to me. It suggests that given additional latitude to explore, we instead take refuge in the ordinary. Or that the present waking lives we experience actually are the best lives possible and that no improvement is durable enough to persist against the erosive forces of human nature. My quibble is not with Watts's brilliant framing, but with the exercise's outcome.

I believe, like Nozick, Watts underestimates interest in more exotic outcomes not achievable in waking life.

He writes to the experienced dreamer who has already experienced lifetimes in the Watts machine:

Let's have a dream which isn't under control. Where something is going to happen to [you] that [you] don't know what it's going to be. And you would dig that and come out of that and say "Wow, that was a close shave, wasn't it?" And then you would get more and more adventurous, and you would make further and further out gambles as to what you would dream.[294]

This is where, I believe, Watts's theorizing breaks down.

I ask: A "close shave" of what sort? A shave against what sharp outcome, precisely?[295]

---

[294] Alan Watts, The Dream of Life (1969).
[295] Suicide in lucid dreams is rare and may even be impossible (the author often experiences lucid dreams he can control and many times has tried to kill himself in dreams in ever-more-creative ways, albeit still without success . . .), but the idea of the omnipotent, yet suicidal, protagonist is recurrent in

Is there any risk truly taken by the dreamer if the ultimate penalty to the dreamer's risk-taking is snapping awake to find herself safely in bed?[296]

I argue the only dream worth having in the Watts machine is one with mortal risk. And because the Watts machine cannot produce real consequences,[297] the idea that people will be ever-more-daring and create the waking lives they have today is incorrect. One of the things that shapes life is death, the risk of dying, even if singularly infinitesimal, is cumulatively appreciable. And this guides our choices.

---

art and philosophy. For contemporary contemplation of whether God can kill him- (or her- or they- or it- if God is a computer on which our reality runs as software) self, see P.F.H. Lauxtermann, *The Paradox: Can God Commit Suicide?* Schopenhauer's Broken World View 197–229 (2000).

[296] Dreaming is, by its very nature, nerfed. It is a playground so well-designed that even what appear to be chasms are either humorously shallow or harmlessly bottomless, blades gleam but do not slice, bullets fly but do not pierce. The worst result is the inconvenience of needing to change a sweaty set of sheets.

[297] Perhaps one can have a startling awakening leading to a cardiac event or other health mishap, but the vast majority of bad dreams (even if the contents of the dream are horrifying) end uneventfully with little more than trace amounts of sweat in one's sheets or the fleeting echo of an *éveil* scream as evidence when the dreamer's experience terminates.

SCENE V, PART VI
Enter a New Machine

[T]he best way to solve the dilemma, you'll find, is simply by spinning a penny. No - not so that chance shall decide the affair while you're passively standing there moping; but the moment the penny is up in the air, you suddenly know what you're hoping.
—Piet Hein[298]

I want to believe Watts is right. It makes the entire puzzle so much simpler to solve.

But I want to think there is more beyond the Watts machine. And, thankfully, there is.

Thinking about these topics on morning bicycle rides around Hyde Park in Chicago, I came to the conclusion another machine was needed, which I'll call the Relief Machine.

The Relief Machine features a direct neural interface that does not require the user to evidence a revealed preference for life or death. Instead, the person logs into the machine (by pressing "begin") and the machine reads the user's "true desire" to live or die and then affects that outcome.

It can be used never, weekly, or monthly, but the risk it will cause death, if the user deeply desires to die, is very real. Constructing the machine to function as I describe requires futuretech (neural interface, reliable memory editing, advanced unsupervised life support, and possibly other technologies), but its basic operation is very simple, similar in core operation to that of the Heinian (as in Piet Hein's 1960s writings) diagnostic.

The screen either reads "begin" or "out of service."

---

[298] Piet Hein, *A Psychological Tip* Grooks 1 (1969).

If the screen reads "out of service," the machine is unavailable for use (this functionality is intentional and later explained).

In the Relief Machine, "real" life ("outside time") pauses,[299] time stops.

The machine installs a "save point" in the life of the individual immediately before she decided to use the machine,[300] to which the individual will return if she decides to survive the experience. In no event will any memory of the experience be available to the user, so every time the user uses the machine, she believes it is her first time.

At this point, the simulation begins.

The machine simulates a calming room of neutral hue and with no contents aside from a comfortable surface on which to think, rest, or do whatever the user likes—the user may sob, sing, yell, or do any activity that comes to mind. There is no requirement for the task and "outside time" is paused at the marker. The user may inhabit this room for minutes or days because the Relief Machine has the ability to stop[301] "outside time," the person's body is not at risk of a Nozick-like wasting death.

The room inside the machine is a perfect, harmless, physical and temporal oubliette, removing the user completely from normal life and dropping the user into a mysterious room. One wall of the room displays the precise time the user pressed "begin" and live footage of various places around the world, illustrating truthfully that time has been paused. Another wall displays messages suggesting, again truthfully, the user is alone, safe, and has as much time as she would like to ponder life and death.

A person is then, with all life's urgency and any threats or crises removed, given calm clarity; the person is not sedated or chemically altered in state, but she is given unlimited time to think about life and living and to inventory all she has done, seen, heard, tasted, and felt. It is in this pause-button vacuum away from the stresses, trivialities, and frolics that are scattered along

---

[299] This is a Q-pause mechanism, as in Q's ability to stop or vastly slow ambient, locally experienced time while Captain Picard makes a decision in at least two episodes of Star Trek: The Next Generation.
[300] This could be considered a Gibsonian "stub" point where reality potentially branches.
[301] Q-pause mechanism.

the typical timeline that the user may contemplate her life, its meaning, its pains or weaknesses, family and friends, pets and favorite destinations on Earth, and other topics that she may deem relevant.

When the user is ready, she presses a button in the simulated chamber and a coin appears. Even if the user has entered the chamber weekly for years, she listens attentively as, to her, thanks to reliable memory editing, it is always the "first time."

The narrator in the simulation announces the coin is perfectly fair, with an equal chance of heads or tails.

The "heads" or obverse side of the coin is a skull and represents death. When the coin is flipped, the narrator suggests, if it lands "heads up," the user will, back on the real timeline, be instantly and painlessly killed.

The "tails" or reverse side of the coin causes the person to wake immediately at the marker, standing in front of the machine. The machine reads "out of service" for a week and cannot be reactivated by the user.

The user is invited to flip the coin, but she is also given the option to leave.

If the user opts to leave, the user is immediately transported back to the marker on the real timeline, where she remembers nothing of the experience and sees an "out of service" message on the screen of the strange machine before her. That's one of two outcomes from three options.

Three options. Yep, read that again; it's not a typo.

If the user opts to flip the coin, things get interesting.

However, there is a complexity: parts of what the narrator says are true, parts are not.

SCENE V, PART VII
A Peek Under the Bonnet

What's the most you've ever lost on a coin toss?
—Anton Chigurh[302]

How the machine actually works is that the coin never hits the ground, just as the person in the "falling" dream never encounters the surface below.

Instead, once the user flips the coin and while the coin is still rotating and airborne, the machine reads the thoughts of the user as she watches the coin gyrating in the air. In so doing, the machine can calculate whether the person truly wants the coin to land heads (death) or tails (continued life).

The machine immediately kills users who are hoping more for heads than tails. The machine spits out users who are hoping more for tails than heads back to the marker on the real timeline, where they remember nothing of the experience and see a disappointing "out of service" message on the screen of the strange machine before them.

Why not just flip a coin? Why did I make this a sci-fi futuretech-required machine?

The pause mechanic is important because the user's deliberation should not be penalized or limited by other obligations. The unsupervised life support mechanic is important because the user's reflection or deliberation period should not be shortened on account of poor health or concern for the body's health while the machine is in use. The memory deletion mechanic eliminates the gambler's fallacy and other biases (including negative recency bias) affecting the wishes of the user.

"Well, gee whiz," you say dismissively. "That's bloody perfect for an undergraduate philosophy class," you say, "but what are we really doing here?"

---

[302] No Country for Old Men Miramax (2007).

We're talking about when.

People with whom I discuss suicide often ask me, "when?"

When is the right time? When is life "done," anyway?

Antoine de Saint-Exupéry once wrote, in a different context, "Perfection is achieved not when there is nothing more to add, but when there is nothing left to take away."

Finding the right time requires thought and reflection from each person. However, speaking for myself, I see everything in terms of hardware and software. There are hardware failures, our failing bodies, our inability to do things we enjoyed when we were young, our shaking hands, or failing senses. Then there are software failures, pawing at the frayed pages of our mental dictionaries for the right word, trouble processing how to use the newest gadgets, wondering when once-simple matters became insolubly complex.

Every hardware or software failure is a small tragedy, sure. But adding them up is pointless. The result is a useless number, which may as well be a random figure on an arbitrary scale.

I'm more interested in life as a matter of user experience, which requires both hardware and software. Life is something that begins with an awesome user experience. The wonder people see in a child's eyes, the brilliant move by the chess player or athlete, or the "aha!" of a researcher in the laboratory—this is evidence of the sublime user experience.

Over time, the user experience begins to degrade.

The simulation feels a few versions behind, and updates don't install properly. (An update might include a new idea but, also, perhaps a new knee or hip.)

To me, this user experience degradation is not beautiful or a vehicle for silver-haired wisdom. It's a cue to the user to think about how much more of the user experience is desirable. At some point, we've gotten all we can from the machine. The real machine, the one we're all experiencing. And certainly other kinds of decline in user experience—for instance, damage to one's financial state or social reputation—can be just as alarming as watching one's body or mind fail.

When is when, then? This may be when a person's body is failing, but just as often, it will be when the user experience simply has stopped living up to the user's expectations. And that's as good a reason to hope for "heads" as any.

SCENE VI
Outcasts Have Superpowers

Appellant was a nineteen-year youth of the black jacket and [L]evi apparel-fashion, unacquainted with his victim, and having a prior felony conviction.
—*The Hon. Harvey M. Johnsen*[303]

People who are discriminated against, outcast, othered, and derided are statistically more likely to end their lives—this includes LGBTQ+ people,[304] BIPOC folks,[305] recovering addicts of various stripes,[306] and other groups often overlooked by mainstream narratives and mainstream culture. But, I assert, this higher suicide rate often *isn't because they feel hated or depressed or sad*, it's because *they're empowered to do things others won't*—including suicide.

They are untethered from the norms and rules and bedtimes and classic rock of the normcore decaf-slurper-inhabited cul-de-sac where each month's calendar begins with an automatic debit of the family checking account for the Camry or F-150 in the driveway. Their olfactory senses and culinary

---

[303] Homan v. United States, 279 F.2d 767 (8th Cir. 1960).

[304] "Young people who identify as lesbian, gay, or bisexual are three times as likely to feel suicidal." *Young Americans Increasingly End Their Own Lives*, The Economist (Dec. 3, 2022).

[305] The suicide rate for indigenous-identifying females is roughly seven times the rate of white females. Suicide rates among Inuit youths are eleven times the Canadian national average. According to Canada's Centre for Suicide Prevention, suicide and self-harm are the leading causes of death for First Nations youths and adults all the way from the youngest age group trapped through age forty-four. In the Australian context, Aboriginal and other Indigenous people are almost four times more likely to kill themselves than non-Indigenous people in the same parts of the age distribution. The Australian Bureau of Statistics reported suicide as the dominant cause of death among Indigenous children ages five to seventeen. For more on possible factors related to economic and housing and opportunity factors, see excellent recent research by the Harvard Project on American Indian Economic Development. Bear in mind, however, the more uncomfortable output from such data-gathering efforts: that the decision to end life under chattel slavery or oppressive conditions or abject scarcity or eternal difficulty might not be the consequence of depression or mental illness but might instead be a rational, reasonable, deliberate choice.

[306] See Frances L. Lynch, et al., *Substance Use Disorders and Risk of Suicide in a General US Population*, 1 Addiction Sci. & Clin. Practice 15 (2020).

palettes are undamaged by Yankee Candles and Celestial Seasonings. They hear Red Hat and think of a Linux operating system, not a Trumpy voter. Their favorite albums are older than their cars, cars with six-figure mileage old enough to have their own driving licenses.

And it's no wonder the less-respected, more-tattooed, perhaps pink-haired, not-famous people of the nonconformist subcultures feel more free to experiment while they explore/enjoy/end their lives; society already disregards most of their decisions as either small and unworthy of attention or unconventional and even threatening to the lifestyle defined by LinkedIn work anniversaries, parenting-by-iPad, American-hetero-football-fan-but-secretly-soccer-curious Sunday television, cheap Tom Clancy patriotism, and high-functioning suburban alcoholism the mainstream portrays as *normal*.

Often, a "normal" suburban Camry pilot wants to end her life but doesn't. She thinks suicide is *abnormal*. That it's *bad*. That it's *selfish*.

She believes this because she's *thought* about ending her life, but she's never ***thought*** about it.

There is an intrasocietal magnetism strong enough to cook a Milgauss[307] that draws many to conform. Cohn, a shy and uncomfortable Jew at Princeton, doesn't even enjoy boxing but earning his middleweight boxing title[308] is really a kind of won whiteness[309] and a way to "fit in" or create social markers of belonging. Belonging is another word for perceived "normalness." But in belonging, Cohn also loses lots of the opportunities beyond the normal citadel's walls.

People "in here" are normal, beyond imagined barriers and razor wire are barbarians who sing hip-hop at karaoke, can drive a car with three pedals, pronounce *terroir* correctly (and not like a scary movie genre), and still own the Doc Martens they had in college. These people, the nonconformists, are *a threat to our way of life*, the normtroopers announce, briefly stepping out from the bunkers whose exteriors are Home Depot vinyl siding punctuated

---

[307] A wristwatch type that stands up to 1,000 gauss of magnetism, hence the name.
[308] Robert Cohn, a Jewish character in Ernest Hemingway, The Sun Also Rises (1926).
[309] See generally Eric L. Goldstein, The Price of Whiteness: Jews, Race, and American Identity (2006).

with moderately priced windows wearing "neighborhood watch" and "we call police" stickers.

If the others kill themselves, *it's because they're weirdos*, the normforcer says. In fact, to kill yourself, *you must be a weirdo*. To even think about it *makes you a weirdo*.

And this normforcer is onto something but doesn't realize those "weirdos" have more freedom than those trapped in lives only remarkable for their arbitrary, self-imposed rules.

How did we arrive at discrediting people who end their lives as, if not insane, abnormal?

How did suicide become a bold-font biographical asterisk calling into question a person's decision-making ability, understanding of the world, or even sanity? Isn't it at least possible it's a greater appreciation of the gravity of the decision, the surrounding context, and the road ahead that leads someone to rationally, calmly, and understandably end life?

Find what matters to you, and only you, and explore it or buy it or experience it. If it's something best done or bought or enjoyed now, don't delay. But how should we weigh these perhaps riskier, perhaps more fun, nonconformist experiences—especially ones that might, with a dash of misfortune, hasten death, even if they are not "suicide attempts" *per se*?

Recall the concept of gradual suicide back in Act I, Scene III.

What if we could somehow quantify how risky, how gradual or accelerated, risky lives are (or, posthumously, were)?

The micromort, invented in 1980 by decision scientist Ronald A. Howard (no, not the Happy Days actor-turned-director who, along with Sir Patrick Stewart, made premature balding cool . . . that's Ronald W. Howard), is a unit of risk equal to a once-in-a-million chance of death. While a skydive adds ten, an attempt to summit Everest is worth between thirty and forty thousand, depending upon your level of experience, your equipment, and the season. In the US, the ambient urban area general risk of murder is between forty and fifty, depending where you live, higher in Chicago and lower in Charlotte. During the COVID-19 pandemic, that virus taking hold in one's body added about three hundred for an unvaccinated elderly person, but only fifteen or so for those vaccinated.

Put another way, eventually the odds of dying will be 100 percent. We will each and all die. But we will approach that point differently, and how we approach 100 percent matters. Each day, no matter what it contains, takes us a step closer to death. As those little micromorts add up, or as we spend down our "time accounts," we are doing things. Those things accumulate into who we are, the mark we leave on the world, the things we're proud of and regret, the friends who will remember us when we're gone.

Every gift you've ever received, performance you've ever witnessed, book you've ever read, or telephone call you've ever answered came from a person who was dying.

More of "life" sounds like a splendid thing.

But life, like alcohol, tastes different once one is on her fourth or fifth glass of it.

Adding up Howard's micromorts gets us to a probability of natural, or even accidental, death. But there is no reason to wait to spend all one million micromorts. Most people are not all that interested in the probability of dying; they are more interested in the value of remaining life. Is the dividend of seeing tomorrow worth the cost of making it through today? That's the fundamental calculus.

In this sense, each tomorrow is like a third card dealt to the blackjack punter hitting on twelve. It may kill him instantly, it may give him tough new decisions to make, or it may put him in a more comfortable position. But walking away from the table isn't always an act of cowardice; it can also be the most responsible option. And each punter is best positioned to make his own decision.

The argument in this book focuses on suicide as a rational decision made by people who have weighed the prospect of death today against the value, obligations, suffering, and intangibles of continued life tomorrow.

As Schopenhauer argued,[310] "as soon as the terrors of life reach the point at which they outweigh the terrors of death, a man will put an end to his life."

But what does this rational suicide look like when made more modern and tangible?

---

[310] Arthur Schopenhauer, 2 Parerga and Paralipomena 156 Cambridge, Cambridge Univ. Press (1851).

ACT VI
Death Is Inevitable
but not
Uncontrollable

SCENE I
It Can't Be Helped
(しょうがない)[311]

He passed calmly and peacefully in his sleep.
—Reassuring and common, but often-untrue, obituarial
narration

I'm a good-enough welder and can occasionally build things that don't self-destruct when they're first used. When I lived in a village in Uganda for two and a half years, I built a variety of projects, from the simple (an *L*-shaped shower curtain rod for the corner shower stall in my cinderblock dwelling) to the sturdy (a makeshift engine hoist to help repair a friend's Landcruiser) to the intricate (a pair of nearly perfectly balanced see-saw stainless steel "valves" to distribute rainwater into buckets from my roof).

But the most memorable thing I built was an aluminum-and-wood killing cone.

To understand what this is and why I built it, we should begin with the first chicken.

Tristan, my research assistant, arrived from the States as most of my friends and colleagues did, via London aboard British Airways 1063/0063 from Heathrow to Entebbe—then onward to the village by car, five hours in the dry season or seven hours in the wet season.

A few days before, I'd gotten some questionable chicken meat from the local market,[312] and I'd resolved to instead buy living chickens from now on, the idea being to slaughter and disassemble them myself on-site. Tristan arrived the same week I began implementing this plan.

---

[311] Japanese: Approximately "it can't be helped" or "nothing could be done." Pron. *shouga nai*.
[312] *Cuk madit*, the local market, literally translates as "big market." No big branding budget here.

My primary form of transport, a ten-year-old mountain bike, became the chicken transporter.

Using stout rubber bands or zip-ties, one can hang a chicken from his handlebars. Inverted *vespertilioesque*, the chicken quickly has blood flow to its head like a fighter pilot pulling too many negative *g*-forces, passing out. The chicken would then sit, limp, for the five or ten minutes needed for me to bicycle home. Once the chicken's "commute" was finished, gently tossing the passed-out chicken onto the dirt surrounding my small dwelling woke it up every time, without fail. It would then run around like a . . . well . . . chicken with its head still attached.

A resolute vegetarian, Tristan was a hesitant and nonobvious teammate for this task of chicken disassembly. Our first chicken slaughtering was needlessly drawn-out and suboptimal. While Tristan held the bird, I killed it on a cutting board outdoors and the process was more disorderly and traumatic than it needed to be; I lacked the finesse and confidence of the men in the market who I'd seen kill chickens with fluid, affirmative motions more like Rafael Nadal's first serve than my audition as an incompetent chicken hitman.

Though chicken meat is chicken meat, I do believe strongly in minimizing suffering of all kinds when possible, including chicken suffering.

After some research and speaking with my friend, Holly, who was building a hut nearby and had thought a great deal about being a *mzungu*[313] in our village area, I decided it best to create a killing cone of (admittedly modernized) local design. This design, essentially a triangle in section (looking down) is a frame of three stabilized wooden pieces (often bamboo, but sometimes local hardwoods) holding a furled piece of metal (usually 18-gauge aluminum scrap) held in a cone shape by a screw or rivet and then fastened (temporarily or more durably) to the frame.

---

[313] *Mzungu* is often mistranslated to English as "European" or even "white man"–neither being helpful or correct. *Mzungu* is more similar to *gaijin* (外人) in Japanese, which comes from *weiren* in Chinese (same *kana*), both meaning a person from outside the familiar sphere, but not indicating that person's origins, color, or ethnicity.

The chicken is loaded vertically and inverted, with its head toward the ground, its shape conforming to the general shape of the aluminum ice cream cone in which it now resides. The height of the cone is roughly the height of the chicken's "torso," so the loaded contraption (excluding the tripod holding it) is diamond-like when viewed from the side, the chicken's feet its tallest point and the chicken's head sticking out the bottom of the cone.

As on the bicycle, the inverted chicken relatively quickly loses consciousness and goes limp in the cone.

Its head, including staring-straight-to-the-sides unconscious eyes, protrudes from the cone's tip.

The chicken is then peacefully vulnerable to its swift, uneventful decapitation. "He passed calmly and peacefully in his sleep" is, for once, for a chicken, an accurate obituary. But it isn't for most humans—those who die "quietly" or "peacefully" in their sleep often actually die lucid, fully conscious, in immense pain, the quietness actually a result of a silent and paralyzing series of cardiac events or the result of liquid filling the lungs and gradually drowning the prostrate decedent. Mistaking silence or stillness for ease and comfort is not the right association to make.

Back to chickens, where perhaps I make this mistake, but against a different set of choices.

While the choice set is rather bleak, if I were asked whether I'd rather die probably unconscious, upside down in a cone, killed by someone who cared somewhat about my well-being and lack of suffering, or whether I'd rather be ripped apart in violent combat while screaming,[314] my final memory the barking glee of three hyenas ready to vie for my delicious internal organs, I think I'd choose the killing cone; I think I'd make this choice even if I wasn't 100 percent sure I'd be fully unconscious upside down in the cone. I say this as someone who woke up to the sounds of hyenas' nighttime murderous sprees outside the wall of my small dwelling more than once . . . and someone

---

[314] Squawking?

very aware a chicken roaming outside my home would eventually have this (or a similarly gruesome) encounter.

My time in Uganda, in a village with a low life expectancy and plenty of ways to die (for chickens but, also, for humans . . .), changed how I think about death. I'm not talking about just chickens or just people, but all death. Perhaps most poignantly, learning the local language taught me a new way of thinking about the future, about fate, and about the aesthetics and ethics of dying. To illustrate this more deeply, I've chosen two phrases to teach you here.

SCENE II, PART I
The Future Is Dark

The future is dark, which is the best thing the future can be, I think . . .
—Virginia Woolf[315]

Anyim col is a common phrase, nearly a slogan, you cannot live in northern Uganda without hearing.[316] *Anyim col* means, literally, the future (*anyim* = future) is dark (*col* = dark), which sounds simplistic and fatalistic, but it's actually very different. *Anyim* is a versatile word; it means the future, but it also means what's ahead in the most literal sense: you use it to instruct a taxi to continue forward rather than turning. *Col* means dark or black, but also means dark like the undiscovered edges of your Sid Meier's Civilization,[317] Final Fantasy VII,[318] or Legend of Zelda[319] map, unknown or even unknowable. *Col* is darkness in literal (meaning black) to poetic (meaning mysterious) senses all rolled into one.

A less common phrase is *wenyo ali malo duogo toa ping*. It means even the highest flying bird will die[320] on the ground. This sounds like ethnolinguistic society wide tall poppy syndrome,[321] but, as with *anyim col*, things are not as simple as they first appear. This phrase is used to illustrate both the inevitability of death and the honor of doing what one can during life (flying

---

[315] Virginia Woolf, *Personal Diary Entry Dated 18 Jan. 1915* Virginia Woolf Diaries in 27 Volumes (digital archival copy) (on file with The New York Public Library).

[316] Though the phrase you really need to learn is the one used to avoid overpriced and aggressively marketed *boda* taxi rides: *amero wot* (I'd rather walk).

[317] Sid Meier's Civilization MicroProse (1991).

[318] Final Fantasy VII Square (1997).

[319] The Legend of Zelda Nintendo (1986).

[320] Translated more literally, returns to the ground, but in a "dust to dust" sense; *duogo* means to return.

[321] Tall poppy syndrome involves an individual (or individuals) who anticipate antagonism or resentment from their high achievement(s) and, as a result, restrain performance or "sandbag" to not achieve as highly as possible.

high); the high-flying bird[322] is not a scolded Icarus or beheaded poppy, but a useful reminder that we have freedom to do what we can while alive and then return (*duogo*[323]) to a peaceful place.[324]

Why am I spending time describing the beheading of killing inversion-sedated slaughtered chickens? Why do I choose these two phrases in some obscure African language to teach you?

The core point here is that, when looking at something foreign, it may at first seem alarmingly doom-soaked or fatalistic (like "the future is dark") but, upon closer inspection, may hold far more nuance. Like the phrase *anyim col*, planning to end one's life may appear from a distance irretrievably dark and pointless when it in fact contains rationale, reflection, and insight.

In the field of statistics, we speak in terms of descriptive statistics versus inferential statistics. In legal analysis, we speak in terms of the facts and the law, with the former testing the latter and the latter offering ways to categorize the former. Can language help us do more than merely *describe* death? Can it help us *analyze* or even *understand* our relationships[325] with death?

Dying is an important event; as the often-insightful George Bernard Shaw quipped, "In the end, the headstone is the only milestone, isn't that right?"[326] What is a headstone but a milestone decorated in words? And the language we use when we talk about things shapes our understandings of those things, our attitudes, our beliefs. *Words matter*.

Language (poetry, song, etc.) is our lens to "see" death because death's earthly companionship is brief, elusive, enigmatic. If I gave you death enshrined and captured in a physical object, perhaps an egg black in color

---

[322] *Wenyo* (sometimes anglicized as *winyo*) meaning bird in Acholi, is probably a very old word predating late branching in the Nilotic dialects, related to *wen* in Lango (same meaning) and *winyo* in Alur (also bird).

[323] Sometimes anglicized as *dwogo*; the transliterated meaning is identical. Thanks to my friend Holly Porter for helping me understand these nuances and challenges of anglicization of Nilotic languages.

[324] The bird in the proverb is not merely metaphorical, it likely stems from a time of animal worship (*lakampiri*) when birds in stories were anthropomorphized as positive or special contributors to the community.

[325] Plural as there are as many relationships with death as there are people.

[326] See George Bernard Shaw ed., Collected Reflections and Essays London, The Fabian Society and Aldwych Press (1889).

as it appears in certain mythologies,[327] how would you hold it? Would it be heavy?[328] Would you *touch* the egg or *hold* it or *caress* it or *cradle* it?

Language is overlooked in our discussions of death, but what are discussions made of if not language? It *matters* whether I *architect* my death or whether I merely *plan* it, whether I *anticipate* my death or simply *know it's coming*. It matters whether I think I will *perish* or *die*.

You can *look at* death, but I encourage you to *gaze upon* it.

---

[327] Stories in the Oyo tradition in Nigeria talk of death as a physical thing contained in a dark pearl, sphere, or egg.

[328] The analogy of physical weight appears often in poetry. See, e.g., Tim O'Brien, The Weight (2013) ("The Weight of death. The Weight of loss. The Weight of injustice.").

SCENE II, PART II
What I Really Learned in Uganda

"Men, Estimated 20 and 23 Years Old, Killed in Farm Equipment Accident
—Local Newspaper Headline[329]

Living in a village where life expectancies are only 50 percent to 75 percent of those you're accustomed to forces you to confront the temporal abundance of life in the wealthiest countries and also the painful, choreographed, extended deaths people in wealthy countries experience. Perhaps nothing illustrates this more quickly and comprehensively than a look at local obituaries—not obits for famous people or notable people, just final blurbs about regular people who died.

In rural village newspapers in the developing world, people simply die. Sometimes it shows up in the local newsprint. The decedent's family may be mentioned, perhaps the family's religion, perhaps an accomplishment. But people don't *die of something* in most of the world, they just die. In the developed and wealthy world, people die "after a long battle with a rare cancer" or "despite hours of best efforts from brave surgeons."

Also, the developing world is a much less safe place. Understanding this is difficult for those who haven't lived there, but many people die because they made an uninformed decision about which water to drink, because a decades-old imported piece of agricultural equipment didn't have a modern safety feature, or because somebody saved $30 by not welding a chain or railing onto a platform opening that was just high enough to produce a fatal plunge.

---

[329] The Independent loc. supp. Kapchorwa District, Uganda (June 3, 2012).

People in poverty, people in the developing world, people living on two dollars a day[330] cannot plan their deaths with any reliability. This world is so unsafe that death is omnipresent and unpredictable.

Part of my argument against physician-assisted suicide in this text is that it elevates suicide to become an inaccessible luxury good because access to physicians, multiple opinions, exotic suicide cocktails, and so on is financially unrealistic for most and unlikely to be covered by conventional insurance; this is true. But there is a separate argument, a strong one, that I acknowledge here and do not know how to oppose: that suicide is *always* a luxury good where accidental or unexpected death is commonplace. Because if death is lurking in every potentially contaminated water bottle, in each shift at one's workplace, in every tse-tse fly that might bite one's neck, then death before one plans or desires isn't just unfortunate, it's very likely.

The village where I lived in Northern Uganda was the epicenter of one of the best-documented and most-studied outbreaks[331] of the Ebola[332] virus. Despite now having over fifty years of knowledge about Ebola (which is, it is important to narrate, only one of the very deadly illnesses intermittently troubling the Continent), our ability to control outbreaks and contain mortality numbers has only slightly improved;

---

[330] For an account of what such lives are like, anthropologically and financially, see Daryl Collins, Jonathan Moduch, Stuart Rutherford & Orlanda Ruthven, Portfolios of the Poor (2009). To understand the longevities of such people from a demographic or actuarial perspective, compare country-level mortality tables to U.N. Population Division, *Crude Death Rate Per 1000 population*, U.N. Doc. POP/DB/WPP/Rev. 2022/F0-1 2015–22 (July 2022). Uganda's published 2020 male life expectancy of sixty-three years embraces the population skew of Uganda toward urban areas with better quality food, water, workplace safety, and so on; rural Uganda's statistic is even lower.

[331] This outbreak was officially reported on Oct. 8, 2000 and it's unclear when the first human carrier died; the outbreak persisted for nearly six months (and was declared over on Feb. 27, 2001). For more on why the cultural factors in this village were particularly important, and arguably made the virus more difficult to combat, see generally Barry S. Hewlett & Richard P. Amola, *Cultural Contexts of Ebola in Northern Uganda*, 9 Emerg. Infectious Dis. 1242 (2003). For more information on this outbreak's timeline and response dynamics, see generally Samuel I. Okware, Francis Omaswa, Sam Zaramba, Alex Opio, Julius Julian Lutwama, John Bosco Kamugisha, Elly B. Rwaguma, Paul Kagwa, & Margaret Lamunu, *An Outbreak of Ebola in Uganda*, 7 Trop. Med. Int'l. Health 1068 (2002).

[332] Ebola is named for the Congolese river valley where it was discovered in the 1970s.

a 2014 outbreak involved a caseload of just under thirty thousand infected, eleven thousand of whom died.[333]

Above: An Ebola infection screening checkpoint. Photo taken by the author.

When I'm sitting at home in Chicago or London, I do not fear Ebola or poisoned drinking water or workplace accidents that might claim my life. What risks I do expose myself to (like the inferior-by-modern-standards[334] crash safety of a 1950s sports car...) are elective and relatively predictable in magnitude; the number of nonconsensual high-magnitude, low-frequency risks I encounter in my career, health, investments, personal life, or really any other aspect is small. In other words, I enjoy enormous latitude in knowing and planning how and how long I will live.

---

[333] See Katherine Marshall & Sally Smith, *Religion and Ebola: Learning from Experience*, 24 Lancet 386 (2015); see also Shaunak Sastry & Mohan J. Dutta, *Health Communication in the Time of Ebola: A Culture-Centered Interrogation*, 22 J. Health Comms. 10 (2017).

[334] "Downright dangerous by modern standards" might be the fairer description.

Meanwhile, back in the village, people face many difficult-to-anticipate and impossible-to-hedge high-magnitude, low-frequency risks across all categories. Yet, there is no word that translates to "risk" in the Acholi language and no word for insurance. When I was working for a multinational Asian bank in the region, I had to explain being an economist by saying *atiyo tic ma wil cato* (I work on buying and selling) and tried to explain the parametric agricultural insurance policy I was designing by saying *lopwur giwilo insurance ki bot beng pi ceng maokato ki rac* (farmers buy insurance from our bank in case the sun is too strong and bad).

The point in highlighting this dichotomy is not to have you, in a comfortable reading chair in a prosperous country, feeling sorry for people in a Ugandan village or feeling guilty for your predictable finances, lifestyle, and longevity. Rather, my goal is to illustrate that only some people live in conditions where planning the "how" and "when" of dying is possible and that, for this subset of fortunate folks, this may not be simply "an" option but "the best" option.

SCENE II, PART III
Planning Death Requires Safe Life

*At least 55 people were killed and more than 100 injured when
a truck overturned in southern Mexico on Thursday...*
—CNN[335]

One can't plan her death reliably if the probability of premature death from accident, disease, or other misfortune is substantial. Meanwhile, if one in New York or Paris or Tokyo wants to set a death date, only slender odds portend this will be interrupted by unexpected fatal misfortune in the interim. Though I advocate that ending life should be a near-universal right, I must admit in this regard, due to other accumulated inequities, a planned death is a type of first-world opulence; requiring physician assistance or physician permission, however, exacerbates this inequity.

Indeed, deciding when to die is not just a "first-world problem,"[336] but a "first-world privilege."

Yet I believe like many other areas (fair treatment of journalists, LGBTQ+ rights, animal welfare concern, funding for theater and the arts, and so on) this can be an area where the leadership of wealthy countries can influence or even change policy positively in less-wealthy countries. If we respect someone's chosen *modus vivendi*, why not extend similar liberal attitudes toward her choice of *modus mori*? Hence, even if it is only realistic for those residing in wealthy countries to exercise this right and die in a planned, consensual, pain-minimizing way, wealthy countries should value making this right explicitly and widely available in order to demonstrate and encourage its availability globally.

---

[335] Karol Suarez, Helen Regan, & Kiarinna Parisi, *Dozens Killed in Mexico Road Accident as Truck Carrying More Than 100 Migrants Crashes*, Cable News Network (Dec. 10, 2021).
[336] "Problem" in this context is often used jokingly, to point to things that are not actually problems or are problems so slight as to be annoyances rather than dilemmas.

Normalizing suicide globally must begin with frank discussions in the wealthy countries around end-of-life being a set of choices residing with the decedent-to-be and an opportunity to better understand, and ultimately reduce, the total amount of suffering in the world. The option to end life must be universal[337] and not purchased through the tenure of the long elderly, the severe pain of the injured, the sadness of the depressed, the wealth of the bourgeoise, or the irreversible decline of the sick. Access must be available as a matter of right, not sprinkled among the masses as a matter of pity or bought only by rich people with access to second and third opinions.

---

[337] Perhaps with safeguards for the very young, the mentally incompetent, and other special cases.

SCENE III
Suicide as a Tailor's Tool to Hem Life's Length

It's complicated!
—Dr. Christmas Jones[338]

As humans, we fashion the tools we need. We fashion cutting tools ranging from scalpels to swords. And psychological tools ranging from scriptural writings to psychedelic drugs. And tools to extend or limit the length of life, from chemotherapeutic treatments to suicide methods.

In a lecture I once attended at the University of Chicago, I was taught humans wouldn't exist today if hands (fists) were harder than skulls. In other words, we would have killed one another in a melee long ago. Instead, skulls withstand blows from fists quite well—damage from rocks or baseball bats or pistols, less so.

I argue also that we wouldn't exist if suicide were an epidemic disease to be controlled or a dangerous idea from which people needed to be shielded. Instead, suicide is merely a tool—not a contagious phenomenon demanding quarantine or a dangerous creature that needs to be locked away.

Imagine a suicide that you believe is bad, wrong, or should be impermissible. Imagine now this is not because suicide is bad or wrong, but because this person's use of this tool to trim one's life expectancy is problematic. Even if I agree with you the suicide you envision is tragic, which I may not, I argue it is user error, and not the tool's flaw.

We can imagine any number of scenarios where a tool is misused.[339]

We do not, for instance, ban 3D printers that can create a variety of contraband or problematic items;[340] we've committed to a societal calculus that

---

[338] The World is Not Enough MGM (1999).
[339] See generally Guido Calabresi, *Products Liability Symposium: Economic Analysis and the Law*, 38 U. Chi. L. Rev. 1 (1971).
[340] As of this writing, 3D printers have been used to produce firearms, faulty imitation vehicle parts,

the merits of additive manufacturing are compelling, even when weighed against its potential for serious misuse.

Many of the anecdotal arguments opposing access to suicide focus on what I'll broadly classify as "misuse and mistake" lines of narrative. In these related, but slightly different, scenarios the decedent does things the narrator or proponent of the argument suggests a reasonable person would regret or change if given the chance.

For instance, perhaps the person is intoxicated or otherwise cognitively compromised when making the decision to end life. Or perhaps the person judges the value of his or her life through a calculus based upon erroneous assumptions or shaky statistics.

Suppose a person believes she has a 98 percent chance of dying a painful and difficult death from HIV-related ailments[341] in 1992, and thus suicide in 1993 seems reasonable but, actually, her HIV would not have progressed into full-blown AIDS by 1993, and research into antiretroviral and other therapies is making enormously more progress than publicly perceived in the early-to-mid-1990s and that person could, in fact, have managed the disease reasonably well and enjoyed decent quality of life had she not ended her life in 1993.

Suicide in 1993 was, then, a "mistake," some would argue. In other words, the same actor with the same reasoning and the same utility calculation as to whether additional days of life are worthwhile would have made a different decision with better information. The decision to die in 1993 was misinformed (or underinformed or the inputs to that decision were contemporarily the best data available but are today known to be flawed).

The core problem with these arguments is that they lead back to the certainty problem. They suggest only an error rate of zero is acceptable and only decisions made with perfect information are acceptable; if the error

---

ingestible pills of dubious content and dosage, and counterfeit luxury goods.

[341] For more on suicide and this particular constellation of ailments, see Adam. W. Carrico, et al., *Correlates of Suicidal Ideation Among HIV-Positive Persons*, 21 AIDS 1199 (2007); see also Y. Conwell, *Suicide and Terminal Illness: Lessons from the HIV Pandemic*, 15 Crisis 57, 58 (1994).

rate in deciding to utilize suicide to end life is 0.1 percent or 1 percent or 10 percent, then we must severely restrict access to suicide for everyone else, with no balancing test in sight.

There is no other choice in our society where we impose such a rigorous standard when scrutinizing the appropriateness of utilization for a given tool.

"But these are life and death choices," the critics exclaim.

Indeed, they are. And this is why restrictions on these choices should be viewed dubiously and critiqued vigorously.

The opportunities for mistakes in the operation of even the best-designed, fail-safe-oriented nuclear reactor designs (the sodium-cooled French design, for instance) are not zero. The opportunities for unforeseen or poorly understood drug interactions and allergies for even the "safest" medications (such as aspirin or non-exotic antibiotics) are not zero. The opportunities for making mistakes in life-or-death activities are not scarce; rather, they are abundant.

In all of these cases, we make one of two decisions or a mix of the two: (1) the value of the underlying product when used correctly is clear and meritorious and thus the product is available despite occasional problems involving misuse or mistake, which we may try to mitigate, but which we cannot wholly eliminate or (2) while the product is not inherently enormously valuable to society, our liberal values orbiting around freedom of choice suggest outright prohibition is not appropriate despite risks posed to the participant.

The first category includes drugs that are quite poisonous or problematic if administered incorrectly, but we are willing to make them available, perhaps with certain safeguards, like availability being restricted to only those with certain diagnoses or characteristics, or distribution being restricted to only packaging that embraces child-proof features.

The second category includes things from casual, unprotected sex to skydiving to so-called "free" climbing (climbing above bouldering heights while not on belay). While reasonable people can agree the risks involved in these activities are significant and potentially life-altering if not life-ending, our general liberal attitudes run counter to prohibition.

Consider, however, that in an environment of prohibition, such as the current environment, the error rate actually climbs because safe, reliable avenues to directing one's death are so severely restricted. This is the error rate that proponents of the "mistake and misuse" argument conveniently omit, but one we recognize in other debates (e.g., the risk of back alley coat hanger abortions versus the comparative safety of professionally administered pregnancy termination).

Such people are deeply concerned the tool of suicide may be mistakenly employed or misused by potential decedents, but show little concern for the misuse of other tools that results from prohibition, such as failed suicide attempts using inadequate dosages, ineffective methods, or ill-informed plans. If preventing suffering is an optimization we value, then we should focus on minimizing the number of initiated, but failed, suicide attempts.

SCENE IV
I Favor Condoned Suicide in Part Because All Alternatives Are Worse

I never found out what happened . . . I hope he died quickly.
—Hazel-rah[342]

If we do not provide predictable and reliable routes to death, then people will try routes that pose more risks.

Imagine a world in which some women are hesitant to have children because there is some percentage chance the childbirth event will prove fatal to themselves (the mother) or the product of the process (the child). Imagine further that other factors, also with low-but-nonzero associated probabilities, also influence this decision, for instance that the child may be afflicted by Down Syndrome or by mental difficulties or by some other set of challenging issues.[343]

One can imagine these possible setbacks as similar to the implications of a failed suicide attempt.

By implementing policy measures that make these undesirable outcomes *more common*, we will not dissuade all childbirth but will create skews in who attempts to reproduce and why. If we instead make reproduction *as safe as possible*, we broaden the number of people who may choose to reproduce by improving their abilities to estimate what will happen when they attempt to have a child. "Someone who is considering whether or not to throw out the birth control pills began considering the values, perspective, interests, and concerns of a mother long before that."[344]

This is what I assert will happen if suicide outcomes become safer and more predictable.

---

[342] Richard Adams, Watership Down 157 (1972).
[343] For further discussion of decision making under similar constraints, see L. A. Paul, The Transformative Experience 151 (2014).
[344] Agnes Callard, Aspiration 59 (2018).

The current state of prohibition leads many to construct plans far outside their own areas of expertise, and sometimes include factors difficult or impossible to calculate: How much acetaminophen is really needed to kill me? When will I likely be found? At that time of day, how long will it take to reach the emergency room once I'm discovered? Could I carry out this plan in a more remote location to both decrease the odds I'll be found and increase the amount of time needed to get to the hospital? How sure am I that emergency services won't discover and attempt to revive me within the forty-eight hours or so during which liver failure may be preventable?

And this illustration involves a plan that is relatively straightforward compared to many.

By prohibiting suicide as a tool to design and plan our lifespans, we force those committed to using this tool to use inferior means to accomplish their aims. While nearly every tool can be used as a hammer and while nearly every object can be a weapon if you hold it right, not every tool is fit for every purpose if we apply even the lightest touch of scrutiny in the general colloquial direction of the word "fit."

Suicide prohibitions actually increase the error rate of suicide generally and enormously amplify attempts' harm to bystanders. I do not mean only the crashing of an automobile at high speed meant to harm Driver One but unintentionally injuring Driver Two and Driver Three, but also the traumatizing of bystanders as a descending decedent strikes the pavement nearby or the incapacitation of a person who given better tools would have successfully ended her life but now is seriously injured, can no longer work, and requires care.

The issue, as with abortion and other matters, is that when safe and accessible and reasonable means to accomplish the aim of suicide are prohibited, people will resort to using alternative, suboptimal means to accomplish the same goal with results that reasonable people on all sides of the larger political debate can agree are tragic. We see this already with the suicide-related misuse of everything from mail-order pesticides to over-the-counter painkillers.

Part of any rollback of society's suicide prohibitions must be accompanied by safe systems for achieving death painlessly and with minimal effect on people nearby. Much as some jurisdictions provide safe injection sites for drug users or safe places for the indigent to sleep at night (even if lawmakers consider injection drug use or homelessness undesirable in some macro sense), we must provide safe places to die and high-efficacy methods to affect death. To do anything else will increase the number of injured and disabled people from failed attempts.

SCENE V
Chosen, Consensual Dying

It is considered useful and enlightening and therapeutic to think about death for a few minutes a day.
—Anthony Bourdain[345]

I am not particularly concerned with the suicide rate. Nor am I very interested in suicide's popularity as measured by how many people expire as planned by the decedent versus how many people die in an unplanned context. Envisioning future states of reality, I care deeply about the *availability* of suicide, not the *popularity* of suicide.

In other words, if the recommendations in this book are taken seriously and the number of consensual deaths stays the same, but within that number of deaths are people who have better access to effective methods, who feel less shame-seeking death, who are not stigmatized by human resources, or forced to listen to a 9-1-1 call on speakerphone during a session with their therapists, I would consider that a huge success.

My goal is not to have more or fewer people die from suicide, but to make suicide more available to everyone and available in a sense it has never been—as an acceleration of death that is as officially and socially acceptable in 2020s or 2030s society as accelerating death through cigarette smoking was in 1920s or 1930s society. And for the tools for suicide to not be hidden away behind prescription pads or locked cabinets, but sold in welcoming environs.

Current policies of prohibition or medicalization produce a now-familiar-to-the-reader scattering of fallout: (1) inadequate certainty of dying or inadequate efficacy of methods, (2) increased injury from failed illicit attempts, (3) conscription of medical professionals into conversations and

---

[345] Roadrunner: A Film About Anthony Bourdain CNN Films (2022).

scenarios for which they were not trained and in which they are not experts, (4) suspicion and scrutiny of people interested in suicide, (5) accusations of mental health defects in those who seek to die and related sabotage of their professional reputations, and (6) one-sided policy interventions limited to prolonging unwanted lives rather than assisting in consensual, desired deaths.

Dying in the future I imagine might be a physical good (a "suicide kit") or a service (a "suicide clinic") and a constellation of activity in this area is sure to evolve in ways difficult for me or you to imagine today. What will not help is crippling the evolution of these goods and services through formal criminal prohibitions, threat of tort litigation (often from the families of satisfied customers where products worked as intended, I might add . . .), religious sanction, normative critique, and accusations of mental health problems.

The prohibitionists may delay the evolution of these systems and routes. They may force people in the near term to live longer than they would prefer or force people to use riskier methods to die than they would like. They may force doctors to revive the happily dead but unhappily alive.[346] They may ensure the final years are extra lonely and extra bleak by convincing society the person who wanted to die is unworthy of stakeholdership in a community, membership in a church, trust in a neighborhood, or respect in a workplace.[347] But, in the end, their arguments against suicide and in favor of limiting the agency of the individual to end life are no stronger or more compelling than when Schopenhauer sat down to write On Suicide so many years ago.

---

[346] For extensive discussion on why reviving people against their wishes, which often results in brain injury or other irreversible harms, is morally questionable, see Dr. Michael Irwin's extensive writings on this topic.

[347] This isolation of those interested in death has forces pushing back against it. In Japan, there are many death cafés where people meet to discuss their plans for dying, debate books and poems about end-of-life matters, and find community around a topic that often is lonely and difficult to raise in polite conversation. For more on this trend, see *A Better Way to Care for the Dying*, The Economist (Apr. 29, 2017).

CURTAINS DOWN, LIGHTS UP
Conclusion

*Bullfighting is the only art in which the artist is in danger of
death and in which the degree of brilliance in the performance
is left to the fighter's honour.*
—*Ernest Hemingway*[348]

Life is not a bullfight. But we each and all have death racing toward us.

We can parry and spin and throw the cape. We can use drugs and pace-makers and ventilators.

You are no Enrique Torres or Felix Rodriguez.[349] And even they could not dodge forever.

You will be gored, eventually. I, too, will be gored.

Death's bull is frighteningly crafty, infinitely patient, and invincible against any *espada*.

As I write this, Colombia is implementing policy that will make it the first place in the world where it is permissible to acquire deadly drugs and end one's life even if one does not have a recognized terminal medical ailment. This is a huge step in the right direction and an exciting experiment from which new learnings will be harvested and new policies born.

Those opposed to this change in Colombia brought up a familiar argument from earlier in this book: How can I trust my fellow citizen with such a momentous decision?

This is the feedback I most commonly receive when I bring up the idea of self-directed or consensual death as something that should be very widely available.[350]

---

[348] Ernest Hemingway, Death in the Afternoon (1960).
[349] Top matadors of Hemingway's era.
[350] Note I say "very widely" and not "universally" to exclude certain special cases, such as the very young

As someone with traditional liberal (perhaps libertarian in the modern context) values, my response is quite simple: (1) I believe the person best positioned to make the decision is the person who bears its consequences and (2) I believe that, absent a compelling argument, the state's interest in intervening in these scenarios is weak.

But I believe we entrust more high-magnitude, low-frequency choices to others than ever before. People can, with a few taps on the glass of their telephones, commit to climb in total strangers' cars or ruin their careers on Twitter. The world is, in many ways, higher stakes than ever; allowing people to pull a trigger or inject a deadly fluid seems less worrisome than it once was. And, in the wake of the COVID-19 global pandemic, death has become a more acceptable topic of conversation and a more universal topic of concern.

Vanity Fair could have chosen any number of things to discuss on the final page of its print edition in October 2020; it was the left-of-center publication's last moment to comment on the upcoming US election and the potential re-election of Donald Trump. Instead of politics, however, the edition closed with an interview with fashion designer Vera Wang in which she was asked how she might like to die.[351] This caught my attention as it seems indicative of a shift in cultural norms.

Just ten or twenty years earlier, asking how a business leader or popular celebrity (I consider Ms. Wang both) would like to die would seem abrupt, rude, and might even terminate the interview. But amidst a global pandemic and in a time when famous people are not just poolside pretty centerfolds and "leading man" men but real people who age and die in our Twitter feeds, ignoring death (or pretending celebrities are immortal) is no longer an option. I found the interviewer's decision to include this question refreshing rather than jarring.

---

or those without the capacity to formulate the intent to die or to consent to die.

[351] *Vera Wang Answers the Proust Questionnaire*, Vanity Fair 92 (Oct. 2020). It is entirely possible the timing of this issue, amidst the COVID-19 global pandemic and prior to the wide availability of vaccines, created an environment in which asking people about dying seemed more timely, appropriate, or polite than it would have in prior epochs.

Today, I view suicide as the only consensual death, the only death over which the decedent can exercise not only control over the speed of death (which one can throttle less precisely by, for instance, taking up smoking) but the manner, context, dignity, and even ceremony of death. Suicide is the only way one can die as planned, when planned, with one's social, romantic, fiscal, and professional affairs as in order as possible. With good communication to loved ones, colleagues, clients, and others, the decedent can end this life in a way that is not only responsible and painless, but altruistic and caring.

Contrast this planned and orderly death to an unexpected natural death wherein, having not had a chance yet to reconcile with an estranged son or to review one's will carefully, one is paralyzed in bed for hours of painful, syncopated cardiac events during which one cannot scream or reach for the comfort of a slumbering spouse's hand just inches away, that spouse deep in dreaming and unaware she will be a widow by morning.

The core of this text springs from several central principles of classical liberalism. Namely, that the default setting in a liberal society is that things are allowed unless explicitly prohibited. Further, that any prohibition on individual agency should be carefully considered and exhaustively debated. Finally, that in cases where a decision is momentous to the individual but likely to have small effects on society as a whole, any restrictions on that decision should be narrowly tailored and imposed only when absolutely necessary and should be taken away from the individual only as a last resort and only with compelling cause.

This having been said, others may be concerned or even shocked by the decision to die when it is talked about openly. Consider, for instance, sending a Google Calendar invite announcing your planned date of death and a preceding "life celebration" cocktail party to a few dozen friends. This might be jarring, worrisome, or even traumatic depending upon how well the audience receiving such an invite understands the context.

Jodi Beggs ✓
@jodiecongirl

pretty sure I just got a google invite for a suicide pact, how's your 2021 going so far

9:44 · 29 Jun 21 · Twitter Web App

2 Retweets **36** Likes

Above: Economist Jodi Beggs feigns surprise about learning the author's planned last day of life via Google Calendar.

Frank conversations about one's goals, achievements, limitations, and ambitions are prerequisite, in my view, to honest discussion's about one's plans to end life. Our conversations with our friends have become so much more nuanced and richer in the recent decades, featuring telephone calls and mixtapes and videos and so on. The idea of an A4 envelope marked "open upon my passing" or a friend learning of our suicides in the broadsheet obits or from the Royal Charlotte[352] seems so antiquated as to be anachronistic.

Why not discuss the plan to end life with friends, rather than merely arranging notification? Why not make a short video or poem or song that encapsulates your feelings about what you've accomplished in life and what may not be able to be accomplished in life's limited bounds? Why not explain how you think about your life's journey and what roles mentors, friends, and others have played?

And these conversations and plenary/preparatory acts, done well, can explain to friends and family why the decedent-to-be is choosing to end life, thereby cushioning the blow to close associates so many suicide-prohibitionist utilitarians estimate to be immutably problematic and unassailably huge.

---

[352] The London delivery of first-class afternoon mail and late edition newspapers.

Ideally, the next phase of our cultural suicide conversation is less about prohibition and prevention and more about access and empathy.

Many forget wines of more recent vintage, of popular acclaim, or of grand lineage can turn to vinegar at any time, sometimes unexpectedly (or by the appraisals of some, prematurely). And so too with lives—whether or not a given life involves health challenges is not the only measure of its remaining value and, in the end, the one living it is the person best positioned to consider its present and future worth.

By excluding physicians from as much of the decision-making process as possible, we can restore the agency of the person wanting to die, whose thoughts can be respected and listened to and heard without accusations of cowardice or feebleness or insanity.

Rather than thinking of suicide as something desired only by a small number of the mentally ill, it can be thought of as an orderly end to life, a way to plan for the future, and a legitimate aspirational thought[353] a successful, healthy person can have.

The sooner we collectively appreciate the reality and diversity of experience, which includes heterogeneity in the reasons we might desire to end life, the sooner we can have frank discussions with one another about how we would like to spend, *and end*, our time here.

---

[353] For more on the question of what aspiration is and why only some aspirations are acceptable or respected in society, see Plato, Alcibiades Major.

A Note on References

As an interdisciplinary text, it is impossible to adhere to the citation standards of the various disciplines and sub-disciplines discussed here.

Example journal citation:

Alexander L. Chapman & Katherine L. Dixon-Gordon, *Emotional Antecedents and Consequences of Deliberate Self-Harm and Suicide Attempts*, 37 Suicide Life Threat. Behav. 543, 550 (2007).

In the above citation, Chapman and Dixon-Gordon are co-authors, the italicized text is the title of the journal article as published with newspaper-headline capitalization, 37 is the volume of the journal, Suicide Life Threat. Behav. is the title of the journal, 543 is the first page within volume 37 the journal article occupies, 550 is the page where a specific quote can be found; 2007 is the first date of publication according to the cover page, corner notation, or masthead of the journal.

Example case citation:

N. Fletcher v. Western Nat'l. Life Ins. Co., 10 CAL. APP. 3D 376, 397 (CAL. APP. 4TH 1970).

In the above citation, N. is a serial footnote number, Fletcher and Western National Life Insurance Company are parties to the action at bar, 10 is the reporter volume, California Appellate 3d is the reporter, 376 is the starting page of the case, 397 is the page quoted, and California's Fourth Appellate District is the court that heard the case in 1970.

Jacket Quote Citations

"People should be free to determine the course of their life, and death is part of that."
—*Easing Death*, The Economist (Oct. 19, 2012).

"The time has come to talk . . . about personal responsibility for managing the dying process."
—Timothy Leary, Chaos and Cyber Culture (1994).

"Americans seem to be obsessed with exercising, doing mental puzzles, consuming various juice and protein concoctions, sticking to strict diets, and popping vitamins and supplements, all in a valiant effort to cheat death and prolong life as long as possible . . . I reject this aspiration. I think this manic desperation to endlessly extend life is misguided and potentially destructive."
—Ezekiel Emmanuel, *Why I Hope to Die at 75*, The Atlantic (Oct. 2014).

". . . I believe there is a paucity of open, honest, and serious discussion of suicide as a topic."
—Tyler Cowen, correspondence with the author dated 14 June 2023 (on file with the author).